MOSTLY MORT...

DR. DON NEWBURY

ISBN-13: 978-0-578-16884-5

Cover Design by Debbie Fraser, Amarillo, TX
Typesetting by Pryce Editorial Consulting, Cleburne, TX
Page Art by Clayton Boyd, Burleson, TX
(His paintings may be viewed in color online,
www.claytonartist.com)
Pencil Sketches by Grant Reid, Comanche, TX

Printed in the United States of America
Printed by CreateSpace

MOSTLY MORT...

*From the 'Way Out' Mind of Dr. Don Newbury Whose Imaginary Uncle Reduces His Chances Of Mind **Ever** Triumphing Over Matter...*

Your attention is directed to a man who hasn't been heard from lately—the late William Hughes Mearns—who'd be around 150 years of age if alive. But he was much alive as an educator and a writer about children, mostly ages 3-8. He lived to be 90, watching and writing down impressions of what they said to each other--without gumming up the works with his own questions. He may have been forerunner of Dr. Seuss, Art Linkletter, Walter Mitty or Elwood P. Dowd. (The latter starred in the delightful play, *Harvey*. It was later an even more delightful movie starring the inimitable James Stewart in the leading role.)

You may recall the first verse of a Mearn's poem, and may swear it had no other verses. It does, but only the first one is imprinted in memory. You'll recall: "The other day upon a stair, I met a man who wasn't there. He wasn't there again today. I wish, I wish, he'd go away."...

My Uncle Mort may redefine “outlandish,” with his zany approach to life landing somewhere roughly between staircases and “whimsy.” If I met him “upon a stair,” I’d bid him stay, seeking help in the pursuit of reasons for folks to smile. And if he were an imaginary rabbit as in *Harvey*, I’d so wish him to be real. If a few smiles don’t occur to lessen frowns in a tough old world, I will have failed. May there also be some important truths shared along the way. If they don’t and I am “booed out of town,” I’ll grab a baton and race to the front, as if leading a parade….

DEDICATION

To our six grandchildren, who brighten the lives of many others. They are: intellectually advanced beyond their ages, competitive in the healthiest of ways, sparkling in personality, comfortable in their own skin, involved in too many activities, advantaged by many friendships destined to grow stronger across the years, committed to God and adored by their parents and grandparents.

They and their parents are: Ben and Brittin, Bryan and Julie Choate, Aledo, TX; Juliana and Kedren, Kyle and Jana Penney, Tyler, TX and Jonah and Addison, Ryan and Jeanie McDaniel, Burleson, TX.

They are featured on annual Christmas cards, sometimes posing under protest… What ho! I came across one just now, so here 'tis:

A CHRISTMAS POSE…
Stair-cased are Addison and Jonah, in back Juliana and Kedren, center pair and in front, Brittin and Ben.

CONTENTS

BY WAY OF INTRODUCTION...

"Handy as pockets on a shirt." This expression—now on life support—sometimes fades to "laugh support." For writers putting words to paper regularly, it is an expression often employed. It deflects spotlights and floodlights—sometimes "low lights"—when authorship admission requires courage—particularly when the barrel's bottom has been scraped.

With this in mind, my Uncle Mort is introduced. He'd prefer, of course, to come on with fanfare, much bugle-blowing and drum-beating. This is not possible, since he's no more my uncle than yours, or any other person on the planet. He is, quite simply, something of a refugee who crawled through a flaw in the fence of my imagination.

If you have been spared the torment accompanying perusal of my weekly Texas newspaper columns since 2003—it may come as news to you that Mort is no more real than the plastic flowers in motel lobbies. Still, he's handy to have around.

Thankfully, most readers have humored me, some even expressing thanks for easygoing, old-time humor, the availability of such clearly waning. Oh, there are exceptions. One reader took time to write a letter, buy an envelope and affix a stamp thereto for conveyance of a terse, suggestive message: "If I couldn't write better than you do, I'd stick the quill back in the goose!"

When I introduced Mort to readers a decade or so ago, he was identified as my "91-year-old uncle." Married to Aunt Maude since 1934, Mort is depicted as being weak of back, strong of opinion, handy with the lip and shots from the hip. He's retired, living way down in "the thicket," and Maude continues to put up with him. He's upbeat, out for an easy buck and quick to embrace "get-rich-quick" schemes. They often result in blow-ups equal to explosions remembered in the old Roadrunner vs. Wile E. Coyote cartoons that highlighted the stretch of films between features at the picture show. Oh, he's much more. Good natured and patriotic, he's well-liked in his little corner of the world where he might be called "eccentric" if folks there knew what it means. He's often found at the domino table at the feed store, and would "give you the shirt off a friend's back."

Someone asked about his mental competency. A psychiatrist who stopped off at the general store one day overheard conversations at the domino table. Mort, of course, was "holding court." The psychiatrist's evaluation: "As long as he's out, I don't think they'll lock him up. But, if they ever lock him up, I doubt if they'll ever let him out." One of Mort's friends spoke thusly: "*Before* God made Mort, I think He broke the mold."

In so many words, perhaps I've created a composite of many of my "real" uncles. I haven't intentionally tried to deceive readers.

Most of them quickly see through—all the way to my imagination—-realizing that Mort lives only there. I admit, though, that for many years, I've received periodic queries from readers asking if Mort is "real."

I've always answered: "Do you want him to be?" That is, if the observations, antics and buffoonery attributed to him cause readers to relax, smile and maybe even sometimes break into laughter, is that so bad? One astute reader called something to my attention that truly had never before been considered. He said he'd been reading about Uncle Mort several times a year since 2004. "He's been 91 years old for at least half-a-dozen years," he laughed. "Does the old guy ever age?"

He made a good point, so I've tried to remember that every July 4—like Yankee Doodle Dandy, Mort was "born"—and annually he becomes a year older. Thus, at this writing, he's turned over 102 on his odometer, still with no end in sight.

He wiggles his ears at gasoline prices, having abandoned his worn-out pick-up truck years ago when the price per gallon slid past a buck fifty. Mort got a deal on a golf cart, and has gotten around thusly all over the thicket for years, bragging about his gas mileage. Maude gets nervous rigors at the thought of hopping on the cart, but does so when she really needs to go to town. She insists, though, that they go when traffic is lightest, never mind that most traffic jams in the thicket clear up when the light changes at the dirt road intersection with the state highway.

She understands him as well as he can be understood. At this point, it is best to extend the umbrella of credibility to include you, the reader. For example, it is left to you to decide whether Maude also is a figment of my imagination, or, you may wonder, only in Mort's mind.

As stated earlier, I find them both to be "handy to have around," often making observations, or blurting out comments, that I, a university president for almost 20 years in another century, find unseemly to say.

Perhaps the best example is Judge Kenneth Starr, former Dean of the Pepperdine School of Law, when named President of Baylor University. Judge Starr, the first BU president with no Baptist heritage, has been best known—and for many, still is—for grilling President Bill Clinton as a special prosecutor during President Clinton's escapades, er, administration.

Mort, often at a loss for cash but never for words, made an observation that may have run through the minds of many Baylor alumni, saying: "Well, if Bill Clinton ever harbored any hopes whatever of receiving an honorary doctorate from Baylor, I'd say he'd best forget 'em."

This book combines many Mort stories, most of which have popped up in my *Idle American* columns along the way. He'll be included there for the duration, as long as I can pound out columns, find home keys, string words together, and corral thoughts—at least occasionally. In short, until the cows head homeward….

Over the years, I've been introduced to audiences many times as the "nation's 'unstuffiest' college president." I consider such a description to be a high compliment; since many of my colleagues—as well as most people I know—take too many things far too seriously. Addressing a convention attended by a couple of hundred presidents, I opined, "If a bomb hit this convention dead center today, it would set education forward by 100 years."

I hope Uncle Mort continues to rub off on me, and on you, too. We all need to find pockets of levity and stories of pastel in an ever-darkening, way-too-serious world. Both Mort and I are admirers of Walter Mitty. That is, we want to go most places on purpose, never forgetting there's much to be said for letting the wind take over much of the time. After all, that's what President George H. W. Bush does, jumping from airplanes every decade or so, even at age 90. Mort and I will stop short of that, but if we run into Walter Mitty, there's no telling what the three of us may decide to do. And hang gliding can't be ruled out....

On behalf of Mort and Maude—as well as members of my "real" family—and those who help me with the nuts and bolts of cranking out a column each week—sincere gratitude is extended. And to my readers, **CONTINUED THANKS**, yes, even in boldface type....

Dr. Don Newbury

Idle American Syndicate

Burleson, TX

UNDERWOOD STANDARD TYPEWRITER

When grandkids ask, I always answer that I learned on a 1950s wood-burning typewriter….

ACKNOWLEDGMENTS

As is the case in all worthwhile projects I attempt, my wife, Brenda, deserves much credit—particularly in matters of judgment, propriety, support, tact and, of course, assistance in the proofing of my weekly syndicated column, *The Idle American.* Her brief career of teaching high school English—abandoned after five semesters for motherhood--spills over into helping me, again and again. She gets punctuation marks properly placed, and helps in other ways to keep retired English teachers reading my stuff from marking it up too badly. Our oldest daughter, Julie Choate, likewise assists.

Since my column began on a weekly basis in 2003—or very nearly that soon—several "pre-readers" have been faithful to proof draft copies prior to publication. Two must be singled out—Laurie Magers, long-time Administrative Assistant to the late—yes, great—Zig Ziglar, king of motivational speakers in our universe.

Finally, a tip of the hat to Vaughn Groom, faculty member at Tarrant County College who is as versatile as anyone I've ever known. Besides "professoring" in the field of computer science, he can blow horns and play the piano, too.

Laurie and Vaughn never miss a week, and all they get is "thanks," the very word I'm using for them here. THANKS!

PART 1

All Around the Thicket...

UNCLE MORT AND NEWS FROM NEW YORK...

Shake any family tree and relatives like Uncle Mort will fall out—or maybe "flake out!" Kinfolks, of course, prefer kinder descriptions, but neighbors who know such uncles best "call 'em the way they see 'em." Their "calls"—like corn shucked right down to the cob—come closest to the truth.

So, his kin describe Mort as an aging conservative who lives near his rural roots. Neighbors are considerably more frank. They call him an old "country coot," tighter than the bark on a tree, and a guy who climbs over gates to save the hinges.

We hear from him at Yuletide for sure and at other times, maybe. We're always glad to get mail from the old home place to sorta "catch up."

Times remain gentle for my old uncle. He refuses to surrender to progress, foregoing even electricity and automobiles. He raises his food and kills his game. Heat and light are from a wood stove and lanterns. He bought a used generator to power up his 12-inch TV, a steal of a price—$4 at a garage sale. (They were asking $5.50)

A fellow selling satellite dishes laughed when Mort asked what he'd take for a rooftop antenna. He pointed to a stack out back, with instructions to take all he wanted. Television is now his window to the world.

Anyway, our conversation the other day was surprising. He had ridden his golf cart into town (claims he makes the 30-mile round-trip weekly on less than a gallon of gas) with zero outlay for licensure, inspections, insurance and speeding tickets. (It's long been his policy to buy NOTHING that calls for monthly payments or has to be fed.) A window sign in town offering a "free cell call anywhere in the nation" caught his eye. The salesman's plan, of course, was to sell a phone. Mort's plan was to talk to me as long as I'd listen.

He wanted to know if I'd heard about "that Westminster Dog Show in New York City." I hated to tell him they've been trotting canines out there annually for 129 years. He was mortified that hounds were passed over and he poked fun at the fastidious grooming of what he called "poofy poochies." Actually, he recognizes only two canine groups—hounds and all the rest. He was convinced that a poodle would have won if the owner hadn't "over-tweezed" the dog's right eyebrow. He prattled on about how dogs look like their masters, and in the "jiggling category," he declared a dead heat between owners and canines as they trotted briskly around the arena.

Then, he railed about an artistic display in Central Park that required a million yards of orange nylon at a cost of $1.3 million dollars daily for the 16-day run. "And that don't count taking it down," he lamented. He claims NYC could save money dismantling the display when the 2,500 dog show entries were released. Then, throw in a few thousand cats. "That should take care of the nylon in no time," he scoffed.

Intentional throat-clearing loud enough to evacuate a circus tent interrupted our visit. Even Uncle Mort realized the phone guy had given up on him and was ready to hand the phone to the next guy in line who wanted a free call.

"I'll write more news on the Christmas card," Mort promised, urging me in his final breath to watch Jerry Lee Lewis on the "hysterical channel." Mort loves to watch Lewis cut loose on *A Whole Lotta Shaking Going On*, claiming that when his hound dogs shake like Lewis does, he gives 'em worm medicine." I was glad the phone guy gave up on Uncle Mort, but I don't think I ever can....

DREAMING AGAIN...

I was sore afraid that bad news was brewing in the thicket when Aunt Maude called. Thankfully, there wasn't, and Maude—unlike her impetuous hubby—assured me that it would be a quick call. She was on a pay phone at the crossroads while my old uncle milled about in the general store.

"I flat out don't know what to do with Mort," she said, "Since the kids gave him the cell phone and told him they'd pay the bill, he's making calls day and night." I winced, understanding the situation as well as one can from a distance. This was the first time my old aunt ever called, so I knew it was a serious matter.

"He's acting crazier than he did 50 years ago when he claimed invention of the hula hoop," Maude said. Oh, I remember it well. When he found out that more than 100 million hoops were sold during the first two years, he argued that it was "his idea first." Never mind that his concept called for triangular configuration. "If my hoop had caught on, the kids could have been gyrating like Elvis before there was an Elvis," Mort snorted.

Maude has stood by Mort for many decades; she knows his quirks. The rest of us know that he'd have to slide several rungs back down the normalcy ladder to be labeled merely "eccentric." Wondering if marbles had loosened, I asked her point blank if his mental state might be shaky.

"Let's put it this way," she answered. "Much about Mort is not at all complicated; instead, it is simple. I mean you can turn a fly loose to fly around in his room, and he's entertained for at least two hours. Add a fly swatter, and he'll be captivated for at least half a day." My advice to her? "Join him in the general store and buy enough fly swatters to last awhile."...

MEANWHILE, AT THE FARMERS' MARKET...

Mort looks forward to Saturday mornings in springtime. He's never been into golf, and gets his fill of fishing and frog-gigging at all seasons of the year. In the spring, however, farmers load up their pick-ups with produce to sell on Saturday mornings. He usually banters the morning away with a guy selling fruit and vegetables from the back of his '73 pick-up parked with 15-20 others on the courthouse square.

My uncle likes to call him "Farmer Jones," a guy who is every inch a business man for sure, and a farmer, maybe. He's always there early, square dab under a shade tree, looking the part of a man barely scraping out a living. The farmer has much of life figured out, with almost all his learnin' soaked up outside the books and way "outside the box."

Mort is fascinated by the farmer's sales pitch. The nester usually has fresh produce in hand, nurturing it as if it's next of kin. When melons and peaches are in season, he's always piddling with one or the other. Their juices drip from his chin stubbled by a three-day crop of whiskers. His overalls hang loosely from his shoulders, often with patches on patches at the pressure points. Scuffed old brogans are survivors of several growing seasons, unpredictable weather and predictable barnyards.

"How's business?" Mort asked years ago when he began his weekly watch. He noticed the farmer's big pockets bulging with coins before the sun was two hours high. "Not bad," he answered, making eye contact that wouldn't let go.

Mort, toying with a melon, asked why he didn't have a better pick-up. "I've got a right new one, but I don't bring it up here," he admitted. He explained that he'd been making Saturday morning sales for 30 years, and along the way, he's studied people from every angle. He knows them well, and has been applying sound sales techniques before experts knew what they were. (By driving his oldest truck to town, he has the "pity" vote from shoppers right away.)

"People don't want to buy produce from a new truck," he explained. "They'd rather think I'm working long hours, barely squeaking by, and that their purchases just might be the ones to help me face another day." He was just getting warmed up. "And they'd rather see me in patched overalls." For all Mort knows, the farmer may wear Dockers, loafers and shirts with pony monograms during the week, perhaps employing hired hands for the heavy lifting.

"Folks like for you to think they know more about farming than they do," he volunteered. "So, I let 'em." He spoke of a woman who bought a passel of produce the previous week. She wanted to know what kind of peas he had. "What kind do you want?" he countered. She said she was mighty partial to Crowders. He joked that she was in luck; his peas had been on the vine just one day earlier. He didn't mention, however, whether "in luck" meant they were Crowders, or just plain peas.

"Within a few seconds, I can spot the thumpers from the clueless at the melon tub," he laughed. "They can thump away the morning, finally choosing one no better than another selected randomly. Or if they ask me, I'll thump for them. Either way, my melons are almost always good." He spoke about the importance of "three-fers." He feels certain that produce priced at 65 cents a pound moves better if offered at "three pounds for two dollars."

The farmer never bragged, really, but came close when he claimed to be a near expert on "guesstimating" weights before produce is ever placed scales that could use greasing. "If people ask for about three pounds of potatoes, I take advantage of the 'about' part, placing 'about' three and a half pounds on the scale." (In the same manner, if they asked for "about $3 worth," the scale pointed to $3.50.) "Not one in a hundred asks me to be exact," he joked, emphasizing that he CAN get within an ounce or a couple of pennies every time. With his tactics, many extra tons of produce have been sold.

"If people have growls in their gullets, they're lookers, not buyers. I call 'em 'Charmin squeezers'," he joked. "I try to get 'em to smile and sometimes one line will do it. "Did a mean old somebody shake your Etch-a-Sketch?" He says that line works every time.

One day, a little girl, maybe eight years old, walked up, her mother in tow. "Young lady, in a couple of weeks, my "Q's" are going to be ready for pulling. Oh, you may not know what "Q's" are—that's what I call cucumbers. And my new cucumbers are going to be the cutest ever grown. I turned the seeds inside out before planting, so the "Q's" will have dimples instead of warts!"

The youngster let out a loud laugh, and a big smile splashed across her mom's face. Though originally headed for the courthouse, they lingered, deciding to buy a bunch of produce instead. Too, they thought they might even hear another joke from a farmer who minds his peas and "Q's."…

TRUTH OR EGGNOG?...

Uncle Mort called to wish us a "Happy New One." He doesn't own a phone out in his wilderness where daylight is piped in, so calls are rare, usually on someone else's dime. But on the flip side, where he abides in the thicket, there's tranquility others mostly dream about, where he's 100% content to watch the rest of the world go by.

Initially, it wasn't expected to be a "special day." His plan was to drive his golf cart to the crossroads general store, where he looked forward to cozying up in a cane-bottom chair. On arrival, though, a fancy car at the gas pump caught his eye. Mort quickly sized up the driver who was flashing a fancy cell phone. The man had no notion that he was being sized up.

"Bet your gasoline bills pin you to the wall," Mort laughed, inhaling deeply. "I'm powerful proud there ain't no charge for sniffing. I come down here to get a few free 'whiffs' whether I buy a couple of gallons of gas or not." His mindless chatter was so much smoke-blowing; he was zeroing in on a free phone call.

"Surprised your phone works all the way out here in the sticks," Mort said. The visitor, intrigued by this Dog Patch-like figure, seemed amused as he tossed Mort the phone. "Try it out," the passerby said. That's when Mort dialed me up. In seconds we finished the "how're you doin'" stuff. Settling back, I was ready for the inevitable ramblings to follow. This time, they were more "hither and yon" than usual; it's quite possible that Mort--eager to get his "fill" of the Christmas season--may have taken on too much eggnog.

Though Mort's mind is not always engaged, his mouth seems always in gear. He's quick to spot opportunities for laughter, usually at others' expense. A few years ago, I kidded that his yakking was driving me crazy. "That's not a drive, it's a putt," he countered, laughing so hard that he almost forgot to change the subject.

"Y'all been on any trips?" Mort asked. I knew this meant he was about to unload on me minute details about his own travels, albeit perhaps decades ago. "I rode the bus across six states," he bragged. "Covered 2,500 miles in six days."

He described the sign at the New Mexico state line that welcomes visitors to the "Land of Enhancement." I was tempted to ask him if the slogan might be "Land of Enchantment," but what would that have proven? It would have been like the time I argued fruitlessly that there is no "Book of Temptations" in the Holy Bible.

As usual, I decided to cut him some slack. Perhaps his five-and-dime spectacles had failed. Or, maybe the pharmaceutical commercials are blanketing shortwave radio, too. Speculation, of course, is pointless. His mind is always made up, and, like the song, "he shall not be moved."

"The pharmaceutical moguls and the tourist bureau people probably are in cahoots," Mort opined. Then, topics shifted quickly. He predicted that attendance will be dismal for the re-make of the movie, *King Kong*. "Why would we want to have the bejeebers scared out of us in a movie twice as long as the first one back in '33? Perhaps they should have called the new one *The Kong Who Would be King* or maybe *Prince Kong* or even *Gong Kong*?"

Then he swung to employment news. "With them pirates taking in after cruise ships sailing around Africa, there's going to be a shortage of marksmen to defend the boats," he asserted. "If I was younger, I'd practice up on my marksmanship and hire out as a tail gunner on a cruise ship."

He had more to say, but thankfully, the driver claimed to be in a hurry, trying to make Amarillo by morning. Said he faced a long road ahead, with miles and miles of nothing but miles and miles. I could imagine his standing on one foot, then the other, fidgeting with his watch and much throat-clearing, letting Mort know, without doubt, that it was time to get his phone back. Mort handed it over, muttering that "no one has to be anywhere."

The befuddled driver stood little chance of making Amarillo by morning. If so, it would be late morning, at best. More likely, the sun would be sliding well into the p.m. side of the sky….

THE NEIGHBOR'S PLACE
Mort needs no fences to make good neighbors. This spread is west of his place about 800 miles, near Santa Fe, NM.

ABOUT THOSE MEDICATIONS...

Mort and Maude have no regular schedule for trips into town. They are close with the dollar, and the 15-mile trip from the country, they claim, is a "costly consideration." Even with the golf cart, a couple of quarts of gas go up in smoke, sometimes literally. That was the case a while back when they stopped by. Maude came inside while Mort jiggled wires, grousing all the while about them not making carts like they used to. (She'd made it clear to him that she had no intention of climbing back on the cart until it was "smoke-free.) "It's bad enough riding on it when it's runnin' right, but when smoke is boiling from the motor, we look like a slow-motion accident looking for a place to happen." I figured we might have to put extra water in the soup for supper to accommodate two extra mouths.

Maude, not one to complain on a regular basis, hates it when they have to explain cart breakdowns to motorists who stop to render aid on the farm-to-market road. "I'm not a golfer, but when we're broke down roadside and he's working on it, I yank a club out of the bag, and act like I'm gonna play a ball several miles out in the rough—if I can find it."

She had a bad case of nerves and was hand-wringing about getting home before dark. I told her we'd have a bowl of soup, and I'd drive them home if need be. Asked about her second "town trip" in the same month, she said each was to see the doctor.

"I'm not used to seeing doctors twice a decade, much less days apart, but my nerves were acting up something fierce; I've been really uptight." On the first visit, the doctor prescribed Valium, explaining that one pill should work wonders when her world falls in. "On the follow-up visit today, I told him the prescription worked like a charm," Maude laughed. "Whenever I feel a smothering spell coming on, I slip one of the little pills into Mort's coffee."...

About that time, I heard the sputtering motor outside change to a steady hum. As they headed for the thicket, I sent along a thermos bottle of hot soup. They scooted away, hoping to make it home before dark. One good thing, their route was east instead of west, eliminating the need for squinting.

Filling the thermos reminded me of Mort's account years earlier. He and a couple of buddies were gigging frogs after it was good and dark in the thicket. One of them expressed amazement about aviation— how heavy airplanes could stay airborne and maintain high speed. Another couldn't understand atomic energy, and how the bombs effectively ended World War II.

"I guess what puzzles me most is the thermos bottle," Mort said. "The thermos bottle?" they questioned. "Yes, the thermos bottle. I can take it deep into the thicket, and open it at lunch time, pouring out hot soup into the cup. And the smoke is still rising from it. On another day, I can take iced tea, and when I pour it, there are still ice chips in the cup."

The friends looked at each other, one asking, "What's so hard to understand about that?" Predictably, I guess, was Mort's quick answer: "How does it *know*?"…

AUNT MAUDE AND UNDERDOGS…

My long-suffering Aunt Maude doesn't usually get excited about sports. For her, typical responses are "How about that?...Do tell. That must have been exciting." She somehow co-exists with a hubby who is a typical, boiler-plate sports fan, with leather-lunged yells for whichever one is in season.

When there's a buzz about one of the nation's smaller colleges, George Mason, making it to the "Final Four" in the NCAA

Tournament, Maude takes sides. "How could I pull for anyone but George Mason?" she asked. "I've always used their jars."

Speaking of underdogs, Dallas Cowboy Terrell Owens might want to contact her about organizing a fan club in the thicket. If such a club ever materialized in Dallas, meetings could be held in a phone booth. (To younger readers: In olden days, there were small booths on street corners. Attached therein were pay phones, into which users could insert coins if desiring to use the phone…) Mort feels the same way about spoiled-brat players, and he cites Owens as "exhibit A." Pointing out that Terrell likely holds the record for workout absences, Mort slapped a "TOAD" label on the season when Owens' rarely practiced. He said this stands for "Terrell Owens Absent Daily." As the season wore on, "TOAD" still applied, with different meanings for the "A." For example, "Terrell Owens Angers Daily"? Or maybe antagonizes, amazes, alarms, anguishes, accuses, alienates, etc.

Owens' arrival in Dallas already was "double-whammied," with the NFL noose-tightening on his unacceptable field shenanigans. This is as futile as taking bunnies from magicians; they simply find other animals to use in their acts.

Rarely has a sports figure ignited such commotion. Media folks around close and far wouldn't buy the company line from team officials, who attempted to whitewash Owens' previous behavior with promises that any day, he'd come of age. Fans didn't take the bait, either. When Dale Hansen, dean of the TV bunch in the Metroplex with some four decades in front of cameras, took a firm stand on the matter, he shelled the corn all the way down to the cob. Even Maude applauded him for "telling it like it is."

When he offered his "unplugged commentary," his words stripped the paint off the dining table. It was clearly "anti-Owens," and response was overwhelming, far greater than to any previous Hansen harangue. Typically, the "pros and the cons" run neck and neck. After 10 days, he received 448 emails, with 441 agreeing with his comments.

"Turns out Hansen was a real prophet, that Terrell Owens was never a fit," Maude said at a quilting party. The other ladies gathered round the frame didn't know any more about sports than Maude, but one of them mentioned Hansen's annual Christmas tribute entitled, *"Thank God for Kids."* They all said they never miss watching his annual tear-jerking tribute. Maude and Mort have long agreed that it is a "must see." Such admission is a watershed moment; they haven't agreed on much across the years….

AND THEN, ANNUAL SPRING CLEANING...

It was March's first Saturday—the day for Aunt Maude's annual challenge: to get Uncle Mort out of the house so she could light into serious spring cleaning. Over the years, she's collected a list of "suggestions," one or two of which always worked. A "can't miss" suggestion includes, "Why don't you play a round of golf, or round up some buddies for fishing?"

She's provided long lists of laughs about her hubby's shenanigans, including descriptions of his golf game. Recalled is the store of his one 18-hole round played under 100 strokes.(Mort called the double-figure day as one worth noting for his "vital statistics," and how it was perhaps a precursor to luxuries of life they'd enjoy later when he made the pro tour.

Maude laughed, saying he'd be lucky to win third place in a four-man miniature golf foursome, then recited what she called "more accurate 'vital statistics'." She lamented that Mort's stats include 7 and a half around the noggin, 44 inches around the waist, 115 around the golf course and a nuisance around the house."

This day, though, suggestions for golfing or fishing thudded. He couldn't even remember where he hid his clubs in protest hikes for senior citizens at the public golf course. "I thought $1.75 was high, but $2 is scandalous," he fumed. Fishing was out of the question, too, since he hadn't untangled the lines that ended a bungled fishing trip a few weeks earlier.

Then the perfect "suggestion" crossed her mind. She'd ask him if he'd like to go to town, share news from the thicket, catch up on political news and play dominoes—all of which could do without ever leaving the general store.

Mort fell for the idea. He double-timed it to check the tire pressure on the golf cart and filled the gas tank to the two-gallon mark. Off he went, negotiating the winding 15-mile route at about the same MPH. He coasted the final 50 feet—anything to save a few drops of fuel, you know. Hearing the shuffling of dominoes before his feet hit the porch made him question why he didn't go into town more often. (The best reason, of course, was that Maude didn't wade into deep cleaning that often.)

A threesome already was playing dominoes, so a fourth player was exceedingly welcome. With his arrival, they could switch to a game of "42." The guys were glad they had drawn straws before he arrived, just in case he showed up. One of 'em winced, realizing his "short straw" meant he was sentenced to being Mort's partner. The county sheriff was "cleaning their clocks" in the domino game. "As much as he plays during duty hours, he ought to be good," one of the guys laughed.

Folks didn't mind losing to the chief lawman, though; it was worth it to hear his stories about law enforcement during the years when alcoholic beverages were available for sale only in distant counties. (Legally, anyway.) Many of his accounts involved bootleggers, who seemed always to have bottles available, usually sold in the shadows or dark of night. Under a nearby sign proclaiming "Near Beer Sold Here," a bootlegger had scrawled: "Real Beer Sold Near Here."…

"I'll never forget the time guys were always getting drunk IN jail," the sheriff drawled. "Turns out they drilled holes in the mortar through the outside wall, then used straws to suck wine from jugs held by their friends in the alley. I saw one of 'em with his face against the wall, and when I yelled at him, he jumped back, with the straw falling inside the cell." Another time, he got a "telephone tip" that a bootlegger had liquor stashes all over his garden, with each bottle covered by a plow disc. "The caller was right," the sheriff said, "But what he didn't tell us was that rattlesnakes also were planted under each disc."

Then, the lawman switched to a quarrelsome night at the radio station. The sheriff was able to settle the issue, but he riled the station owner in the process. "When I sign on in the morning, I'm going to give you 'Hail Columbia,' and I'm going to rail against you until they vote you out of office," the nettled radio guy screamed. The sheriff claimed he'd "had lots worse burrs than these under his saddle blanket. Still, he turned the radio on when at 5:30 a.m. the next day when the owner signed on. After playing the National Anthem, the owner said, "Go back to bed, sheriff, I changed my mind."…

Hours passed quickly as the sheriff continued "clock-cleaning" at the domino table, "rolling on" with his stories. Mort was sad when lengthening shadows meant it was time to go home. He figured that at least monthly, he ought to suggest "sweeping out" to Aunt Maude while he goes into town to conduct some business….

RED PLANET CAUSES ROYAL BLUSH...

It's a well-accepted probability that one man's trash is another man's treasure, and garage sales held by millions of Americans each weekend provide ready proof. Mort and Maude frequently poke through garage sales in the thicket, and a while back, he bought a "$100 telescope for $1.50."

After viewing the usual constellations for several nights, he took note of a friend's email that a couple of weeks later, the earth and Mars would be closer together than they've been for 5,000 years. "Just think," he mentioned, "It could be 60,000 years before they're just 35 million miles apart again!"

It was more than a coincidence, Mort thought, that there would be such a marvelous astronomical event at the very time he'd come into ownership of a telescope. His mental wheels turning, he suggested a cook-out for the whole community. They'd have Mars Bars for dessert and a contest for storytellers to see who could tell the biggest space "whopper." And they'd arrange for Age of Aquarius background music. Invitations went out, financial help for the event poured in and the evening went swimmingly until the very end—when the friend who'd furnished the initial email notification requested a "point of personal privilege."

Then, a flush-faced guest said, "Actually, the two planets align this closely every 15-17 years." Further, he pointed out that the date Mort thought to be current had already occurred—three years earlier! However, it was a nice summer evening for a cook-out. As they say, a "good time was had by all," and Mort promised if he ever got into computer usage, he'd keep Snopes' web address close at hand….

HEARING WHAT HE WANTS TO HEAR...

Tuned in to the rhythms of the thicket, Uncle Mort doesn't mind being "tuned out" to news from the outside world. In fact, he prefers it. When his hearing aid batteries are running on empty, he never hurries to replace them. With or without the hearing aid, he hears more than he wants to.

So, it's easy to understand why he's happy to "make do" with his old black and white TV. It bothers him not that the picture sometimes rolls, and that the antenna is seldom pointed "just right." He knows also that even so-so reception depends greatly on favorable atmospheric conditions. "Just think how many political announcements I miss," Mort bragged. "Far as I can tell, a heap more promises are made than can be delivered, and a passel of losing candidates—folks who felt like 'the little engine that could'—couldn't." Claiming that most of the "slung mud" dries before it rolls into the thicket, he seems generally aware of campaign goings-on. Taking the "little engine" analogy a bit further, he predicts that the losing politico's "huffing and puffing" could put us on track for a new definition of "loco"-motion....

It's a daily occurrence for Mort to change the subject at warp speed. For example, he said he was "considering the switch to a strict vegetarian diet. "If I do, I won't eat anything that has a mother," he said....

MORT AT THE COUNTY RODEO
He claims to be the rider in this mid-1950s painting; Maude thinks it's more likely that he ran the concession stand.

GOLF: MORE HUMBLING THAN WE THOUGHT…

Honed to a fare-the-well are hundreds of memories of Mort and his "42" buddies who meet more "on purpose" than by chance at the general store. With no plans to buy anything—except soft drinks, maybe, this foursome seated around a butcher block table on cane bottom chairs. Yeah, they spent big chunks of many days killing time around the table.

Down deep, each one of 'em sorta hopes Santa this year might see fit to bring them a brand new set of dominoes. The ones they're using are chipped, scratched or otherwise marked, creating distinct advantages for the players who memorize the anomalies. And they all do! After shuffling, they close their eyes tighter than a bank vault, just in case. If anyone peeks and goes straight for certain memorized dominoes, all "yell" breaks loose.

The game stops for few reasons, one being on those rare occasions when drivers get lost and stop to ask for directions. Mort and his cronies always offer "tsk-tsk-tsks" to commiserate with such visitors, whom they encourage to fill up with gas in case they get lost again.

There's a lone gas pump in front of the store; it's regular unleaded or nothing. Mort often springs into action, wiping windshields to get tips. Sometimes he whips up yarns to tickle motorists' funny bones, like he did the other day. "Man, we've never had so many geese flapping their way south," he said. "Do you happen to know why those V's of geese have one short row and one long row? Because there are more geese in the long rows," he cackled, slapping his thighs.

A recent errant motorist tossed his morning newspaper into the trash barrel, and when he was out of sight, Mort and his cohorts fished it out. It was the freshest news they'd read in days. This time, though, none of the headlines grabbed their attention, but a tiny story on the sports page did. Mort nearly got the vapors laughing about Jimmie Johnson, the crown prince of NASCAR racing, breaking his wrist in a fall from a golf cart. "Well blow me down," Mort said. (In "thicket talk," this is the rough equivalent of "Shiver me timbers.")

Mort expressed the same sentiment of surprise when he heard about Dick Cheney shooting a friend during a South Texas bird hunt. Mort, between convulsions, said racing fans would not be surprised if Johnson were injured roaring around race tracks at 200 MPH, or even on a freeway. But such accidents might be at warp speed. His injury, though, was sustained at a charity golf tournament, where carts move more like snails than "warps."…

He figures that NASCAR will add new rules, making sure that their participants in golf tournaments have designated drivers for their carts. "This may be more important than changing the rules allowing a 'designated putter'," Mort laughed. Oh, but the story gets worse. According to the *Citrus County Chronicle*, Johnson was sprawled on top of the cart when a sharp turn—taken at perhaps 5 MPH—did him in. "What was he doing up there?," Mort questioned. "You're 'sposed to sit under the canopy to stay out of the sun, not on top to get more rays. Sounds to me like the whole kit and caboodle may need Breathalyzer tests. There may be more swigging than swinging going on."

When on his soap box—that's most of the time—Mort claims he won't go anywhere on his golf cart without seat belts and airbags. (So far, no one has questioned—but all have wondered—if he has the only cart in the world so equipped.) And, when he's got a full head of steam, Mort has offered consultant services to help NASCAR with safety issues.

He's convinced that Johnson is the beneficiary of some "blind hog luck," since the accident occurred during "off" season. The wrist should have plenty of time to heal. Oh, he'll miss the X-Games in Paris, but since his right hand is fine, he can still show up there to back-slap and flag-wave if needed.

No, the world is not a complicated place for the few people remaining in the thicket, and that goes double for the foursome seated around the table. The guys finish playing around sundown, having enjoyed many laughs between shuffles. As good-byes are said, one player salivated at the thought of Christmas treats—"sweetening the air from a mile away," as he put it. Another was ignored when he tried to show new pictures of his grandchildren. A third player said of his four grown children: "We have three brilliant daughters and one almost-average son."

Mort jumped on his cart, fastened the seat belt and puttered toward home. He hoped he wouldn't run over something in the evening shadows, or be pursued by a varmint running faster than his cart. He smiled, certain that even if he took a turn too sharp and tumbled to the terra firma, it wouldn't make the newspapers. His mind drifted to Johnson's post-accident news conference, where Mort would have loved to ask, "Other than that, Mr. Johnson, did you enjoy your golf outing?"...

DENOMINATIONAL CORRECTNESS?...

For most of us, it's a perfunctory assignment—way short of "rocket surgery"—like husbands grocery shopping from a wife-prepared list. But EXACTLY what's listed, in the size and amounts shown—nothing more, nothing less. Any deviation requires an explanation, signed by the grocer or his designee. Aunt Maude's instructions were 100% clear. The only difference was that Uncle Mort was to pick up EXACTLY 50 postage stamps at the post office—50—no more and no less. She handed him a $20 bill, telling him to spend the remaining 50 cents to top off the tank in his golf cart.

The old couple had a clever plan concerning holiday greeting cards. They DO NOT send Christmas cards, even though they relish receiving them. If the senders also mail birthday and anniversary cards during the year, they then qualify to receive New Year's greeting cards from Mort and Maude. She writes personal notes on each card sent, wanting to be "the first to wish you a Merry Christmas next year."

Mort was muttering about buying 50 holiday stamps as he entered the post office. (He knows when it is safe to mutter. When Maude is rattling off instructions, he doesn't say a word.) In this case, he knew if there happened to be a stamp or two left over, they could be slapped on envelopes for bills paid by mail.

His smile twisted to a snarl a moment later when the clerk asked, "What denomination?" Face reddening, veins bulging and eyes darting around the lobby as if searching for a soap box, Mort repeated the question: "What denomination? Is that any of the government's business? You government people are taking political correctness too far. Now you're trying to drag the church into your 'denominational correctness' stuff," Mort said.

The clerk thought she had seen and heard it all, but here was a new one to add to the list. She faked a cough, cupping her mouth to conceal outright laughter. Realizing Mort was just getting revved up, she took the easy way out, keeping her mouth shut and her ears open.

"I can get petitions signed at every church in the county," Mort snorted. "Churches will not put up with such government intrusion." Then it dawned on him that he was smack dab in the middle of a government building. For all he knew, hidden devices might be recording every angry word he muttered. In an instant, his tune changed.

"If you must know," Mort softened. "I'll take 8 Baptist, 12 Methodist, 4 Catholic, 6 Church of Christ, 2 Lutheran and 1 Episcopalian. Let's see, that's 33," he figured. He decided to finish out the list with 10 non-denominational and 7 "undecideds," asking if there were any special stamps for "back-sliders."

Then, it was the clerk's turn for head-tilting. Realizing the expression may have been new to her, he defined it, figuring he could count it as missionary work, sort of like handing out tracts. "Back-sliders are professing Christians who take one step forward and two steps back; I know a lot of 'em," Mort explained.

Claiming that backsliding is the bane of all denominations, he said that during the depression era's dry-land farms, the practice even dictates the specifications for clothing orders placed by churches. "Farmers all needed overalls, and preachers knew how to order them," Mort said. "All the overalls were ordered with double-strength knees and quadruple-strength seats."

He went on to say that double-strength knees were needed since "they spend so much time on their knees praying." As to the need for quadruple-strength seats, Mort's take was that "they spend twice as much time backsliding as they do praying."

Then the clerk started laughing, as did the dozen folks in line. There were "high fives" and "Happy New Year" wishes. Mort climbed back on the golf cart, head back into the thicket without stamps and the gas tank untopped. Oh, well. He could handle Maude's rant, and repeat the mission on the morrow….

WHEN PUNS STRIKE OUT...

For the millions of us who live in towns the size of county seats and larger, much of life is taken daily in large gulps. The tiny numbers of folks who'd never willingly give up living away from it all often have different perspectives. For them, news oozes into the thicket like sorghum syrup from a cold jug. They pick the news bits that strike their fancy.

They choose their own pace, caring not their lives are devoid of one-hour photo processing. In fact, they still call cameras "Kodaks," and remember as if yesterday the many times they mailed roll film out of state for processing. Weeks would pass, fruitless trips to the mailbox made and prayers offered that photos shot during the holiday season would arrive before the NEXT holiday.

Digression—that slippery slope—may be forgiven if admitted within three paragraphs. Consider yourself apprised. The longer we live, the more side roads beckon. I try to stay on the pavement, but keep in mind that I've learned from the master—Mort loves the side roads, too.

When he phoned recently, he was breathless, explaining that he had just three minutes left on his calling card, so he needed "to do all the talking." (Dominating conversations, of course, is nothing new to Mort.)

"I'm going to home in on Texas Tech Basketball Coach Bobby Knight, Texas Governor Rick Perry and a pun contest I didn't win," he began. I had no clue where the conversation was going, but was semi-eager to learn, and Mort was totally eager to enlighten. This had to be one of his most random of days.

He asked if I'd read about the Big 12 boss coming down with a reprimand on Coach Knight for berating a game official. He allowed no time for a simple "yes" answer, rolling on as if he was certain I knew, and he was right. I knew. Reprimanding Coach Knight is like adding another quill to a porcupine. It was a "keen observation," I wanted to say, but was cut off after "keen."

Then he zeroed in on the Texas lottery, explaining it this way: "If I wanted to win the lottery, I'd just raise the window," Mort said. "The odds of buying a winning ticket and one blowing in through the window are about the same."

He didn't figure Governor Perry had much chance of gaining public support for his new proposal to sell the lottery operation to a private concern. "I understand the odds of winning the lottery jackpot in Texas are one in 26 million," he mentioned. "And I'd say the governor faces about the same odds in getting a majority of folks to agree with him on selling the lottery." Mort's calling card was about to belly-up in less than one minute. We both knew it. It had crossed my mind that if the call ended in mid-sentence, we might have to drive down to the thicket to find out about the pun contest Mort DIDN'T win. (I didn't even know that my uncle liked puns, much less ever composed any. We live and learn.)

His speaking pace went from a "southern slow" to a "yankee hurry." He was challenged by a pun-writing contest that offered nice prizes, including shotguns, fishing gear and camping equipment. Putting on his thinking cap, he tried hard to follow instructions carefully. "They said entries had better chances if at least 10 puns were submitted, so that's what I did," Mort began.

With seconds left, Mort's voice lowered in sadness. Hurriedly, he explained how he'd spent the better part of a week writing what he thought were 10 good puns. Since Maude helped him "smooth 'em out," he thought surely at least one would win. "But no pun in ten did." (With that, the phone card expired, so Mort didn't hear my laughter peak on the laugh meter.)...

ON THE SUBJECT OF BEST FRIENDS...

Mort has a way of showing up at the most unexpected times. When he skids to a stop with his golf cart smoking and takes the porch steps two at a time, it usually means one or all of the following: 1) Aunt Maude has had enough, suggesting—if only in body language—that Mort might want to go to town for awhile, 2) The fish aren't biting or 3) Anger has reached a boiling point, and he's ready to ingest tin foil and spit out roofing nails.

Saturday morning, it was "all of the above." Maude was busy with spring planting, an annual project far too exacting to interest Mort. Depth and placement of seeds bored him greatly, and she had dozens of other "musts" if he were to help out.

His sentences came out in gasps. Within seconds, he was venting on state legislators, figuring they may be distant kin of Will Rogers, since "they never met a tangent they didn't like." Then, he paused to make coffee, filling the pot to the 10-cup line, so I knew I'd better settle in for a heap of listening. "It don't take much water to make good coffee," Mort opined.

He conceded that many legislators had good raisin', but somehow start "majoring in minors" once they reach Austin, plunging "full bore" into minutiae that doesn't need laws, just a "heavy coat of common sense." On this day, he was in a snit about new laws aimed at dog owners. "Lawmakers' priorities are rarely impeccable, and giving dogs a bad time is about as 'peccable' as it gets," Mort said. He figures canines are now under siege, and they probably weren't even consulted when the "man's best friend" was coined.

"One of these days, dogs are going to demand a recount, and then folks will realize this friendship thing is a one-sided deal," Mort snorted. “If canines vote, we’ll be lucky if they consider us mere acquaintances.”

He feels they have many reasons to be peeved, claiming they’re being served tainted food and all tangled up in leash laws. “Shouldn’t happen to a dog,” he kidded. He wasn’t through, chomping at the bits to continue a litany of other front-burner items that had many verses.

Mort mentioned topics of poverty, immigration, environment, energy, school finance and much more. But taking center stage with him was legislation underscoring that dogs’ bites are always worse than their barks. He unfurled stacks of proposed legislation aimed at dog owners. It shined light into darkest corners, including “what they knew and when they knew it” gossip.

Severity of punishment would no longer hang on “first-bite” details. It would now include detailed historical information, such as the date of each dog’s first fang-showing. “Could be that some dog owners will be so scared, they’ll muzzle their pets all the time instead of risk litigation and the possibility of a felony conviction, hefty fines and even jail time,” Mort explained. He paused to stroke Ole Bullet, his hound dog that often accompanied him into town, perched on the passenger side of the golf cart.

“I really love dogs,” Mort said. “And they’re due a fair shake. Bullet helps me a bunch and is as smart as a whip.” He told about a heated argument a few days earlier with a farmer who maintained that pigs are smarter than dogs. “Ain’t no way,” Mort swore. “I ain’t never seen no seeing-eye pig." (Bullet nudged me, making sure I recognized this as a cue to laugh.)

Mort shifted gears, opting to reflect on bygone years instead of blistering the government for current faults. He recalled the depression era, when neighbors got rid of their dogs because food was so scarce. Mort urged them to simply feed the dogs turnip greens. When his friends said their dogs wouldn't eat turnip greens, he responded, "Mine wouldn't either the first three weeks."

As he poured his final cup of coffee, I asked Mort if he'd heard about the new Internet contest called *American Idol, Dog Version.* Entries were expected from throughout the nation. Mort wanted to know if the contest had the approval of the legislature. I glanced at Bullet, who was flossing his teeth. Then, he started howling a tune that sounded much like *How Much is that Doggie in the Window?...*

MY UNCLE IN MOURNING...

When I drive in East Texas, my car, like a horse headed for the barn, veers toward the thicket. Mort and Maude have lived there all their lives in the deepest part, right next to the swamp. Their setting is as rural as it gets. No one passes their house going to town. I usually stop by to say "hello;" it is something of a joint greeting, offered with feelings of both obligation and curiosity. This day, Maude was putting new elastic in Mort's black arm bands—the ones she made for him years ago when it became obvious that he liked to wear his sadness on his sleeves. "I just wish he'd quit wearing them to the general store," Maude said. "Guys there keep snappin' 'em, pokin' fun at him for taking sports too seriously." She said her hubby was in post-season mourning for the Dallas Mavericks and early-season sadness for the Texas Rangers. For Mort, the arm bands signify a heart at half-staff.

I dreaded the prospect of hearing his harangues, but felt obliged to look for him out back, where he was fiddling with his golf cart. (He would have taken a dim view of my leaving without at least a quick "hello.")

Had things been going well, he would have bragged on a flour sack half-full of crawdads. He would have joked that the crawly creatures are suckers for raw bacon, and how they don't notice the kite string that will lift them from the shallows.

On previous visits, he licked his lips, talking about what wonderful gumbo Maude had prepared for lunch. Then, he'd abruptly change the subject, saying, "If I think about gumbo, my mouth starts watering, and I don't want to dilute it none." This day, he started talking straight way about the Mavericks and Rangers.

He spoke of how fortunate he was to see games on his 12-inch black and white TV. "I think it would have been too painful to watch Dallas' pitiful play on a big screen in color," he winced. Further, he was weary of hearing Texas Ranger ads touting baseball, particularly the one with the tagline: "You could use some baseball." He thinks the ad writers are 180 degrees off on this one. "The way the Rangers are playing, that's the message fans should be sending to management," he suggested.

Mort said he would wear the black arm bands all summer, eager to tell his friends about the adornment. Most of his conversations will be at the little league field a few miles away. There, kids play for free, are loyal to their teams and feel fully rewarded, win or lose, if they get snow cones at games' ends. "There's much to be said for amateur sports, " he asserted.

He told me stories he'd heard at the little league field a night earlier. "We grandparents got off the subject of baseball to unlikely names for churches," my uncle said. "One mentioned 'Little Hope Baptist Church' near Tyler, and another spoke of 'Halfway Baptist Church,' equidistant between Plainview and Olton."

One grandma stayed on the church theme. Her five-year-old grandson overheard a conversation about "pounding the preacher." She explained that church members offer gifts of staples like flour, sugar and corn meal—foodstuff measured in pounds—to welcome the new parson and his family. The grandson was present for his first sermon, and was not impressed. Breaking silence on the way home, the youngster said, "Maybe an 'ouncing' would have been enough."…

TRUTH IN LABELING & 70TH ANNIVERSARY CRUISE

Mort's blood pressure rarely changes. Resolved to life at its simplest, he keeps his cool. And he's made it for more than 70 years without air-conditioning, with most food raised in his backyard garden in the thicket. Game and fish, mostly fried, have provided protein, and a 50-foot antenna drags in enough signal for a fair picture on his 12-inch, generator-powered TV. He is, one could correctly surmise, as current as he wants to be.

He's rarely riled, and words like "cholesterol" and "trans-fat" have crossed neither mind nor tongue. When he discusses "high definition," he points to his dictionary up on the top shelf of the bookcase.

When life has him buffaloed, he takes his dogs on an all-night hunt. Or, if time is short, he skips rocks across the river. I asked him once if he ever jogs. "Nope," he answered. "I get my exercise serving as pallbearer for my friends who jog." And, when nobody's dying, he says he can always "jump to conclusions."

Mentioning his dogs called to mind his recollection of seeing Elvis Presley early in the singer's career when he appeared in Tyler. "He was wriggling all over the stage at the Oil Palace," Mort said. "I hope he makes plenty of money so he can spend every other day at the chiropractor's office."...

During our visit, Mort reminded me that he and Aunt Maude have a 70th wedding anniversary coming up. He said she's always wanted to take a cruise, so this might be a good time to take her. I concurred, offering to drive them to the cruise port. I easily envisioned their taking to cruising like viewers to *Duck Dynasty*. He seems always to be the "designated talker," so on the ship, he was bound to find captive audiences.

Still, he seemed most interested when I recounted details of our cruise aboard the Wind Surf, a vessel with "MSY" designation—

motorized sailing yacht. He cocked his head with heightened interest when I spoke of the magnificent churches in Barcelona. There, one has been "under construction" since the 1880s, with completion in sight by 2030. "Man, that's a long time to be paying out a building pledge," he joked....

He asked why a sailing ship needs motors. I explained that they are helpful when the wind doesn't blow, or if it's from the wrong direction. "On our route from Lisbon to Barcelona, we faced strong headwinds for six straight days," I explained. "We wondered if we'd see the sails at all, but on day seven, the captain said he would "order them up no matter what, even if it meant going backwards." He said he was not consulted when the vessel was pictured on colorful brochures with billowing sails that guests expected to see during the cruise.

Mort seemed interested in my comment that cruising broadens understanding as well as horizons. Old-fashioned goodness can be found in many places when eyes are kept peeled. When our ship docked at the beautiful island of Malaga, we noticed several teens kicking a soccer ball alongside the boat. Later in the evening, half a dozen crew members with rescue poles acted quickly when the ball wound up in the drink. As it was drifting away, instead of scolding the kids for playing on the dock, they fetched the ball, returning it to the teens, and their game continued.

It was a magical moment of international good will, and we savored it, watching ship personnel from the Philippines and Indonesia helping Spanish youngsters keep the ball in play—and them off the streets. Yes, Uncle Mort agreed that a cruise might be a great way to mark 70 years of marriage….

PROPHET IN HIS OWN MIND…

When Mort is wrong, it usually takes a long time to get him to the mat, and when he finally "hollers uncle," it is under his breath. For decades, he's poked fun at kinfolks trying to grub out a living in West Texas. "About all you can count on out there are the wind blowing and mesquite trees growing," he has kidded, urging them to join him and Maude in the thicket.

Here lately, though, he's grown quiet. The wind he criticized is now producing electricity from wind turbines attached to towers erected on the mesas, and researchers now think mesquite trees are potential automobile fuel sources. Uncle Mort says it'll seem strange calculating miles per cord instead of miles per gallon. Some of his West Texas relatives dream of cashing in on windmills and mesquites. And they're pondering the possibility of changing the name of their neighborhood—from Billy Goat Hill to Angora Knoll.

Mort and Maude make it to the senior citizens' center occasionally. She leaned heavily on him recently to make the trip, mentioning they could both do well to visit on "salad luncheon day." He agreed, adding that he wanted to be on the safe side, so he'd ask them to "hold the E-coli." It may have been more than the prospect of salad attracted him. It also was "nose and ear hair maintenance day."

One day, longtime Houston Oilers Coach O. A. (Bum) Phillips spoke at the center. "I had thousands of fans who loved me in Houston," he said. "Unfortunately, one of them was NOT the owner!" Talking about rushing star Earl Campbell, he mentioned a sports writer pointing out that he failed to complete a one-mile run one day in practice, and what did Bum plan to do about it? "I won't ask him to carry the ball when it's third down and a mile to go."...

ON THE LOOKOUT FOR JOKES...

Mort is forever bragging that he's all-around town for all-around service. Sounds like a cure-all, or at least a delivery service. In his stumbles, though, he chances across some mighty unusual situations, some almost crying out to be "storied."

Last deer season, he saw three fellows on a hunt. A slain deer lay nearby, and they were arguing heatedly about which hunter fired the fatal shot. Mort stopped by and examined the animal, asking, "If one of you is a preacher, I can tell you straightway that he's the one who brought the deer down."

Sure enough, one of the hunters admitted, "Yes, I'm a long-time preacher of the gospel." But, he wanted to know how his being a man of the cloth would be a clue that he also was the marksman that felled the deer.

"Easy enough," Mort said, "The shot—like your sermons—went in one ear and out the other." In Fannie Flagg's *Fried Green Tomatoes*, the little Alabama town of Whistle Stop seems like a place where everything goes 'pert near right, almost never bad wrong, and food is served up fresh and fried at the café. In the book and movie, the community was aflutter about rumors of a new store coming to town, leading one character to mention that if they could get a picture show, they'd "never have to go into Birmingham."

Well, the thicket—a community with only a general store and rural services" so primitive the village's name doesn't even start with a capital letter—is kept "stirred up" by the Walter Mitty-like world of my Uncle Mort. He feels comfortable spending big chunks of time each day bragging about whatever to anyone who'll listen. Most visitors to the area stop at the general store to ask directions. Few arrive there "on purpose."

Such was the case a while back as Mort motored toward the store. A cloud of dust was overtaking him from the rear, kicked up by three motorcyclists who looked mightily like "Hell's Angels," or at least novices in training.

"I was rolling to a stop, and the three guys parked their bikes 'circle like' round my cart, snatching bandannas from their heads to hold over their noses until the dust settled," Mort said. "When I cleared the dust from my eyes, I couldn't believe the size of these guys. If any two of 'em had stepped on a scale with a half-ton limit, it would have tilted," he joked. "They weren't 'broad of beam,' they were 'broadest of beam'." He avowed the skin of three cows went for their leathers, and their bikes were outfitted with Mack truck springs and industrial strength tires.

The bikers went inside, heading for the soft drink machine; they chug-a-lugged, speaking in a brogue rarely heard in East Texas. Thinking them to be Scots, Mort asked, "Do you gents happen to be from Scotland?" One of 'em, a corrective sort, answered, "Man, it's Wales. It's Wales."

"Beggin' your pardon, sir," Mort offered. "I'll ask the question again. Are you whales from Scotland?....Mort chortled heartily—maybe the most robust laughter since he stumbled into an unlikely joint meeting of the Masons and Knights of Columbus. That's when he caught them red-handed—gathered in record numbers to swap secrets!...

ABOUT THOSE BOWL GAMES...

A proven survivor of primitive life in the thicket, Mort sent Thanksgiving greetings in a note delivered by the bread truck driver who lives in our neighborhood. I knew Mort would call around the first of the year, if for no other reason than to re-cap the bowl games. Sure enough, when the new year was but a few hours old, he called.

"Most of the games were as predictable as the sunrise," Mort opined, zeroing in on the University of Texas game. There, a young man said to be a member of the UT "football operation staff," treated Longhorn Coach Mack Brown like a step-dad. Mort re-set the scene, where the live ball was bouncing crazily toward the UT sideline.

"That kid, who turned out to be the coach's step-son, has been playing too much fantasy football," Mort laughed. My uncle joined the rest of us in amazement as the staffer inched toward the ball, as if to "shoo" it away from the sidelines, toward the eager clutches of a Longhorn player.

Officials called on replay cameras—for 12 minutes, no less—to determine if he touched it. The point should be forever moot. The offender, along with several coaches and dozens of players, accompanied him on the field of play. "I blame the NCAA for the kid's boo-boo," Mort asserted. "Rules are rules. When coaches or players cross restraining lines, officials should flag 'em for unsportsmanlike conduct. Forget the warning stuff."

Mort said that teams might need to consider hiring a coach to monitor restraining line encroachment. "This reminds me of what the late Abe Lemons said years ago when he wanted to name two additional members to his coaching staff," my uncle laughed. "Lemons, one of the most colorful of all basketball coaches, claimed what his team really needed were a psychologist and a hair dresser."

My uncle switched gears. He was still talking football, but now about a UT-OU game played in Dallas a half-century ago. Only in recent years has Mort been able to laugh about the escapade, when all was in order for him to be an eyewitness to the Longhorns' battle with the Sooners.

For years on end, he had listened to the game described expertly by the late Kern Tipps, arguably radio's all-time best football analyst. Mort's friends in the thicket, tired of hearing of his hopes to one day see the game, took up a collection.

They bought him a train ticket, booked a hotel room and provided a game ticket. Upon Mort's arrival in Dallas, revelry had already begun. It was everywhere, and he was an immediate joyful participant. He wobbled toward his hotel when the hour already was wee.

When he waked, the clock showed 9 a.m. He thought there to be plenty of time for room service breakfast and a quick read of the Saturday morning newspaper. A half-hour passed. Mort was flustered; he called room service again, asking why it took so long to scramble eggs. "Oh, we've got the eggs ready," the attendant answered. "But SATURDAY papers aren't easy to find on SUNDAY mornings."…

THE PAPARAZZI IN THE THICKET…

Sometimes phone calls from my Uncle Mort call for considerable dissection. A recent one did when he asked if the word "paparazzi" is singular or plural. It seemed to me that an "I'm not sure" answer might be safest.

"It's definitely plural," he cackled, adding that there's "no need for singular designation for meddling photographers who travel in packs." Again, he was certain that his foresight is better than the collective 20/20 hindsight of the rest of us. "If you ever run into just one paparazzo, let me know," said my uncle before turning serious.

"We learned how to handle those guys when they showed up at Cut 'N Shoot 50 years ago," Mort said. "They thought they'd barge in here to get the goods on good-old-boy Roy Harris when he was training for the world heavyweight boxing championship." He said none of the "stalkarazzi" had ever been in East Texas, and got so interested in frog-gigging that they forgot all about why they were there in the first place.

Rambling continued. (Those lacking sensitivity might call it babbling.) He spoke of organizing East Texas plumbers as honorary members of the Tony Romo Fan Club. There were audible groans when he announced the name: "Romo Rooters." (They thought this was nearly as bad as a survey he'd conducted earlier concerning support for Cowboy Marion Barber. He called it "The Barber Poll."

Then, Mort waxed poetic, quoting his altered version of late sportswriter Grantland Rice's poem. Here's the way he put it: "For when the One Great Scorer comes to write 'against the Cowboys' names, he marks down that they won or lost, and how Romo played the game."

A BRIDGE NOT TAKEN
Locals aren't scared of warning: Load Limit: 1 Tractor or 2 Golf Carts. Paparazzi may decide to swim across...

PAID POLITICAL QUACK?...

To be wakened an hour before alarms jangle on the first day we've "sprung forward" to Daylight Savings Time borders on the inhumane. Slumber interruption at an hour when sleep is deepest is about as welcome as an FAA inspector at a stockholders' meeting of Southwest Airlines. And it's even worse when the raucous noise seems comparable to the sound emitted by the AFLAC duck with one foot in a mud puddle and the other in a light socket.

I wobbled to the window, and there Mort stood—on top of his golf cart—both jaws puffed as he blasted away on a duck call. Headphones were dangling from the canopy, and eight-track tape players were still in their boxes. Signs were plastered all over the cart reading: "Honk if you're tired of political campaign commercials."

It was a sight equal to the farmer's wife spotting the three blind mice. Mort's vehicle of choice has always looked like what it is—a golf cart. He'd always pat it, kick a tire and then brag on miles per cup of gasoline. This day, it was dusty, looking like it had been used in too many Shrine parades.

"I know it's early, nephew," he began. "But when I see a clear path to a fast buck, I have to get high behind." (Aunt Maude, back at home in the thicket, claims her hubby's "fast buck" shenanigans typically turn into plug nickels, and slow ones, at that.)

He asked if I'm as tired of radio and TV pitches from political candidates as he is. My mind, reeling with the ongoing spiels that clog the airways, was weary. I was only half awake, but my emphatic answer was easy: "Yes!" I told him of my regret that presidential elections fall on leap years, giving all candidates an extra 24 hours to spend gazillions of advertising dollars. Mort nodded knowingly. "And there's so much sameness in those 30-second appeals."

Yep, we learn the names of campaign treasurers by heart, and that the candidates always smile, say their names and admit they've "approved the message." Who cares who the treasurers are, and should message approval be determined by voters instead of candidates?" Mort wondered.

"I was ear-deep in paid political announcements the other day, but thankfully, the very next ad struck my fancy," my uncle said. "It was for a duck call so authentic that it attracts decoys." That explained the raucous noise that had awakened me, but it didn't explain the headphones and tape players. "I wanted to strike while the iron is hot, and that's why I'm here early today," he sheepishly continued. "I need your help."

Slowly, the picture was clearing. Mort explained how he'd "made a killing" on eBay, getting dozens of headphones and eight-track players for a quarter each. "When I heard about that duck call, it came to me in a flash what to do," he bragged. At this juncture, what he thought he needed was a repetitious recording of the duck call on eight-track tape. Our fingers "did the walking" through the telephone Yellow Pages.

"The AFLAC people are no dummies," Mort joked. "They've figured out that a majority of folks truly enjoy hearing duck quacks." Mort's plan, of course, was to peddle the "quacking tapes" to people whose tolerance for political announcements was used up. He figured people would stop on the highway, if not out of curiously, perhaps—just perhaps—they really enjoyed hearing ducks quacking repeatedly. Anything is better than political ads, he reasoned.

"I'm gonna offer a package deal of a 'quacking tape' with an eight-track player, both for $20," he beamed. Back in the thicket, Maude was wincing at this, another hair-brained Mort deal. Or, she may simply have shrugged and gone back to bed….

SLIMMEST OF ODDS...

There's nothing to support it, but a fascinating contention looms nonetheless. Lottery critics say if you want to win the lottery, you need to buy lots and lots of tickets, even if one has to borrow the cash to do it. Dreamers, we mortals be, always fantasizing whether we could strike just the right pose in the picture showing the 10-million-dollar winner. Odds may be similar on how a museum accident may lead to a man's decision to remove a wedding ring he's worn for 80 years.

The gent is my Uncle Mort, who chanced to read Steve Blow's column in *The Dallas Morning News* despite it not being on his Sunday afternoon agenda to do so. He was on his golf cart—headed for the general store on a "non-agenda" mission. He figured there'd be enough cohorts present to discuss global warming, immigration and/or dwindling whooping crane numbers. (At a previous general store confab, his foursome recommended padding the numbers simply by teaching regular cranes to whoop.) Probably, though, the afternoon would be whiled away at the domino table.

He claims he was "zooming" along at about 10 MPH—10 times faster than a cruise ship in tow—when a newspaper blown from a speeding convertible shrouded his face.

Mort easily sputtered to a stop on the shoulder of the road. He unrolled the newspaper from his noggin, and a column headline caught his eye: "Scary finger injury has a ring of truth." Columnist Blow explained how a visitor to Dallas' Perot Museum of Nature and Science lost a ring finger during a vertical jump to determine how participants "measure up" to athletes' leaps. His wedding ring caught on something. He came down, but his finger didn't.

Blow went on to tell of several mishaps each month where wedding rings are caught in machinery, on basketball goals or numerous other objects. This set Mort to worrying; "what ifs" crowded his mind. No longer interested in seeing his buddies, he headed back home. Perusing an encyclopedia, he learned that women have worn wedding rings for centuries, but grooms have commonly worn them only since the end of World War II.

He was pretty sure he could remember to avoid taking vertical jumps in museums, but he feared getting his ring caught in other ways—maybe while pitching horseshoes, baiting fish hooks, saddling horses, sky diving from planes or repairing his golf cart. How, though, could he convince Maude that continuing to wear his wedding ring could be hazardous to his health?

He likewise questioned himself. Would he feel "less married"? (Mort always claimed that he "wrote the Constitution for his marriage," but that he's accepted all of Maude's amendments.)

He began by showing her the column. They "tsk/tsked" in unison, shocked that so many accidents each month claim ring fingers. As they nodded in agreement about possible dangers, Mort decided it was the right time to seek permission to remove his wedding ring and keep it forthwith in their lock box. He was surprised how quickly she agreed. However, she added one proviso: His nose ring stays in place 'til death do they part.

It's common for Mort to worry about things about things over which he has no control. He's always enjoyed telling about a woman on the adjoining farm who is a world-class worrier. Years ago, she fretted greatly about visiting San Francisco, afraid the fog would prevent her seeing the Golden Gate Bridge, the bay air wouldn't be fit to breathe and that she might get hurt riding the cable car.

Well, she saw the bridge perfectly, and she took deep breaths of crisp bay air. Yet, she feared getting on the cable car. If her foot chanced to contact the rail, would she be electrocuted? A young Californian explained that unless she swung her other leg over the wire above, she had nothing to worry about.. .

Mort smiled, mostly at the thought of his neighbor's silliness, but also at his own. How could he ever entertain the possibility of putting his wedding ring away? He'd take his chances on continuing to wear it. That's a heap better than riling Maude, who at such time might vow, "With this ring, I thee sue."

He headed back to the general store, hoping there'd be one laggard there ripe for a "clock-cleaning" in checkers….

NEW THOUGHTS FROM AN OLD GUY…

I'm guessing my uncle's "forward thinking" for the new year more likely is akin to "slumgullion stew," or simply a "hodgepodge" of thoughts he's carried forward. His ideas are a "mish-mash" of miscellaneous ingredients rolled together, some of 'em dating back a half-century or so. Included in the current mulling of my old uncle are truths, half-truths, what he's heard, what he *thinks* he's heard, and "hoopla" about government health insurance. Altogether, they are light years away from reality. "Slumgullion" fits about as well as anything. Again this year, truth is stranger than fiction, and it's growing ever tougher to tell 'em apart. Mort believes the man passing himself off as a hand-signer for the deaf at the Mandela funeral may deserve the prize for "most convincing."

"Millions believed he was 'true-ern blue,'" Mort claims. "Turns out, his left hand didn't know what his right was doing, and vice versa. He was mighty convincing, though, so surely there's a spot for him in the front office of the Dallas Cowboys." He compared the signer with a TV wrestling showman from the 1950s called "Gorgeous George." Mort claims the late wrestler was as handy with clever lines as the signer was with hand motions. "GG," his carefully-coiffed dyed blonde locks always in place and glitzy well before Liberace came along, claimed: "I don't think I'm the best wrestler who ever lived…I don't think I'm the most handsome man on the planet…And I don't think I'm the smartest man who ever lived—BUT, what's my opinion against millions of others?"

On a dime—the coin on which Uncle Mort always turns—he asked me if I knew how he could contact the ad people at *Duck Dynasty*. I suggested that he try Googling them. (He probably thought my wife and I visited their place during a recent visit to Louisiana.)

"I've got an idea they can build a segment on--or maybe turn into a product--that might sell millions," he claimed. Then, he follows with, "Don't you want to know what it is?" I am trapped, with little choice but to ask. "I'm working on a duck call so authentic it attracts decoys," he claimed. "That ought to line up real straight with *Duck Dynasty*." It was pointless to challenge him; maybe he really is working on such a duck call. However, the ticket for this idea was punched by my friend, C. R. (Choc) Hutcheson in Lubbock.

With his yarn, he was awarded first place in the Burlington, Wisconsin, Liars' Club Contest back in 1961. Paraphrased, here's what is written on the certificate on the wall in his home: "For years I have been working to perfect a duck call. The first time I blew it, ducks swarmed in from all directions; the sky was black with them. I cut loose with my pump gun, killing my limit of six ducks with six shots. What is so strange about that, you say? Well, when I picked up those ducks, three of 'em were decoys!"

Muttering about the government's claim to offer low-cost group insurance, Mort said it only applies if the whole group gets sick. Then, he told me about helping Maude make lye soap out back of the house in a huge wash pot. "I'm proudest of the label," he bragged. "Our soap is both bacterial and anti-bacterial, whichever you want it to be." I asked him how it could be both.

"Glad you asked, nephew. The researchers can't decide, either. Some scream 'bacterial' is the way to go, and others are just as vocal for 'antibacterial.' I'll swear that no bacteria have been added. My escape clause will be 'except for the germs stirred up on the dirt road from cars driving past the hog pen.'"

Few people ever argue with Uncle Mort. It's just not worth it. My guess, though, is that before he's gone very far into the new year, he'll wash his hands of the lye soap project, perhaps favoring new lyrics for a song to help determine how long we should wash. "I know the 'Happy Birthday Song' is working pretty well, but it's really hard to remember how many verses to sing," he chuckled….

AUNT MAUDE IN DREAMLAND...

The greeting card people missed quite a photo op a few nights ago down in the thicket. The sun was surrendering to twilight. The darkening sky was aflame in orange on the horizon, and in the thicket, azaleas ruled. At their peak in blossoms and fragrance, they provided a colorful backdrop for Uncle Mort and Aunt Maude. The old couple was whiling away the final wisp of daylight in their porch swing with talk exceedingly small.

Swaying slowly, they took in the wonder of spring flowers and sweet smells of the season. Reflective on 80 years of marriage, they chatted, their voices soft against a backdrop of frogs croaking in chorus and armies of chirping crickets. Fireflies, as if in recess for leisurely games of tag in flight, lazily drifted in and out among Aunt Maude's prize-winning daffodils. The blossoms have hung around longer than usual this year, but they never outlive their welcome. "In your wildest dreams, did you ever expect to wind up with a husband like me?" Mort asked. "You've never been in any of my *wildest* dreams," she answered.

Maude often describes her hubby as being "misdirected." (This is preferable to saying he doesn't have a clue.) A while back, she sent him into town with a grocery list. He found all the items, save one. He couldn't find EVOO, and, in the grocery store as on the highway, could hardly bring himself to ask for help. The store manager scratched his head; he wasn't even sure they stock EVOO. Then, it dawned on him what Maude needed for the recipe: extra virgin olive oil. Neither one has spent much time in front of the TV watching the food channel.

Oh, that woman has always had a mind of her own, and it's usually set in concrete. Years ago, she hired babysitters to care for their youngsters so she could go to the daycare center to voluntarily babysit children whose mothers hired out in the neighborhood to babysit. Finally, she realized that it was a losing deal. In the early going, cooking wasn't her thing. "Once she had a 24-hour virus, and the next day received a get-well card from McDonald's," Mort recalls.

She's always been a top-notch opportunist, first in line when such positioning counts. In recent years, she has been first in line at the courthouse on the day of the couple's wedding anniversary. "Never hurts to check," Maude maintains, "to see if our marriage license has expired."

The couple finds all the ingredients for happiness in the thicket. Maude has her garden and flowers, has taken to healthy cooking in recent years and loves to quilt and crochet. "And any day I can get Mort out of the house, whether he's fishing, puttering around out back or running around the thicket in his golf cart is a good day," she laughs. Often, of course, Mort goes far afield on the cart, sometimes even to the airport.

These days, Mort is deeply interested in safety issues pitting the airlines and the FAA. Barking by officials on both sides of the issue has reached high decibels. Mort is listening carefully and taking notes, wondering who knew what and when they knew it.

Oh, he doesn't fly, but Oscar, his neighbor one farm over, does. Oscar plays a tuba in a shrine band that parades about all over the country. Mort often volunteers for "pickup and delivery" to the airport. What a pair they make, Mort in the driver's seat blowing on his duck call, and Oscar on the back seat "oompahing" tuba accompaniment.

Mort thinks the issue of airline safety is due more scrutiny. "When Oscar was due back the other day, I called the airline to get arrival information," Mort said. "The lady asked me which arrival information I wanted—the time or the odds." Upon arrival, Oscar was wide-eyed. "Before I boarded, I downed two double/double mocha-mochas," he laughed. "I wanted to be so wired that I wouldn't worry about the plane's wiring."

After the landing, they waited a full 30 minutes for the tuba to appear on the luggage carousel. It never did. While they were completing the missing baggage claim, it was found on the plane. "It had fallen into a crack in the fuselage," Mort said. "And just think—a few weeks ago, airline honchos thought paying fuel bills was their biggest challenge….

UNCLE MORT AND SILVER LININGS...

When he's really steamed, my uncle becomes a different person. His glasses fog over, his voice shakes, and Aunt Maude fears his blow-up might boil into a full-scale smothering spell. During his phone call from the thicket, I heard a crackling voice that might have reached 8.5 on the Richter Scale. It would have melted butter on a day-old waffle.

His shape wasn't bent out by high gasoline prices. Or the presidential race. Or the wretched three-digit temperatures on the weather charts. His anger wasn't centered on global warming, world hunger or wars across the seas.

He was heated up because of threats to eliminate a heat source that he says should have millions of Americans riled up. "When the government tells us not to eat jalapeños, school is out, last straws are broken, and Katy's door is plumb 'unbarred,'" my uncle fumed.

He claimed scriptural backing. "Man don't live by bread alone, but he might make it if you throw in jalapeños," he chuckled, admitting that he'd paraphrased a bit. There was a long pause, then a big sigh. I instantly sensed that the "regular Mort" was back on the line. "My brain's whipping up a great plan that can make me a bunch of cash," he bragged.

"It'll take more than a salmonella scare to shoot down this scheme," Mort said. (In the background, Aunt Maude winced. When her old hubby schemes, she knows that a boondoggle usually isn't far behind.)

Mort said that a few days back, when tomatoes were thought to be sources of salmonella, he bought a boatload of green ones "on the cheap." His plan? Trade the tomatoes for a load of jalapeños offered in "fire sales" down South. "I'm gonna scrub 'em up, and then scrub 'em down, and they'll bring five bucks apiece when advertised as being both disease-free and organic," he predicted. Texans ARE going to have their jalapeños.

Uncle Mort, known for subject-changing--sometimes between syllables--started rambling. Next, he took on the feds, laughing about the plan to retire one-dollar bills in favor of one-dollar coins. "It's costing the government nearly two cents to make a penny and close to a dime to make a nickel, so no telling how much it'll wind up costing to make a dollar," he insisted. "Inflation being what it is, maybe a modified expression soon will describe down-and-outers who don't have two dollars to rub together."

He then addressed the Dallas squabble about putting the zoo's 22-year-old elephant out to pasture. One suggestion was to accept the offer to send the elephant to Tennessee. "If they do, Al Gore might re-route the elephant to Mexico," Mort said. The old-timer also had a unique "take" on Starbucks' shuttering 600 stores, just when he'd "learned to pronounce a few of the drinks' names."

What's the deal on all this coffee news? Only a few days before the Starbucks' announcement, Procter and Gamble decided to sell its Folgers brand to Smucker's in a $3 billion stock deal. Mort claimed to be "squarely between the horns of a 'ponderment'" about the transaction. (He explained that a "ponderment" differs from a dilemma only in that the latter has a reasonable expectation for resolution.)

He opined thusly: "Smucker's may have waked one day to smell the coffee. And maybe on that same morning, P&G decided that the days are numbered for any of us to have a "best part of waking up."

My uncle then told the story of an eight-year-old neighbor girl who delivered "special coffee" to him and Aunt Maude. He took a sip, noticing a tiny plastic soldier bobbing in the brew. "Wow, this is special coffee," he laughed. "Sure is," the youngster said, "The best part of waking up is *soldiers* in your cup!"

Mort ended the conversation with a quick switch back to jalapeños. He turned serious, bragging about his "new invention" that might vault him into wealth and fame. The new "invention"? Jalapeño popsicles. Mort's always coming up with half-baked notions that make Aunt Maude's hair hurt. This is his first "on a stick" project, however….

ROUND-UP OF REFLECTIONS...

Miscellany rules as summer winds down, and the Olympics heat up. With Beijing's "smogginess" roughly six times that of Los Angeles', it's a good bet that the "condition of air" is a major topic of conversation among Olympic participants. Two women, reportedly members of the USA's curling team, offered hair spray when they heard two others bemoaning a "bad hair day." What a misunderstanding! The complainants were actually lamenting a "bad air day." We should forgive them—words filtered through air masks lack clarity.

Mort often worries about back-burner issues that sometimes aren't even "pilot light warm." Now, he's warning friends that cranes are "headed for extinction."

I challenged him with strong statistical support: "Whooping crane numbers have grown by six fold in three decades." We were on different tracks, as usual. "I'm not talking about cranes that fly," Mort clarified, "I'm talking about cranes that fall."

His friends chuckle when he admits to being "headstrong;" One of his friends said it best: "More than likely, most people in the thicket think Mort may be 'headweak'." For example, he's convinced he knows why the Dallas Cowboys took the train ride from training camp down to San Diego for the season's first exhibition game. "They can blame the loss on 'rail lag,'" he joked, but a five-hour train ride after a loss "feels" much longer.

Mort also informed me that he believes there are three kinds of working men. I braced myself, hardly knowing what to expect. He continued, "There are a few men with their names on buildings, many with their names on their doors or desks, and hoards of us with names stitched on our shirts."

My uncle told me about the preacher who had "hoof and mouth" disease, explaining the parson "refuses to visit and can't preach a lick." Our conversation ended abruptly when it was his turn to shuffle the dominoes….

"Hold the mayo. Hold the mustard. Hold the catsup." Sounds like orders to a short-order cook, right? Wrong! It's the Dallas County sheriff's cancellation of packaged condiments for jail prisoners. With a budget awash in red ink, it's a $150,000 lick at a $6 million shortfall. Historically, similar actions haven't set well with inmates. They've been howling about jail conditions since locks were installed on cell doors. The late Lew Sterrett, for two decades Dallas County Judge whose name now adorns the justice center, had a word for the protestors, in the form of a suggestion: "Those who don't like the Dallas County Jail should commit their crimes in some other county."...

Those crunches we hear all over the country are coming straight from the budget sheets. Most agencies, institutions and organizations show negative balances. The American Ballet Theatre in New York City may be the exception. Its annual budget includes $350,000 for shoes—that's $7,500 per ballerina. It's pointless, I guess, to suggest that they take old shoes to the cobbler. When "pointy-toed" shoes are gone, they're gone....

Our nation cries out for "feel good" stories, and, God be thanked, they're still around. Maybe we should all look harder for "larger than life" figures. Often, unlikely heroes step forward. Consider Neil Sauter, a 24-year-old Michigander who was saluted for completing an 830-mile walk. Earlier this year, he walked across Michigan's Upper and Lower peninsulas. Oh, I failed to mention that this cerebral palsy victim made the walk on stilts. And that he raised $16,000 for United Cerebral Palsy of Michigan....

Accidents in Texas and New York that typically result in obituaries had happy endings. Near Fort Worth, a man survived a 40-foot fall into a hole at a gas field drilling site, and in Manhattan, a 12-year-old girl survived a 14-story fall down a chimney. Firefighter Derek Izzo was lowered into the hole to rescue the "wedged" victim. Sporting a barn door-wide smile when it was clear that the victim had been spared serious injury, he was asked if he drew the assignment because he had the most experience. "Nope, the least seniority," he answered. Authorities in New York said that the youngster lucked out because of the makeup of the final two feet in her 180-foot fall--soot and ashes. Sudden stops rarely are so cushioned….

AN AGELESS WONDER...

When Mort accused me of "dealing loosely with the truth," I knew the facts were stacked heavily in his favor. Were I not in his close circle of kinfolks, the charge might well have been one for bald-faced lying. "You've been writing about me in your column for four years," he blurted. "And from day one, I've been your '90-year-old uncle'."

He opined that it's one thing to round numbers off, but even then, he recommended periodic updating. "Particularly when you missed my age by a couple of years at the git-go," he scolded. "Charlie Brown hung around comic strips for a half-century, 'maturing' from age four to age eight in that period." Adding that he's "not Charlie Brown," he closed the thought with a classic "good grief" exclamation. He threw in an additional comment that some of my columns are like soap operas—where it takes a woman three years to give birth prematurely. He added that it shouldn't matter a whit whether he's a real person or merely a figment of my imagination. He warned me of my duty to "at least get his age right."

I was reminded that July 4th marked another "Mort birthday," and yet another chance to get his age wrong. I half expected him to break out candles. He'd already broken into song, desecrating George M. Cohan's patriotic "Yankee Doodle Dandy" ditty.

When he bragged about being "a real live hero of My Uncle Sam," I was mulling over numerous past references to "my 90-year-old uncle," and I was defenseless. My old dad, describing times in tight places, called it "hubbing it." And I was in a tight place; again my old dad was on target. Mort was right, too; I should always list his age correctly. I pledged to do so in the future. Hoping for a subject change, I asked him about his political feelings.

"I've digested dozens of long speeches at both national conventions," he responded. "Most speakers have 30-minute slots, so they spend the first 15 inspiring us, and the last 15 talking us out of it." Aunt Maude confirmed his claim. "The more he digests, the more indigestion I get," she laughed. Mort is a basic conservative who wants government to defend our shores, deliver our mail and leave us alone, claiming this sobering thought to be entrenched: Every presidential election year, one of the candidates is going to be elected.

He asked what I thought about a growing number of handguns authorized in public schools. "That should give Mary's lamb second thoughts about following her to school," I answered. Mort agreed that pets "making children laugh and play" could quickly transform lambs into scapegoats.

I remember a convenience store, where a sign placed boldly under a one-way mirror worked wonders. It read "An employee holding a sawed-off shotgun stands behind this mirror one night each week. YOU guess which night." At the school, maybe all employees could wear signs, proclaiming that "One of us has a concealed weapon. YOU guess which one."

My uncle asked me about interesting people I'd met recently. Pleasant memories included the soon-to-be second grader who was exceedingly eager to get back into the school grind. "Over the summer, I've forgotten lots of my words I learned last year," he admitted….

DAWNING OF A NEW CENTURY...

Rarely have I heard Uncle Mort so excited. I'm used to his calls with news from his faraway world where country road lifestyles have changed little across the years. I thought he'd give me the rundown of "thicket thinking" on the presidential race, but as usual, I was 180 degrees off course. Behold and lo, he was on a technology kick this time. The "warp and woof" of his litany concerned the "what'll they think of next?" stuff.

When Mort told me a neighbor faces prostate surgery in upcoming days, his voice raised a couple of octaves with these seven words preceding an exclamation point—"And a robot's going to do it!" He was breathless, and I knew that Mort's personal "take" on the procedure would follow just as surely as there is cotton on both ends of Q-Tips.

"Don't jump the gun on me, nephew," he warned. "The last time I saw the doctor, he opened a package of Q-Tips that didn't have cotton on either end." The doctor figured "they rubbed right up against 5 o'clock Friday at the factory."

The patient really wanted to know what Mort thought of such surgery. He's used to offering second, third and fourth opinions—and often well beyond that. "Just make sure the robot's moving parts have seen the business end of a grease gun within the last month and that it has fresh batteries," my uncle suggested. "Be sure to leave your magnets at home, and if 'made in China' is printed on the robot, tell the doctor you'd sooner take your chances with home remedies." Mort's final thoughts were that the robot's parents may have "starred" at the first automated car wash. Maybe his "grease gun reference" has been brain-locked for the past 50 years.

BIRDS IN THE NEWS...

Many is the time I've heard him talk about the thicket visit of the late Al Capp—creator of Li'l' Abner—during the golden days of cartooning. In the final years of his life, the outspoken Capp traveled around the country making speeches, typically answering questions "planted" in the audience. Two favorite queries were whether his wooden leg was bothersome and why he had such a dislike for Jane Fonda. (Capp lost a leg in a trolley accident at age 9, and he was a constant critic of the anti-war activist.)

His unchanging answers were well-known. 1). "My leg's never a problem unless I forget to grease it," and 2). "I have nothing against Jane Fonda. I'd send her a dozen roses tonight if I knew which jail she was in."

On a technology roll, Mort switched to chip implants, warning that if they're sticking them into Arizona cactus and into birds, humans are "bound to be next." I'd read about the Fed's plans to implant electronic chips into the giant Arizona cactus plants to thwart thieves who are digging them up in the dark of night, then re-selling. "If you get a new cactus and your garage door opener goes nuts, the dog starts howling, your pacemaker acts up, or UFO's hover overhead, you'd better abandon desert landscaping pronto," Uncle Mort warned.

The "bird thing" was news to me. Mort was in awe of the migration of plump shorebirds called "godwits," which migrate each year from Alaska to New Zealand. This time, the "wow" was on my end of the phone line. He spoke of how the three-pound birds—some of them with electronic implants—fly NON-STOP to their winter home in New Zealand, monitored all the way by satellite. Some span the 7,242-mile distance in as few as five days, losing half their weight in the process. (Ecologists say that the birds expend energy at 8-10 times the rate they do at rest, easily more than the six-fold output of Tour de France bicyclists, human pace-setters in the energy department.)

"Come spring time, they fly the same route back to Alaska," Mort revealed. "I believe if I was a godwit, I'd just stay in Hawaii year-round, settling for pleasure flights between the islands."

Before we signed off, Mort jumped to acorns. My assumption that it had anything to do with swine or lipstick thereon was dead wrong. "I'm talking about ACORN with capital letters," he said. "It's an acronym, nephew," he mumbled, adding something about how he was "always having to educate me."

A bit miffed, I informed Mort that the probability had not escaped me that folks in this group seem to be big targets for voter fraud, and that the letters stand for "Association of Community Organizations for Reform Now."

"All I know is that ACORN is setting squirrels back a hundred years," my uncle concluded, "And blind hogs even further."...

GOING FOR GOLD...

Stories about survivors of "Black Friday" abound. You know who you are, and you know what I mean. You "bit" on the advertising lure—sinker, line and hook—that you should abandon your bed around 2 a.m. to join the chase. Everyone is out that day after Thanksgiving to save a bundle on gifts as the Christmas shopping season officially begins. My hunch is that you perhaps save a half-bundle, but still have more than half a list to check off 'tween now and the big day.

Uncle Mort called the other night, labeling himself "frenzied" about gift plans for Aunt Maude. They've gone awry. For my uncle to make such an admission is big indeed. His "frenzied" would be comparable to total hysteria for the rest of us. He hates shopping in general and long lines in particular. He figured that a gift of gold would be a wonderful present for his wife of 75 years. "Maude would have loved it," he chirped. "But my dentist put the quietus on it. He said it wouldn't be cost effective to remove my gold tooth."

Mort said there is a "silver lining" in his ill-fated, "gift-on-the-cheap" scheme. "You've mentioned what a great conversation-starter that gold tooth is," the dentist reminded, "but I just don't think a gap there would be nearly as interesting." The doc advised Mort to keep an eye on gold prices, and if they keep on going up, the tooth might make a nice gift for her summer birthday.

Don't expect to see Mort in the shopping lines. At least, not yet. He's going to suggest to Maude that they draw names this year. That way, he's got a 50/50 chance of drawing his own. As we approach the festive season, let's take note of two toy world giants who made their exits this year. What are the odds that founders of companies that manufactured all-time favorite toys would expire months apart?

Dead at 82 was Richard Knerr, inventor of the Hula Hoop, and also claimed by death was Betty James, 90-year-old head of the company that makes the Slinky, an item with gross sales of hundreds of millions of dollars around the globe. Though both toys quickly achieved "must have" status when unleashed on the world more than a half century ago, their origins differ greatly.

The concept for the Slinky was born when a spring from a mechanism on a World War II naval vessel bounced around the deck. The Hula Hoop (sometimes called "hoola hoop") craze didn't blossom until it was manufactured in plastic configuration. Earlier, they were made of bamboo, and popular only in Australia.

Ah, but pages must be turned back much further if we're to learn when the hoops first whirled. A song mentions walking like an Egyptian. Well, I'm here to tell you that researching ABOUT Egyptians isn't easy, either. One could go loopy poring over this stuff. Originally, the hoops were made of twisted grapevines by Egyptian youngsters some 3,000 years ago. More specifically, it is believed the very first ones were fashioned by young Egyptian herdsmen. Once the herds were settled for the night, the guys fought off boredom with fruit of the vine, and eventually the vine itself. It is said that the night air in those olden days was fouled by the odor of cigarettes made of grapevine.

Though historical references are sketchy, it is believed that these creative herdsmen may have concocted the recipe for "Grapette," a soft drink introduced in the 1940s. Egyptian hieroglyphics also reveal passages that were mute across the years until "herd" in the smash Broadway/movie hit, *The Color Purple*. And some musicologists think they may have written several popular songs that made it big in the 20th century, including, *I 'Herd' it through the Grapevine, Deep Purple* and *Flying Purple People Eater.* Enough already! Too much, in fact. All these

Egyptian "facts" could be the stuff of dreams. Or maybe I'm just recalling spiels reeled off by Uncle Mort. They said he was awful bad about smoking grapevines back in the day….

UNCLE MORT TO THE RESCUE…

Aunt Maude, a woman of few words, decided long ago that life is more pleasant if she lets Uncle Mort handle talkin' for the two of 'em. She understands him to the degree that he can be understood and ignores the rest. A while back, her passing observation explained much about her hubby's storehouse of opinions that often fly headlong into the face of facts. It all goes back to the day of his birth," Maude said. "Mort was delivered by an absent-minded doctor who held him up by his hands and spanked his face."

My aunt's theory explains a great deal about his bent to challenge conventional wisdom at every turn. He's never had any use for conventions, and precious little for wisdom. Kinfolks claim that Mort "means well." This comes across as a worn, throw-away expression—in the same harness with "his heart being in the right place."

These thoughts came to mind a few nights back when Mort called, excited as a Somali rebel graduating valedictorian at a pirate school. The "chase cut to," he was breathless when he asked if I have a cutting edge, souped-up cell phone called an "E-Berry," and if I did, to "get rid of it immediately."

I was as dumbfounded as the heavily-taxed guy who said he wished that whoever said "taxation without representation is tyranny could come back and see what it's like with representation." What, in the name of Joe Biden, was my uncle talking about? Immediately I realized that I needed to think in reverse to line up with my uncle's brain waves.

His next statement explained much: "Our neighbor got one of those new-fangled phones, and he said he'd received an alarming blackmail on his 'E-Berry'." I figured immediately that he might be the victim of "backward recall."

But I didn't. Trying to untangle his made-up mind would be as big a project as construction of a wall on the U.S.-Mexico border. Further, I doubted that my mentioning that maybe the neighbor received "an email on his BlackBerry. Yet another can of worms would be open, always a precursor of much wriggling.

It was apparent that Mort wanted to talk about more than "E-Berries." No political party is conservative enough for him (his middle name is "Attila"). So probably I shouldn't have mentioned VP Biden.

"I've wondered about him from the 'git-go,'" Mort huffed. "The man may be charitable, but his giving record suggests otherwise. He's claimed an annual average of $369 to charity in IRS filings for the past decade."

Mort guessed the VP would have dropped that much into Salvation Army buckets. "Our preacher talked about church-giving last week," he continued. "I guess his talkin' about giving 10% of income figured on gross instead of net would have been wasted on Mr. Biden."

Remembering that Mort's "fact-finding" and recall typically are "all sky west and crooked," I considered interrupting. (It occurred to me to suggest that maybe decimal points were misplaced, and that Biden's annual charitable giving might actually have been $3,690, or even $36,900.)

Thankfully, I didn't. Whadda you know? Numerous "Googlings" of respected sources support Mort's claim. (Broken down further, the figure represents less than one-half of one percent of income.)...

I reminded Mort that one's stance on charity is a matter of choice and not a requisite for holding public office. "You still might want to write Mr. Biden a letter, telling him what you think," I advised. "Haven't you heard what it's gonna cost to mail a letter next month?" he questioned, adding that he had protested the new rate to his postmaster..

"Government guys usually have warped answers, ready-made for dispensing," Mort laughed. "When I asked him to verify that it's really going to cost 49 cents to mail a letter from the thicket to Washington D.C., he said I was looking at it all wrong. He said that by the time it gets there, the cost will be only a penny a day."...

GREENING OF THE USA...

I heard a story about a yard man who sheepishly thanked his employer for a gift of whiskey he described as "just right whiskey."

The employer asked what that meant. The worker repeated the "just right" description, adding, "If it had been any better, you wouldn't have given it to me, and if it had been any worse, I couldn't have swallowed it."

I feel such ambivalence when driving down I-20 in East Texas. At a certain exit, my conscience pulls at me to veer off onto the state highway, wind down a farm-to-market road, then finally to a briar-canopied lane to my Uncle Mort's place.

The practical side of me asks, "Do you really want to add at least an hour to the trip?" The hour is best-case scenario. That's driving time, with a few seconds to scribble a note and slip it under the screen door if Mort happens to be away. But, he's might near always at home, brimful of news from the thicket, suitable for sharing. He then prattles at 250 words per minute, with gusts to 300.

If I understood him better, I'd drop by more often. If I understood him less, I'd mark him off, figuring that he'll be hauled off by authorities at any time. Mort brings to mind the man in a little town who was three feathers short of a war bonnet. Friends in the thicket say Mort spends a great deal of his time in a state of "amiable incandescence."

Dropping by a few days back, though, was a no-brainer. I knew another birthday was at hand, and that a previous commitment would prevent our attending his party. We got him one of those "sorry-we-can't-be-there, but-want-to-be-the-first-to-congratulate- you" cards. The card and two-dozen bottles of gen-u-wine Dublin Dr Pepper in hand, I tried my best to drive down the absolute center of the lane, conscious that no matter what, the dust would cancel a fresh car wash. Maybe, though, I could steer clear of briars that threatened to do a number on my paint job if I veered the slightest bit, left or right.

He often trots to meet me, full of "howdies," then asks Aunt Maude to make a fresh pot of coffee and serve us some of her palate-pleasing teacakes. Last week, though, it was a quick "hello," with curtness rarely seen in my get-rich-quick uncle. "I'm too busy to mess with you today," he said, barely looking up from what appeared to be a tedious chore. He was scooping livestock feed from 50-pound bags, dumping it into freshly-printed bags he'd ordered from the Metroplex. On them were these words in bold print: Burpless Cattle Feed.

"I'm tellin' you, nephew, we live in a world where most people who used to view green simply as a basic color now think 'pert near everything needs to be green. I heard over the radio that the radicals now think that our atmosphere is polluted with methane expelled in cattle burps."

Uh-oh. My uncle was up to shenanigans again, claiming sole "heirship" of the latest get-rich-quick scheme. He believed the printing on his new bags would increase its worth. He called his "new" feed the new-and-improved "burpless" variety. I reminded him that it could be extremely embarrassing if the cattle people challenged him.

"There ain't gonna be any problem, nephew," he assured. "Farmers are working 18 hours a day just to break even. I saw a bumper sticker just the other day that said 'Show me a successful farmer, and I'll show you one with a wife who has a job in town.' Farmers are stretched thin, and they don't have time to stand around listening for cattle burps." I stood there, dumfounded, happy at the prospect that this would be one of our rare, short visits.

As I drove away, I thought about the card my wife bought the other day for the couple's 77th anniversary coming up in August. The message? "May you have as many more anniversaries as you want."...

A CHICKEN WAY OUT...

It was something of a hybrid event, partly "connived" by loving relatives and the rest perhaps attributable to a perfect alignment of the stars—or at least a coincidence of the calendar.

Now, several days removed from Labor Day, on which fell my 72nd birthday, I can better objectify the observance. In the moment it felt like contrived chaos, rubbing right up against a maelstrom of monstrous proportions.

I am grateful for yet another birthday and for most of its activities. Besides, it is the first time in almost seven years of column-writing that I've had a grand opportunity to use "maelstrom," a favorite word during theme-writing years of yore.

Let me begin by reiterating my long-held belief that we are fortunate indeed to experience life a few bites at a time. Those who wish to see ten years up the road are urged to reconsider. And, we who take baby steps toward the future think it best to seek 10-hour views of our tomorrows, 10 days at most. During a 40-year career in higher education, long-range planning, which educational experts insisted was of paramount importance, made my eyes twitch.

Luckily, I did not know what lay ahead on "birthday eve." Driving toward Fort Worth, I was grateful for a spate of speeches that had taken me to far-flung parts of Texas for four speaking engagements in as many days. Wearied in voice and body but near-giddy in spirit, I perked up as the city's skyline appeared, signaling that the comforts of home were but moments away.

I broke into a smile, warmed by the thought that Chick-fil-As across the land offered free sandwiches on Labor Day for all patrons sporting shirts with their favorite team logos. That meant birthday lunch plans already were in concrete. The prospect of tasty sandwiches, sans cost, conjured imagery akin to a warm fireside moment. The next morning, however, my dreams were reduced to mush.

It never occurred to me that my uncle would remember my birthday, or weasel a ride to the Metroplex with the bread truck driver, or even be aware of the free sandwich promotion. When he burst through the door, I knew that whatever plans I had for a quiet day were gone with the wind. "Lunch is on me," he joked, herding 15 family members—all three daughters' families, including their six children, then ages 2-8—into three cars.

You're getting ahead of me, and that's okay. Mort, in the lead car, took us straight to Chick-fil-A. He ushered the whole bunch through the door, handing out team logo shirts to all who needed them, including a few to puzzled patrons who had no family connection.

He "pushed" the merits of ice water, of course, since water is free. Moving four tables together, Mort was immediately the maestro, orchestrating the "Happy Birthday" song, and much else. Dozens of patrons—folks who didn't know Mort from the energizer bunny—joined in. He emptied his backpack stuffed with candle-bearing cupcakes Aunt Maude had sent along. As Mort ignited the candles, the store operator stood vigil with a fire extinguisher.

Decked out in green with the energy of a leprechaun, Mort was everywhere, refilling drink cups, joking with patrons and finally drawing stares when, with the slightest bend of knees, was short enough for the play area. He is believed to be the oldest patron ever to zoom down the slide.

Then, the diners were "hooked" on Mort's handful of "Austin Madness" bumper stickers from his extensive collection. An older one, pushing Austin's Sixth Street, read: "Keep Austin Weird." One urged to "Keep Georgetown Normal"; another, simply "Round Rock Rocks." Pflugerville's got the biggest laugh: "Between a *rock* and a *weird* place."

Two hours later, Mort said his good-byee, hitching a ride back to the thicket on an eastbound bread truck. (I heard him putting the con on the driver to take an alternate route so he could sneak a peek at the new Dallas Cowboys stadium.)

As we left, we surveyed the debris at our tables. We prayed there would be enough room for it at the landfill. Stats on the day, for Chick-fil-A in our town, anyway: 2,890 sandwiches given away. And that's no lousy chicken joke….

MY UNCLE ON OXYGEN...

Uncle Mort unquestionably has the largest "alibi collection" on the planet.

"I've banked on alibis to wiggle out of predicaments since Hector was a pup," he laughed. "The way I figure it, alibis and fibs are first cousins. Liberal dependence on both keeps us off the slippery slope of outright lies." I felt yawns coming on as Mort rambled. My eyes widened, though, when he offered an alibi for the Dallas Cowboys' 7-6 football win over the Washington Redskins.

I had heard him offer alibis on thousands of subjects over the years, but this was the first time in memory he'd made excuses for a win. He blamed the Boys' poor offensive showing on oxygen deprivation. "If they had lost, they could have blamed it on a bunch of schoolkids determined to make the Guinness Book of World Records," my uncle maintained. My curiosity piqued, I was determined to hear him out. He was happy to oblige, explaining that earlier in the week, a crowd of 4,626 Arlington eighth-graders gathered at Dallas Cowboys' AT&T Stadium to learn CPR techniques shown on the giant screen. (Guinness officials have confirmed this to be the largest CPR training session ever held, topping the old record by almost a thousand.)

"Those kids dang nigh pumped all the oxygen out of the place, causing the Boys' offense to be light-headed," Mort surmised. "I'm shore 'nuff glad that their defense sucked it up."

I attended a high school football playoff game there. Add me to the list of people overwhelmed by this $1.2 billion venue which is billed as the largest covered athletic facility in the world. It is surreal, commanding more attention than the glitzy ads, or, for that matter, play on the field. And, as cameras pan the stands, smiling, hand-waving fans ham it up for their "15 seconds of fame" as they watch for their pictures on the big screen.

The old claim is that you "can't know the players without a program." At the new stadium, you can't know the score without binoculars. It has four scoreboards—one for each quadrant. Surely they sent the wrong ones; these seem better suited for a junior high school field. Eyes squint to locate the 'boards marked as "home" and "away." The long and the short of it is that they are tiny in a cavernous place where "big" reigns.

When fans realized that there was no "American flag for America's team," they set up defiant squawks that caught the attention of team brass. On Thanksgiving Day, as the Cowboys shellacked the Oakland Raiders on the field, Old Glory was hanging from the rafters in both end zones, and the place was alive with movement, color and excitement.

CPR training or not, this wonder of the sports world takes the breath away. Everyone should see it. If the thought of donning football pads or band uniforms doesn't compute, maybe you can sign up for CPR training.

Coming to mind is the story of the leather-lunged Texan, on a crowded airplane. Nudging the man next to him, he asked, "Where you from, son?" The man answered "Chicago." The Texan, acknowledging the "great lakes up there," boasted that if we "had the great lakes in the Metroplex, it'd be a whole lot bigger'n Chicago." The vexed "victim" had the last word, suggesting: "Why don't you move them?"

Admitting that he didn't know how to get the job done, the Texan was instructed to "get a giant straw." A what? The Chicagoan ended the conversation with this rejoinder: "Put one end of the straw in Lake Michigan, and the other end in the Metroplex. If you can suck half as hard as you can blow, you'll have 'em there in 30 minutes."…

JERRY JONES IN A CAMEL SUIT?...

It's getting tough for a camel to find a tent that doesn't already have another dromedary's nose in it. Uncle Mort is convinced that the trend is true throughout culture. "It's everywhere," he contends. "Too many folks are pushing envelopes to the absolute edge, even at AT&T Stadium." Upon further review, he says there's a "multidimensional" nose-under-the-tent drama playing out at the stadium. At the center of things, of course, is owner Jerry Jones—in a camel suit.

My uncle believes this time Jones may have gone too far, getting caught up in three-dimensional video board technicalities when there should be more attention paid to his "one-dimensional team."

The 3-D video "trial run" in the early going fizzled about as badly as the team did. All 90,000+ fans were handed throw-away eye shades, but the desired crisp 3-D effect they were supposed to deliver was blurry. They shut the thing off early in the third quarter, opting for high definition pictures seven stories tall on the $40 million board. Sports writers and pundits are having a field day with the 3-D efforts, some calling for the distribution of "rose-colored" glasses, others for black lenses.

There are reasons to vote "yea" or "nay" concerning the glasses. On the "plus" side, fans showing up with bloodshot eyes can do so undetected, and the glasses will also be handy for fans preferring incognito status. On the flip side, when they don't like the way the players play, coaches coach or referees "ref," their eye-rolling might as well be in a mine shaft.

A Cowboys coach was fiddling with a pair of the shades when he left the stadium, and accidentally bumped against a little old lady, sending her to the ground. "No offense, no offense," he offered. "You certainly haven't," she huffed.

Mort seems sure, though, that Jones will come out on top—eventually. "He's called cunning and he's called shrewd," my uncle said. "Them who're against him like the first description, and those favoring Jones like 'shrewd' best. Look 'em up in the word book; the definitions are mighty similar."

Here's the way Mort thinks the deal will play out: Before long, they'll get the video thing straightened out, and the 3-D will be so sharp that fans will go "ga-ga." He figures the next announcement will be that Dolly Parton will be at the stadium in concert, and there'll be an extra charge for the third dimension.

I may need to start giving Mort more credit. He's "bulldog stubborn" when he gets on a case, and he recently cracked one over in East Texas. It seems that a grinch in the community was deflating yard Christmas figures far and wide. Mort caught him "red-and-green" handed, and a common-sense judge found him guilty as charged. He faces 100 hours of community service, in addition to repairing and re-inflating all the figures he damaged. If he's just got half the hot air Mort has, well.

I'm batting .500 repairing yard ornamentation my wife labors over. This year, the lighted yard angel with moving wings stood motionless, a broken plastic piece in its straw-like shell. I was able to glue it back in 20 minutes, but "ungluing" my fingers took nearly four hours.

We hope to visit Mort and Maude soon. Their little house is devoid of glitzy decorations, but it smells so much like Christmas. They always have a live cedar tree Uncle Mort cuts himself, and basic adornment consists of strings of berries and popcorn. Visitors get their fill of apple cider and are treated to a glut of Mort's stories. They're non-stop, and the pump requires but little priming. It's fun to watch them open presents, too. Even then, the rules of frugality apply. Maude carefully unties the ribbons, putting them away with the undamaged wrapping paper for reuse next year.

The old couple doesn't complain. As their stock of medicine mounts, storage is becoming a problem. So, they're giving themselves practical gifts this year—"his" and "her" medicine chests.

Makes sense to me….

THE WIND BLOWS IN TEXAS

Uncle Mort says he's yet to see a windmill that didn't need a good greasin'...

PART 2

A Twosome for the Long Haul…

FIRST THINGS FIRST...

With a new calendar still thick with pages, it is tempting to extend more patience to my uncle, stopping just short of taking as gospel whatever falls from his lips. He is famous for yapping away, often in his shadow-box sparring with silence, sometimes even flailing away at long pauses. Only his appointments with sleep makes possible snippets of silence for which the region is otherwise known.

Now he's claiming to be "full of fix-up analysis" concerning the turmoil in the Texas Tech football program, and the "tragic death of the University of Arkansas hog mascot." If his intent was to pique my interest, it worked. "I've moved these issues to the top of my list," Mort sputtered. "To give both of them due consideration, I've put aside plans to organize a torch-light march on Washington. Me and a few other East Texas toughies have a single demand: That all members of Congress take a page from the NASCAR handbook—the one requiring drivers to wear decals of sponsoring corporations.

If they'd do that, we'd at least know who our D.C. leaders are driving for."

He expressed sadness about the brouhaha at Tech. Mort thinks there are few winners, with all parties significantly diminished. "We're suffering from information overload, hearing way too much stuff from every direction," he moaned, "and some of it is probably true." He contends the ugly scenario in Lubbock could be the springboard for "national reconsideration of higher education priorities by 'big-school, backboneless presidents'."

Mort, with one more brand to burn, made another strong statement: "When I hear the words 'coach' and 'agent' linked together, I wince." Continuing his ramble, he said that "all the 'coach hiring/firing news' these days reminds him of the musty line about how people who enjoy obeying laws and eating sausage had best not watch either of them being made. He thinks big-time coaches' contract sagas should be added to the list.

The phone cracked; maybe a swarm of mosquitoes buzzed through the signal. Talking faster than ever, he lamented the "untimely death of Tusk II," Arkansas Razorbacks' 500-pound Russian boar mascot. The porcine seemingly "gave his all" for the team in its 20-17 conquest of East Carolina in the Memphis, TN, Liberty Bowl. The remainder of his conversation came through in bits and pieces, but here is what I deduced, subject to possible correction later.

Mort thinks the Pirates' ace field goal kicker, Ben Hartman, was victim of a "hog hex." The team's all-time leading scorer, he kicked game-winning field goals in six previous games, including four as time expired. Against the Hogs, however, he missed on four, including three of 39 yards or less in the late going. He had booted a school record 77 straight extra points, and in the 2008 season was voted "best under pressure" by opponents in Conference USA. Hecklers may have chanted "shanks a lot" to this nationally-recognized kicker who'll have nightmarish memories of his final collegiate game.

Mort mentioned the word "tuckered" as he re-thought his "hog-hexing" theory. "Why he probably over-worked his heart," my uncle analyzed. (Tusk II was pronounced, hmmmmm, "un-alive" just two days after the game. Though there was no autopsy, swine flu has been ruled out. Some Arkansas hecklers noted that the mascot had served four years, so technically, his eligibility expired at the same time he did.)

Razorback rooters are heartened that his little brother, Tusk III, is ready to assume the mascot role. (Detailed info at wholehog.com.) A final thought on the subject is that maybe we've been using the "old South" expression wrong for decades. Should it be "root hog AND die?"

Quarterbacks and field goal kickers get closest scrutiny. Hard-nosed fans want perfection, their piercing critical spotlights on these players' every move. Years ago, an eastern sportswriter covered a game in which a vaunted field goal kicker muffed three chip shots in his team's one-point loss. Hecklers claimed that the kicker attempted suicide. He supposedly measured a rope carefully before securing one end in a stout oak tree. Standing on a stool, he slipped the noose around his neck. All that remained was kicking the stool away, but he missed. . . .

MAUDE TO THE RESCUE...

Details of Mort's life have been duly chronicled, perhaps in too much detail, and of his wife Maude, not so much. Actually, she's stronger'n garlic, too. During their recent visit, Mort fell into mid-afternoon slumber, dozing off in front of a crackling fireplace. We laughed, figuring we'd have to wake him for dinner. While he dozed, we launched into "chit-chat" at much lower volume and half the speed Mort chooses.

Maude asked if I'd heard of Groucho Marx's long-ago radio show, *You Bet Your Life*. Turns out she and Mort were contestants in its—and their—early going. "I got to answer Groucho's question about what to mix with water to get soap suds," Maude beamed. "I answered, 'lye'." Marx, the dean of radio wise-crackers, joked, "That's a lie, but we're going to give you the $50 anyway."

Groucho probably never heard of lye soap, Maude figured. "I've used it to put out washings during all of my 'put-together'." She contended that she could make this soap in her sleep. "Mort starts the wood fire and brings water to a good boil in the wash pot before I take over."

Maude was ready to 'come clean" with more detail than I relished. She told about jabbing the clothes with a broom handle, rinsing and hanging out to dry—unless she thought it was "coming up a cloud."

I thought about our across-the-street neighbor who was gleeful when her dozen-year-old washer and dryer were wheeled out, surrendering to a shiny, state-of-the-art pair. (She wondered if she might qualify for membership in the "everything green" bunch.)

It hasn't worked out that way. She should have been forewarned by Thomas Becon's line in 1553. The quote, even with its quaint spelling, holds true: "All is not golde that glittereth." (Becon may have stolen the quote from Alain de Lille, a French theologian in the 1100s who warned against holding "everything gold that shineth like gold." Authorities maintain that "fool's gold" is the only kind that actually shines, but that's a topic for another time.)

Let the nightmarish chapter begin. Soon, the washer vibrated excessively, once bouncing into the wall. It left a softball-sized hole and broke the soap dispenser in the process. With a few months of warranty remaining, my neighbor was confident that repairs would be made with dispatch. Sure enough, the repairman replaced the dispenser without charge. Before leaving, though, he offered several suggestions, including the placement of socks and such in a mesh bag. Another rep on a subsequent visit recommended the placement of a rubber mat under the machine. He warned her to avoid washing heavier items such as bath mats and beach towels, and to try half-loads. Still a third "alleged fixer" offered mournful words: "You've got one of the worst models ever," and that she'd "be better off with a set 10 years old," because they "made 'em better in the old days."

Maude had heard enough. She walked briskly across the street, clearly on a mission. My neighbor needed encouragement; her warranty had expired and "washer woes" were mounting.

My aunt preached "simplify," offering to give her a wash pot and the lye soap recipe.

"You'll love the 'smell and feel' of line-dried clothes," Maude promised. "And remember, all lemons don't grow on trees. Sometimes faulty products rub right up against 5 o'clock Friday at the factory."

My neighbor jotted down Maude's suggestions. Some scribbles included: "No moving parts (unless broom handle and pliers used to repair clothes line are counted). No more waiting for service calls. No more 'on hold' sessions of nothingness after the recorded voice explains 'how important her call is.' No longer need to wedge ironing board between washer and wall to protect the latter." Sadly, she wished for her old set back—the one that never once needed repairs. She wanted so much for the faulty washer to be back on the showroom floor where it had languished on display just 16 months earlier. (Later, she learned an additional pertinent fact: the retailer no longer carries this model.)

"It reminds me that the people in the loan department at the bank ain't the ones writing the advertising jingles," Maude said, smiling....

COUNTDOWN ON THE WAY THINGS ARE...

A few days after the Super Bowl, I bade "so long" to the Interstate, knowing that the sun-splashed highway would be visible only with headlights upon resumption of my travels a few hours later. It was time for my semi-annual visit to the thicket where Uncle Mort and Aunt Maude have been residents almost a full century.

I wanted to get Mort's "take" on current affairs, and to watch Maude shake her head in wonderment. Everyone has known for decades—and Maude's been privy to the probability since they were wed nearly 80 years ago—that Mort spends his waking moments trying to outsmart the world, or a large portion thereof.

He was taking his grease gun to the accelerator of his golf cart when I interrupted. "I try to grease this sucker every five years," Mort moaned. "Been reading about car-driving people having trouble with accelerators. The only time 'recall' is mentioned around here is when I'm trying to remember where I left the grease gun." He was punch-pleased that even if the pedal sticks, he can either jump off or keep it between the fences at top speed of 10 MPH until the tank empties.

I made the mistake of asking about the moans. "Down in my back, nephew," was his answer. "It's getting tougher to load a 50-inch TV on my golf cart the day before the Super Bowl, and then return it to the store two days later." Oh, no! This vignette reminded me why the clerks run the other way when Mort enters the store to make sure they still have the "48-hour-no-questions-asked return policy."

Then, he switched to the game. "I never dreamed I'd profit from New Orleans winning the Super Bowl," he bragged, "but I've come up with a book that's bound to make me rich, particularly in Louisiana."

He showed me the manuscript of *How to Speak 'Who Dat' in Ten Easy Lessons.* Truth to tell, it is a replication of Pig Latin, a "language" born of boredom many decades ago and seldom used today.

"In words beginning with consonants, the initial consonant is moved to the end of the word followed by 'ay'," he explained. "So, 'Saints' would be "Aints-say." (There are a few more rules, but reading them invites eye-crossing.)

On one point, Mort and I agreed. We nodded that it was common to hear "Sooner Nation" referring to University of Oklahoma football and "Red Sox Nation" commonly heard synonymously with Boston Red Sox baseball. We decided on the need to "practice up" for similar application to New Orleans Saints football. Where shall we place emphasis? "WHO-dat Nation?" "who-DAT Nation?" Or maybe "who-dat NATION?"

About that time, a woman—a bona fide representative of the United States government—entered the backyard, startling Uncle Mort. He isn't used to having two visitors at once. Pad in hand, she began her spiel. "Every decade, the government tries to find out how many men, women and children live in this country," she explained. "I'm plumb sorry, ma'am," Uncle Mort apologized. "But you've done come to the wrong house, 'cause I don't know."

I figured it was time to wind my way up the country roads to the Interstate and get back in the race. I wondered if my accelerator would stick, if I could remember Pig Latin without buying Uncle Mort's new book, and if the census lady was still laughing. I thought of Mort's insistence to omit "marching" from the Saints' famous song. "They didn't 'march' in," he contended. "The Saints 'passed in,' 'kicked in' or even 'barged in,'" he said. I thought of the post-game shot of teary-eyed MVP quarterback Drew Brees, hugging his infant son. I think he "soared in."…

MAUDE'S 'BLUE MOON' PHONE CALL...

It was a "once in a blue moon" telephone call. My Aunt Maude, who usually has about as much use for a telephone as a meteorologist has for a Farmers' Almanac, rang me up. Ever the meticulous planner, she called to make sure we had Uncle Mort's birthday bash on our July 4th calendar. I assured her that we'll make the trek to East Texas with pleasure and considerable anticipation.

A person devoid of guile, Maude might otherwise have called to make a twin-barbed jab at my double-barreled forgetfulness. For at least a couple of decades, I've mailed both birthday greetings and Happy Mother's Day cards to Maude; this year, I forgot. She'd sooner believe the cards were lost in the mail than to blame me.

I asked her if she enjoyed Mother's Day. Her response sounded like the one last year and the one before that. She had whipped up a country lunch for a couple of dozen kids, "grands" and "great-grands," topped off—as always—by saucer-sized slices of world-class strawberry pie. Then, the outdoor crowd tossed horseshoes and pitched washers. Inside, some whiled away the hours playing "42"; others were busy printing names on snippets of paper to be drawn at day's end for Christmas gifting.

There was a dull roar with four generations present, and, when daylight hours gave way to history, the couple's treasured twilight hours in front porch rocking chairs beckoned. "We stayed out extra late," Maude said, "counting bird sounds when we could hear them above the cricket choruses. We lingered in the rockers for two hours, holding hands the whole time—him holding his and me holding mine."

If the devil expects to get Uncle Mort into a corner, it won't be an "idle mind/workshop" kind of deal. The old guy's mind is always spinning. Maude claims that he has more ideas in a day than most men do in a lifetime, and some of 'em are good.

"He had a hard time deciding which tee-shirt to slip on this morning," my aunt said. "One of them read, 'You have mistaken me for someone who cares.' The other, 'I'm just like a pool shark, except I miss too many shots and scratch too often'."

Maude said his latest project is a plan to use solar energy to power his golf cart. (The cart has been the couple's vehicle of choice since gasoline prices went north; that's when Mort put his rickety old pick-up on blocks right behind the hen house.)

His inspiration came from a news article detailing plans for an airplane capable of circling the globe solely on solar power. "If they can build a plane that can do that, surely I can make solar power work on my golf cart that putters around the thicket," Mort reasoned.

When Maude handed Mort the phone, I knew the remaining minutes would be taken by his hop-scotching over topics far-ranging from hither to yon. He was "wired" to roll on about solar power, dead certain that it could have been used in American homes for decades.

"The power company heavies didn't ride in on a turnip truck," Mort said. "They aren't pushing solar power because they don't know what to do with customers who get behind on their bills. They can't figure out how to turn off the sun!"

Finally, Mort wanted to let me know about a landmark on the Interstate highway that'll be helpful for folks trying to get to the home place down in the swamp. "They've put up a new billboard," Mort bragged. "It reads: 'Tattoos—While You Wait'." Mort figures those three words might provide comfort for customers who think they have to go through miles of government red tape to see if they qualify. "I was a little surprised they put up a tattoo pitch," he mentioned. "I thought they might choose one to promote the merger of FedEx and UPS, and the obvious new name, 'Fed-Up'."…

WHAT IFS AND AN OLD SHOE...

Uncle Mort sometimes goes a "fer piece" on trails where rabbits fear to tread. When his fascination and imagination engage, his mind whirls into nooks and crannies not found on maps. "Sometimes he spins enough cobwebs for a ten-year spider crop, leaving me to do all the chores without a lick of help," Aunt Maude fretted. A tiny news item caught his eye; his mind shifted into "what if" gears.

The headline hooked him like a catfish after dough bait: "World's Oldest Leather Shoe Found in Armenian Cave." He laughed, "I thought I had old shoes, but compared to that one, mine are brand new."

He had a hard time visualizing a 5,500-year-old shoe that predated the pyramids by a thousand years. Mort's prattle about the discovery heightened. When he mentioned hitch-hiking to Armenia, Maude told him to "stuff it." He spoke of buying the shoe, then organizing a needle-in-a-haystack search to find its mate. "No telling what a pair of ancient shoes would be worth," he reasoned.

Had it stopped there, he might not have been banished to the barn for continuance of his pipe-dreaming. "This could even make saddle soap a hot item," he added. "I've got a trailer load I bought for a song years ago. News of leather hanging around this long, coupled with budgets crimped by the recession, could have folks 'saddle-soapin' shoes they even forgot they own," he grinned. Then he thought about how he might react the next time he's labeled "common as an old shoe." He wasn't sure if he'd smack 'em upside the head or extend thanks for recognizing his caveman lineage.

Mort's dreaming didn't end there. He imagined ad tie-ins to Buster Brown shoes and stock purchases of Mother Goose rhymes. "Genealogists will come out of the woodwork to trace the oldest woman ever to live in a shoe," he joked. Maude, gathering eggs nearby, realized that Mort's babbling was unfair to the horses and cows. "They probably hate his prattle, too," she thought.

She decided to try to get his mind off the subject with an old hiccup remedy. Maude reminded him that the 6 o'clock news had begun on TV. They watched President Obama signing a document; Maude wondered about the BIC letters on his pen. "My guess is, the letters stand for 'Because I Can,'" Mort cackled. At bedtime, Maude carefully hid the newspaper clipping about the old shoe. "Out of sight, out of mind," she figured.

The next morning, she got up first, like always, to prepare a wonderful breakfast—the kind Mort always claims to be "as good as any he had ever lapped a lip over." Featured are mouth-watering biscuits the size of lily pads, made from scratch, of course. He also loves the sausage patties, eggs and butter she churned a few days earlier—all of this topped off by a final biscuit oozing rivulets of butter and blackberry jam. "I eat it as fast as I can," he explains. "If I look at the food too long, I drool so much I get behind on shoveling the food in." He pours another cup of coffee, adding, "It don't take much water to make good coffee."

After the repast, they retreat to cane-bottom chairs on the front porch, about the time the sun's shadow hits IX on the sundial. Maude, her mind in yesteryear mode, starts talking about doctors' endorsement of running barefoot. Then she makes an unlikely proposition: "Want to race to the mailbox?" He does, and off they go, dust flying down the 100-yard path. They arrive at exactly the same time, laughing heartily. They wiggle their toes in a bed of mint;

he tears off a sprig for afternoon tea. Mort and Maude, hand in hand, walk slowly back to the house, humming—well, I guess it was a duet—"I got shoes, you got shoes, all of God's children got shoes."…

A BIRTHDAY AND SARAH PALIN...

Uncle Mort, having completed 98 years of living, faced a fistful of unexpected pre-birthday decisions. Usually, his impalement is no more serious than the "horns of a dilemma." This time, it was more nearly a rack of antlers, like the points on a full-grown East Texas buck.

Learning that Sarah Palin had scheduled a stop in East Texas, Mort fretted that plans for his big birthday party would go awry. His angst rubbed off on Aunt Maude, who made it clear from the "git-go" that she would like to go to the Palin rally at Tyler's Oil Palace.

The thicket was abuzz with the news that the political figure would include a Texas stop, sandwiched between appearances in California and Virginia in a span of 48 hours. Aunt Maude was caught up in the excitement, forgetting momentarily about a plethora of priorities for party preparation. Sakes alive, there was so much to do before Mort blew out the candles on his July 4 birthday cake.

Then she thought about logistics. Her "druthers" changed when she thought of "riding shotgun" on Mort's golf cart. She envisioned the sun beating down from a July sky on the 90-mile ride to Tyler; her make-up was bound to be a mess long before arrival. And almost surely there'd be embarrassment for the wind's re-arrangement of posies on her big straw hat.

At the same time, Mort had a smothering spell. He learned that admission was $35 a head; parking would set him back another $8. He was miffed at the prospect of buying a couple of corn dogs, since the tab included no food. His eyes crossed when he calculated gasoline cost of some $15, not to mention a critical need for new tires on his golf cart.

Knowing financial arguments wouldn't sway Maude, he chose another tack, citing bad tires and the danger of driving late at night—particularly at "his age." Then he mumbled about the difficulty of bouncing out of bed for church the next day.

Downsizing to the "promise mode," he vowed to make a nice sign for the Palin speech. Maude liked the wording: "I Can See November From My House," realizing that the claim was a stretch. Sometimes they can't see as far as the end of the current month. He humored her with an iron-clad assurance that he'd mow the yard—front and back—and "make good" on a six-month-old promise to take down the sagging outdoor Christmas lights and finish heavy duty leaf raking. The offer to buy Maude enough denim for a new skirt sealed the deal.

Truth to tell, Mort doesn't care much for crowds, particularly when they have large numbers of lawyers. "Most of 'em are politicians in the larval stage," he claims. (A few minutes earlier, he asked if I knew why lawyers are buried in graves 12 feet deep. "Down deep they aren't bad.")

That night, Mort went to bed, his Big Chief tablet in hand. He fell asleep in minutes, tossing aside wadded up sheets of paper. Before "beddy-bye," Maude rounded up the trashed notes.

She knew immediately that Mort had been winnowing thoughts for his "impromptu" response at the upcoming party. (His "throw-away lines" included: "standing straight at 98," "still taking nourishment," "in good shape for the shape I'm in," and finally, "over, and over, and over the hill.") Suddenly, he sat up in bed, saying he'd thought of a great line: "I'm still vertical and ventilating!"

Maude gave him a peck on the cheek and then shared a secret; she'd baked an unprecedented quadruple-chocolate birthday cake. Mort sauntered out to the front porch, taking in a full measure of the fresh night air. He heard thicket sounds that poked holes in the darkness. On his knees by the rocking chair, he offered a prayer of thanksgiving and a plea for rain to cool the parched land.

"I always ask God not to bother with rain on both the 'just' and the 'unjust'," Uncle Mort opined. "If He favors the 'unjust' with a gullywasher, I'll make sure the 'just' get their share from Maude's teakettle." He howled with laughter at a story he'd told a thousand times. Never mind that his "audience" included only critters of the thicket. They paid him no mind, long considering him to be one of their own.

Going home from the rally at the witching hour of midnight, the old couple had several hours to talk. At the same time, Sarah Palin was on board a sleek jet plane, heading for her next engagement. Soon, she would be bounding up the steps at another venue. Mort, hoping to have slept in, will be dragged to church, even if by the ear, probably far more painful than the one Maude plays the piano by….

MID-SUMMER POTPOURRI…

July can be both hazy and crazy, and my Uncle Mort's 98th birthday party down in the thicket fits both of the rhyming words. Pride-swollen that he used only six of his ten minutes allotted for candle-blowing, he blew the extra time rambling through his "impromptu response."

Though a far cry from the "over the top" party NBA star LeBron James orchestrated to herald his change of address to Miami, the party was backdrop for Mort's surprise announcement that even stunned Aunt Maude. His wife of 80 years usually can finish his sentences, interpret his dreams and predict his excuses. (She even knows how many grunts precede his deepest snoring, and how many kicks it takes to slow him down, mute him completely or at least re-direct the noisy blast to the opposite wall.) This time, her "peepers" were pie-sized at the party with her partner's paunchy pals.

Mort announced that come September, he'll enter the "writing side" of literature. He's already nailed down the title—*Mort's First Hundred Years of Potpourri*—and now is on the homestretch "assembling the words between the covers." He predicts that use of "potpourri" in the title will send many of his friends scurrying for dictionaries.

His marketing plan calls for an initial printing of 50 copies, all to be given to kin. A month later, another 50 will go to friends, and the next 50 will adorn the "please take one" table at the senior center. Then will come his publicity raves that his "best-seller is in its fourth printing in just four months!" His "pronouncement" barely dented conversations around the punch bowl concerning basketballer "King James," however.

Mort's flock "has no truck" for the manner LeBron chose to harness ESPN for infliction of an outright infomercial. The team owner just wishes that James' play for the Cavaliers had been as "cavalier" as his exit. One guest summed up James with the old axiom that "there but by the grace of God walks God." Someone else offered a pair of intriguing thoughts: 1) that LeBron and British Petroleum may share the same PR firm, and 2) that if the star ever writes a book, a title suggestion is *Humility and How I Alone Attained It.*

One attendee predicted a big drop-off of King James Bible sales in Ohio, but offered a plan for Cleveland's inventory of LeBron's bobble-head dolls. "They can add hatpins and peddle them as 'voodoo dolls' next season." Another guest said his jaw dropped lowest when James predicted the "road to history begins now." Maybe James was thinking of the "pathway to hell" being paved with good intentions. (This quotation is attributed to Saint Bernard of Clairvaux, almost a thousand years ago.)

One party guest was reminded of his recent dream about Heaven. "I dreamed that new arrivals are shocked to find that all streets are not paved with gold, that most of the streets aren't even paved and that they're expected to help pave them."

Mort predicted the Miami Heat will become to the NBA what the Yankees are to major league baseball. "Miami will become the team fans love to hate," he said. Meanwhile, much of Ohio wept with tears of flood-stage proportions, sad that no professional sports team from Cleveland has won a title in almost a half-century. "The last time we won, the telecast wasn't even in color," one fan lamented, remembering that the "vertical hold" knobs on most sets were worn smooth out.

Mort cocked his head about LeBron's promise to "take the Heat to a different level." Reassured that Miami remains situated at sea level, he wondered if the Heat will yell down at us from the sky, or "gurgle up" from the Atlantic Ocean? He laughed about "keys to the cities" given to James by South Florida municipalities, noting that in Cleveland, "they've changed the locks."

My uncle admits his views of James will change if the star should decide to underwrite the cost of my uncle's book. (Mort is already busy jotting down quotes that'll be "suitable for framing," as well as for embroidering.) Such nuggets will include, "Artificial intelligence is no match for natural stupidity," and "People who insist on a 'business as usual' approach to life soon will be out of business."

In fairness to LeBron, though, it should be mentioned that four years later, he retreated to Cleveland "with class." And early in the season, fans will remove the word "Prodigal" from references to the King….

MOVE OVER, BEN FRANKLIN...

Anyone stumbling upon my Uncle Mort's place would be taken aback by ill-arranged clutter in stacks, piles and barrels all over the yard. And the barn is in the same shape, its inventory of his junk replacing agricultural trappings decades ago. He has a sweeping acronym for the whole mess—"PIP"—or, projects in progress. Luckily, few people ever see Mort's eclectic collection through arrival there by accident. One has to visit my kinfolks' place on purpose; no one passes it on the way to town. I've struck out trying to describe it. It's kinda like the digs of TV's "Sanford and Son." Unlike them, though, Mort spends much more time collecting than he does dispensing—and he considers much of it, uh, indispensable. Aunt Maude, one year his junior, sizes up their homestead this way: "If a tornado hits our place, it'll cause $100,000 worth of improvement," she laughs. He's at it again with lots of new stuff—a rusty weathervane, a kite with key attached, a reinforced butterfly net, and an assortment of electrical coils and batteries. Had Mort worn a white wig, waistcoat and tall black boots with shiny buckles, he would have looked like a modern day Benjamin Franklin, trying to harness electricity.

Guess what? In a way, that's what he was trying to do. Learning that up to 7% of electricity is lost in transmission, Mort is determined to "recapture" it. "We're already paying through the nose for the stuff, so if I can figure out how to reclaim some of the lost juice, maybe I can re-sell it."

My eyes rolled as he rattled on about plans to bottle it, crate it or somehow cram it into batteries. Again, Mort was in dreamland, envisioning a sky crowded by trillions of dollar marks fluttering toward him. He continued with his theory: "Maybe lightning bugs are looting the 'lectricity. That may be why they're disappearing from the planet. Some of 'em may be getting too much of the juice, leading to death by zapping," he continued. (At least that explained the modified butterfly net. No doubt he planned to catch as many lightning bugs as possible to "unzap" 'em.)

When Mort's babbling switched to "his invention" of crystal radios, I wilted. His neighbors who believe him probably also buy Al Gore's line about his inventing the Internet.

Nose sniffs aren't often connected with rescue operations, but on this day, mine detected something special that called for a quick get-away from my "sideways-thinking" uncle. The aroma wafting through Maude's kitchen window was unmistakable. A delectable pineapple upside down cake was in transfer from the oven. My opening of the screen door coincided with her robbing the cake of an over-sized slice hanging over the side of the saucer.

Without my saying a word, Maude flashed an understanding smile. "Mort means well," she said as she almost always does. "But he can't put in flashlight batteries on the first try and is as clumsy as a buffalo on an ice rink when he changes a light bulb." She went on about considering it a small victory when he's occupied by long stretches in the yard. That way, she can stay inside, enjoying the World Series.

"If he happens to figure out how to recover electricity from lightning bugs, more power to him," she joked. On that note, I bade farewell, making sure not to forget that other big slice of cake she'd wrapped for travel. It would go down well on the morrow. As I drove away, I wondered if Mort would later try to frisk glowworms for their ill-gotten gains in their electrical heists....

OLD HOME PLACE
Soon after first phase of renovation...

ON TAKING OF TURNS...

Rarely does a single word—"turn"—morph into so many uses. Satellite navigation systems screaming "turn, turn, turn" account for some increased usage .It's kinda like words such as "wiggling" and "writhing" that came into repeated play when Elvis Presley's concerts were reviewed, usually in more detail than his vocal offerings.

In our youth, we "took turns" in spelling bees, and many disputed playground games were righted by teachers who always came down on the side of "turn-taking." When sick folks' conditions deteriorate, they take "turns for the worse," creating the remote possibility of a u-turn that shouldn't be wagered on.

The late Joseph Schott, an FBI agent in Fort Worth for 23 years, was mystified by a memo concerning his boss's planned highway route from Dallas Love Field to Austin. The year was 1959, and J. Edgar Hoover wanted to visit then House Majority Leader Lyndon Johnson, an aspiring presidential candidate. The directive ordered "no left turns" during the entire trip.

Schott learned later that in California a few months earlier, Hoover's chauffeur-driven limo was rear-ended during a left-turn attempt. Thus the decree for future trips, and the intriguing title for Schott's hilarious book, *No Left Turns.*

Strange turns, by both players and baseballs, were plentiful when a couple of over-achieving teams, the Texas Rangers and the San Francisco Giants, made it to the World Series.

Granted, the Rangers' bats turned to jelly during what retired Dallas sportswriter Blackie Sherrod called "The World Serious" during a big chunk of the 20th century.

Ah, "what-if's" abound, but a few different turns in a couple of games might have made huge differences. Rangers' second baseman Ian Kinsler may still be shaking his head about two big "what-ifs." One of his long drives to deep center hit the top of the fence, and with a slightly different turn, might have bounded over. Instead, it bounced back into the park, reducing a four-bagger to two. Another time, he beat out a grounder, but inexplicably turned left toward second instead of choosing safe harbor to the right. He was easily tagged out. Mort said Kinsler's base-running blunder reminded him of Moses' descent from Mount Sinai.

"When he got down off the mountain, it's too bad he made a wrong turn," Mort contended. I thought of challenging him, but thankfully remembered that his mind is a lock without a key. "Yep, whether by chance or not, old Moses took a wrong turn," he continued. "If he'd turned left instead of right, they'd have the commandments and we'd have the oil."

Oh, well. It was great fun to follow this merry band of Rangers who added to the season's delight with their "claws and antlers" gestures, all-for-one, one-for-all attitude and unbounded energy. Little wonder they warmed fans' hearts with songs, poems and stories making the rounds about this memorable season. Books and movies will follow.

Kudos go to the Texas baseballers who seemed never to take themselves too seriously. And hats off to the Giants, the self-proclaimed "cast of misfits." They were "fit enough" during baseball's final week to warrant the label of world champions. Cast of misfits? Maybe, but they fashioned a wonderful season for Ranger fans.

Though detailed newspaper coverage of the World Series was warranted, I cringed when front pages of Metroplex dailies were dominated by World Series stories. And they used big headlines I thought to be reserved for the Second Coming.

There are many wonderful memories, some of which will surely center on TV shots of disgruntled New Yorkers filing out of Yankee Stadium in the eighth inning on two consecutive nights against the Rangers. As one local preacher put it, "We beat the heaven into the Yankees." Meanwhile, like it or not, the Dallas Cowboys now face a few weeks of spotlight scrutiny. Sadly, they're already done to a "turn," written off, and "twisting in the wind."...

MORT AND IVORY TOWERS...

In a land of make-believe, I'd prefer to think of Mort as a "foster uncle," with hope that he might soon be adopted, taking his opinions, suggestions and cockamamie schemes along to "bless" some other family. I was down to my last nerve one time when my old uncle stepped on it.

"I never thought it could happen, nephew, but you are partly responsible for the demise of elephants as they lumber ever closer to extinction," he blathered. I was tempted to throw the phone, but didn't because curiosity trumped my disbelief that Mort—usually affirming—had accused me of contributing to "pachydermicide."

I protested vehemently that I'd never even shot a rabbit and didn't figure Kodak shots of elephants could be held against me. He "deaf-eared" me, rambling on. "You were a part of the gang responsible for keeping the 'tusk market' pumped up," Mort analyzed. "I've heard all my life that college presidents live in ivory towers, and now we learn that for some of 'em, this isn't a figurative statement." Armed with private college presidential salaries from a *Chronicle of Higher Education* study, Mort figured that it would take a freight car load of elephant tusks "just to make one boilerplate, run-of-the-mill, garden variety ivory tower."

I'd read the report. It dawned on me that Mort was on a "goat-getting gig," comparing my modest, long ago presidential salary with much bigger contracts now in play for most presidents. Assuming a "me no Alamo, me no Goliad" stance, I laughed at him, pointing out that my 18 presidential years were way back in the 20th century. "When I served, presidential salaries at most institutions were 'in context.' If I'd built an ivory tower, it would have been made with Ivory soap, and maybe equipped with flotation devices that would come in handy for college presidents. Some of 'em are in over their heads and don't even know it. They'd have to hope Tom Brady had nothing to do with inflating them, but that topic is way more convoluted than the worms writhing in cans."

He kept the pressure on, citing three salaries that averaged more than $2.3 million last year. "That's tall cotton, nephew," he laughed. "How was your cotton crop?" Picking up on his analogy, I admitted to have served in fields often ravaged by boll weevils and long-term drought. My total compensation in a 40-year career amounted to about one-half of the $2.3 million annual figure he threw at me. "Your boards probably got what they paid for," Mort joked before asking me to retell a story I'd shared with him years ago.

I knew exactly which story had crossed his "elephant-like" mind. At a board meeting in my early presidential years, a trustee posed a serious question. I expected to buy some response time by asking if he wanted an "educated guess or a gut reaction?"

"What makes you think that you are intellectually or anatomically qualified to render either?" the trustee questioned. It dawned on me that if I wanted to shift topics, I'd better wedge in a timely interruption.

"How 'bout them Cowboys?" I asked. That did the trick; I braced for his cockeyed football ramblings. "Coaching is tough," he admitted. "It's the only profession I know where autopsies are performed *before* they die."

A fan of Jason Garrett, Mort suggested that the coach wear trifocals during games. "That way, even if the Cowboys' play turns to a 'mess of pottage' on the field, he can watch 'em with his head held high," he guffawed. Mort, weary of the oft-heard speculation about what candidates "bring to the table," concluded: "It ain't about Thanksgiving, and has nothing to do with chess, checkers, dominoes or poker. What's important is what they bring to the football field."

He spoke of a coach who sprang to the podium when his hiring was announced. As bulbs flashed and microphones lined the lectern, the new coach claimed to be "fired with enthusiasm."

He was a miserable failure, posting a 0-30 record for three seasons. When sent `packing, he mounted the same podium, with the same media folks chronicling the moment. "I appear before you just as I did three years ago," he said. "*Fired* with enthusiasm."

I dozed off with dreams of bloated presidential salaries—varying greatly in our wobbling world—of price tags on ivory towers and of ever-widening and deepening of moats around same….

MAUDE PUTS HER FOOT DOWN...

Thanks to timely intervention of Aunt Maude, Homeland Security was able to cross off a potential problem at Super Bowl XLV. Oh, Uncle Mort meant no harm. But, if he'd carried out his scheme, probability of gumming up the works loomed large.

Maude said Mort had been acting strangely for several weeks. His plans came into sharp focus on the eve of Groundhog Day when he dozed off—his nightly ritual—while watching TV news. As Mort's snoring reached full bore, his Big Chief tablet fell to the floor.

Open to the front page, it revealed his plan to "get rich" at the Super Bowl. Maude, drinking in details, flatly vowed that Mort would

NOT attend the game in Arlington. I don't know if she planned to confine him in leg irons, lock him in the barn, tie him to a tree or put double-strength sleeping pills in his Ovaltine. Had I read the details Mort had formulated, I'd have restrained him, too.

We've known for decades that Mort—along with National Football League brass—would have graduated with highest honors from the P. T. Barnum School of People Fooling. Who could deny Barnum's contention that a "fool" is born every minute?

With so much Super Bowl experience under their belts, honchos of the NFL have found that Barnum hit the nail of truth squarely. They've determined that a quarter-million or so fans will show up to pay money for just about anything the league wants to sell. Football fanatics are drawn to THE GAME screaming, "Feed me!," and the league is happy to accommodate. The NFL has layers of trappings for both attendees and a vast TV audience, including a football game! All Mort wanted to do was "piggy-back" on the NFL. At least that's what Maude learned upon reading details of his nefarious scheme.

On the "to do" portion of the list, Mort wrote of affixing "Thicket Emergency Vehicle" signage to his golf cart, his only means of conveyance. (It would take six hours at top speed to make it to Jerry World, assuming a slight tailwind.)

He reminded himself to "shine his helmet"—the one he wore in World War II—as well as his "Honorary Deputy Sheriff" badge. Mort borrowed a stethoscope and portable oxygen bottle to legitimize his appearance. He scrawled reminders to "wear dark shades and a press pass around his neck." Further, he'd hang a walkie-talkie and a billy club from his belt and "be sure to bring along a marks-a-lot."

Mort thought his "get-up" would get him past the ticket-takers at the plaza party, where fans paid hundreds of dollars to stand outside the stadium and watch the game on jumbo screens. Once admitted, he'd spend the first half drawing fake knot holes on the stadium wall with the marks-a-lot. During the second half, he figured it would be easy to identify fans whose refreshment excesses had eased them into a state of warm lubrication, or, as he put it, "amiable incandescence."

He'd line up sober helpers to man the fake knot holes. They'd then charge fans $50 for one-minute views. Fans would welcome the offer, amazed that anything sold at the Super Bowl would go for a mere half-hundred. Mort dreamed of wheelbarrows overflowing with cash.

"I don't need to worry that they don't see anything," Mort analyzed. "They'll think there's something wrong with their eyes. The NFL will wonder why they didn't think of it." Mort envisioned hundreds of thousands of fans telling their grandchildren about how they "saw" Super Bowl XLV for just fifty bucks. This serves to remind millions of baseball fans claimed to have been eye-witnesses in Atlanta Stadium for Hank Aaron's home run that vaulted him ahead of Babe Ruth.

He figured his scheme to be a "no-brainer." If it turned to mush, he'd apply the well-known theory that it's easier to apologize than to get permission. Kinfolks are congratulating Maude for "putting her foot down," even if it meant Mort missing the biggest game of the year.

Realizing attendance at the game was a high priority for her husband, Maude arranged for a neighbor to record it. When Mort wakes up—gaining at least a modicum of the common sense he manages on his good days—she'll make sure he's invited over to see the game, perhaps as early as the last week in February….

MONEY ON THE RUN…

Uncle Mort continues his "business as usual" approach to life, presidential race or no presidential race. Recently, he announced that he "ALMOST had good news," based largely, it seems, on mail he received from Starbucks.

"At first, I thought I had won a free drink. Sadly, I misread the letter. It turned out that all I'd won was a free Starbucks' franchise." (He made a good point, with sales going down and price per ounce going UP!)

Mort didn't talk long—said he had to go check on an adoption. He signed up for the "adopt a highway" program. Mort provided an intriguing reason for deciding to help with cleanup of our highways. "The 7-Eleven stores are now selling coffee in red cups (Republicans) and blue cups (Democrats), so I believe I can spend a couple of hours picking up cups and may have an inside track on how the presidential race will turn out. Promising to "keep me posted," he figures his call on the presidential race will be as valuable as the TV news anchors' typically turns out to be.

I never expected to see a business that might rival my uncle's self-confidence. But my wife and I did during a visit to Mary Ann's Deli in Fairhope, AL. It fit his general attitude to a "T," reading, "If our food, drinks and service aren't up to your standards, we suggest that you lower your standards." They've been serving up food since the early 1980s, so few diners have found it necessary to lower their standards.

Speaking of standards, Mort and fellow workers once ordered breakfast at a short-lived café in the thicket. "Make sure I get a clean plate," Mort requested. Upon returning with the orders, the server asked, "OK, who gets the clean plate?"

The news recently chronicled the death of Paul Newman, and cockles in hearts across the nation were warmed by thoughts of a life well lived. He died at age 83.

His was a magical life. Newman was married to Joanne Woodward for 50 years, and was fully engaged in philanthropy outside his entertainment career. Newman, an actor, film director, entrepreneur, humanitarian and car racing enthusiast, was unaffected by his many successes.

He gave $250 million to charities, most for terminally ill children. All profits from Newman's Own, his brand of grocery items that began with salad dressings, have been directed to such causes. They will continue to benefit these charities. He was a "cool hand" indeed….

HAPPENINGS AROUND THE DEPOT...

From time to time, Mort gives me a rib-jabbing, asking if I saw so and so in the newspaper. More than once, it has been about sparks flying from the Texas School Board of Education concerning textbook selection. This background provided a springboard for an off-the-wall question, and walls, I guess, are as good a place for questions to spring from as anywhere.

Whatever, it gave him a chance to drag out the old joke about the smart monkey given copies of the Darwinian *Theory of Evolution* and the *Holy Bible.* He read 'em both, becoming, as Mort put it, "dizzied by ambivalence." Poor animal couldn't decide if he was his brother's keeper or his keeper's brother." (That old story turned the joke grist mill faster than anything since the Scopes Trial.)

Anyway, it set him to thinking about how he'd wanted to visit Dallas for years before ever setting foot in Big D. Members of the Lions Club, where so often he bummed a free meal, tired of his constantly talking about Dallas. They came up with a way to shut him up, or so they thought.

They passed the hat, collecting money to send him to Dallas on the train, and there was plenty of money for lodging and food needed for a week or more. The only request of him was to provide a program about his trip to Dallas upon return.

He was literally a "speaker of few words" when he stepped on the podium. "About the only report I can give you about Dallas is that I didn't see it," he confessed. Why? "There was just so blamed much happening around the depot!"...

'THISA' AND 'THATA'...

There are bits and pieces of columns perhaps worthy of recall, and commencing here are such items. (I usually call this "Mother Hubbard" material, which, like the pioneer dress of old, is said to have covered everything, but touched nothing. Here goes.

Mort usually picks up old newspapers left behind at the general store, which also hosts domino games during most waking—and some sleeping—hours. I was somewhat surprised to learn that he's read hundreds of Ann Landers columns, saving some of them in a picture album.

He was most excited when one of his fellow domino players wrote her a letter, and, of course, wanted to read it to me, verbatim. "Dear Ann. I have a jealous wife. Every evening, I like to go out for a walk, and she thinks I'm going out to see other women, so she hides my dentures." He signed it: "Gumming in the thicket." Ann wrote back, "Dear Gumming: Be thankful you've got the kind of wife that you do. She's trying to keep you from biting off more than you can chew."...

Speaking of writers, few humorists—in this century or any other—will ever measure up to the late Erma Bombeck. Quite simply, she was as good as it gets. I, and several million other Americans, read her regularly without fail. Once I wrote her a note, thanking her for sharing her experiences with us.

A few weeks later, she responded. Somewhere, I still have the note. Typed on an old Underwood upright typewriter—and on copy paper (the kind of rolls they used to have in newspaper offices)—she said, "I'm so sorry to be so late responding to your kind letter. I'm further behind with my correspondence than I am with the laundry." To further authenticate she had written a personal response, she signed the letter with a copy pencil, "Erma." She is keenly missed....

Years ago, Mort overheard a conversation at the general store. It was started by a yankee who was yammering about having visited Dallas, describing it as a "fair-sized country town." Hair rose on the back of his neck when the visitor continued to put down Texas, observing a vast area "devoid of culture."

After the guy left, Mort could have kicked himself for not bragging about Van Cliburn being from Kilgore, a few miles away on the other side of the thicket. Unable to get the matter off his mind, he decided not nearly enough had been done to recognize this renowned figure. He set out, on his own, to schedule a performance by Van Cliburn. It would be held at the high school. Signs were placed in business windows, a piece ran in the newspaper and radio news carried accounts of the upcoming performance.

Alas, it was to be on a Saturday night in February, and a winter storm gripped East Texas. The temperature hovered around 10 degrees, roads were ice-covered and a cold north wind howled. "I had to put several bales of hay in the back of my pickup to get enough traction, but we were going to have the program, no matter what." Only about a dozen people dared get out. Mort greeted them warmly, then, presenting the star of the evening, apologized for the weather. "I know the weather is a fright, and we certainly don't expect your complete repertoire this evening, Mr. Cliburn. But would you be kind enough to SANG us two or three songs?"…

❧

Uncle Mort says it's been so dry in the thicket, he caught a string of tick-infested catfish. He also has to trot out the old line about trees down there whistling for dogs. Oh, yes, and the drought was blamed for putting a damper on his birthday party.

"Maude baked a great, big Kansas-shaped cake," he explained, perhaps not thinking most of us can easily conjure mental pictures of a rectangle. "The volunteer fire boys said she'd best not put the 100 candles on the cake, the drought being what it is." Burn bans popped up everywhere—yes, even on birthday cakes for adults and older—and one politico in the area says it is so dry, he can't even "water down" the truth.

❧

My uncle says he's an "honor graduate" of the school of hard knocks. He doesn't need a diploma, said he, to deplore NFL footballer Michael Vick for his "dog-fighting ventures" that cost him 18 months in prison, as well as the respect of many fans. Mort said if the Philadelphia Eagles had gone for a nickname with one additional letter, they might have been called the "Philadelphia Beagles." In a subject-swapping mood, Mort switched to the 40th anniversary of man's first moon walk.

"Old Alvin Dark was quite a prophet," he claimed. Dark was manager of the San Francisco Giants when Gaylord Perry was a rookie pitcher in 1962. It is said that in that year, a sportswriter asked

Dark what he thought of Perry's chances of ever hitting a home run. "Man will walk on the moon before he hits a home run," Dark predicted. Wouldn't you know it? Seven years later, on July 21, 1969, Apollo XI made its lunar landing. A few minutes later, Perry blasted the first of his six career major league homers….

"Whoa" has been a handy word for my uncle, both around the farm and on the edges of technology he tip-toes around. That's the way he's brought horses to a stop, and also the way he's drawn a line in the dirt in opposition to much so-called "technological progress." Oh, he sometimes borrows a cell phone, and about the only technological term he's comfortable using is "the battery is down."

One of his most embarrassing moments involved use of a telephone more than 50 years ago. The instrument was attached to the wall of a neighbor's farm house. The neighbors were cutting a watermelon when the phone rang, so Mort answered it with the usual "hello." The operator said, "Long distance from New York." Mort answered, "It sure is," and hung up….

My friend Melinda, editor of the *Albany News*, can identify with Mort "back then," as well as with cell phone users now who wind up red-faced. She won't soon forget when she fumbled what could have been a golden moment of spontaneity worthy of note in her newspaper column. Zoned in for a guest preacher, she heard his admission of envying some congregants who have "heard the voice of God." He said he'd never had such an experience, and that there had been long, dry periods when he was uncertain of God's direction for his life.

At that precise moment, Melinda's cell phone rang. She scrambled to turn it off, then immediately regretted doing so. "I so wish I had handed the phone to the preacher, saying, 'I think it's for you'."…

Some of the world's best laughs occur on the telephone; many rich sources for laughter are never revealed, however. Receptionists have some of the best "you ain't gonna believe this" stories.

In my hometown years ago, a receptionist at an optometric practice routinely answered phones with this cheerful greeting, "Dr. Smith and Staff." My aunt—I always called her Awalt— let me speak to Dr. Staff." On another day, there was a call for "Dr. Smithenstaff."….

Only in recent years have I learned that Mort and Maude have a niece who is a long-time rancher who has tended a large spread in West Texas for more than 60 years. They say she's way short on book-learnin' but, like Mort, has what one day will be terminal degrees from the university of hard knocks. "She knows ranching, forward and back, and has little use for brain trusts sent around the state, particularly from Texas A&M," Mort said. "She thinks they live in the rarefied air of academia with being able to identify the most obvious aromas—okay, odors—out on the range. When such folks have "Ph.D." after their names, they are even more suspect.

She told about the time coyotes were doing a number on sheep, decimating herds over vast areas. They engaged an A&M "expert," and the meeting drew standing room only crowds. She went to the meeting with considerable reluctance.

"We've got wonderful news for sheep ranchers," he said. "We've developed a potion at College Station that is working wonders. You simply dip raw meat in it, then throw it out on the range. Coyotes eat it, and they become sterile."

Hands on her hips and teeth gritted, she'd heard enough. "Send him back to Texas A&M," she fumed. "He don't even understand the problem. The coyotes ain't attacking 'em, they're eatin' 'em. We ain't interested in their romantic propensities; we want 'em graveyard daid, right now!"....

During his long life, Mort has heard much music. Dancing? Probably it would be correct to say that he's "mostly observed," but then, who am I to say? He's always quick to identify outstanding vocalists and big-band names from yesteryear.

When Mitch Miller died at age 99, Mort spoke long and often of one of his favorite musicians. In the days of my youth, my life was one of wine, women and song. Nowadays, it's Metracal, the old gal and 'Sing Along with Mitch'."...

Mort has always maintained there is more to life than music, citing history, for example, and how important languages have been. Tabbing him the "wise ruler," he credited Charles V with this gem: "I speak Spanish to God, Italian to women, French to men and

German to my horse!" He's also the king who said, "Italian is the language for opera, French is the language for love; German is the language for war, English is the language to train horses and Spanish is the language to speak to God."...

During long stretches of time, Mort ignores staple conversational topics like the weather, sports and "getting ahead" (or behind). He sometimes calls his life "on the fringes or perhaps outer space," but claims the right to dip back into talking with we commoners as readily as changing lanes without signaling.

For example: Upon re-visiting the general topic of baseball, he began dissecting the base-running of a certain major league star. Joking about how longtime sportswriter Blackie Sherrod (of Dallas and world fame) liked to call baseball's ultimate series the "World Serious," my uncle described the errant base-runner as having lapses of fantasy rarely interrupted by reality. To soften the observation, he might—or might not—add that the athlete has a mind sometimes "turning to jelly without use of a recipe."...

Mort is forever bragging on kinfolks who have "made it big" in various professions, gigs or sidelines. (I've never given in to asking if any of these had to do with blimps or bubblegum. Nor have I asked if any of them have "made it small.")

He did share of one guy—maybe a fourth cousin—who was in real estate, however briefly. Mort claims that finally, the man was "weighed down by terms he never quite understood." One day, for example, he had a ready answer when the client asked the width of a lot advertised for sale. "It is 80 feet wide," the kin informed. "How deep?" This query got him. Finally, he answered, "Well, all the way to hell, I guess." (Maybe he was preoccupied with thought about a recent billboard message that hit home in Texas during August: "The devil called, and he wants his weather back."

During one of his sobering moments, though, Mort can be "right on:" The problems we face today are largely the result of people who work for a living are now outnumbered by those who vote for a living."…

Mort still wears homemade shorts to this very day. Aunt Maude confirms that she's turned 'em out by the hundreds, on a treadle sewing machine for 40 years and an electric model for the last 40. Mort says they are "roomy and comfy," and inspired a poem he sends out as requested. It reads thusly: "It's easy to grin, when your ship comes in, if it's just a small boat or a yacht. But one that's worthwhile is one who can smile when his shorts creep up in a knot."

My uncle was always slow to endorse anyone for anything—politically or otherwise. There were a few exceptions, one being baseball great Nolan Ryan. He would cast a vote for Nolan, even if he were running for king. I mean he's seen Ryan talking about foundation cracks "being bad" on TV commercials, usually followed by a trot outside, where he swears he sees cracks in the foundation, real or imagined.

He's even tried to rally a "Ryan for President" following. "He would take good care of our nation," Mort said. "In fact, why not call it 'RyanCare', except I'm afraid too many people would confuse it with 'ObamaCare'." Mort contends that "ObamaCare" has significant precedence, none of it encouraging. "The Romans weren't too wild about 'CaesarCare,' Egyptians took an even dimmer view of 'PharoahCare' and 'KingTutCare' never got off the ground."

Despite Rick Perry setting a record for tenure as Governor Texas, Mort never figured he'd get any further on contentions that required considerable vote-getting. ('Course this, like anything else, Mort admits to getting to bottom lines before wet paint signs have been removed, and if they offer Olympic jumping trials, he's "all in" because of his considerable experience in reaching conclusions by jumping to them.)

He thinks Perry ought to simply "walk away" from the ordeal of presidential campaigning. He recommends Perry "take up painting." I questioned whether he might most enjoy landscapes, seascapes or still life." Mort countered, "I was thinkin' barns, deer blinds and fences—right after he slaps a second coat on that rock by the hunting camp gate." (Aside: It was such a temptation to mention "Cain Mutiny" and "Perry-less seas.")…

LIFE THROUGH SQUINTED EYES...

From time to time, I bear down on an iron-sure fact: Any way life is sliced, squared, quartered or sneezed at, I am my Uncle Mort's nephew. Maybe that's what I've inherited from him—at least this may be the most desirable trait that comes to mind—is his tendency to view life through squinted eyes.

His mind's eye was in "squint mode" upon learning about a new study suggesting there are merits in running barefoot. "We started running millions of years ago," Dr. Daniel Lieberman said, noting that during most of history, runners have run shoeless, "landing" toward the middle or front of the foot. For the past few decades, cushioned shoes have been introduced to absorb heel impact. Nike, of course, is in crisis mode, spending billions of dollars to convince runners that periodic "improvements" justify steady price escalation for state-of-the-art running shoes.

Anyway, I asked Mort what brought him to town. Looking toward the ground, I could plainly see he was barefoot, so for all I knew, he came from the country to protest carefully-pitched ads by Nike and other shoe giants. Again, though, I was wrong.

"I see my dermatologist today," he grinned. "The doc says I have more skin tags than skin, and he removed enough of 'em to tag store-wide price markdowns at Wal-Mart." I groaned; he rambled on. "Did you hear that Glen Bell, 86-year-old founder of Taco Bell, died?" He said the fast food pioneer, with 60-plus years in the business, had 5,600 franchises serving 37 million Americans weekly. What I hadn't heard is that he also was a founder of Der Wienerschnitzel, the big hot dog chain. "If I'd had to learn to spell 'Wienerschnitzel,' I'd have started thinking outside the bun, too," Mort joked.

I hope I haven't warped Mort's intent to "stay current" despite no formal higher education—unless one counts the weekend class he completed at Texas A&M University on treating snakebites. Another time, he was a dropout in a non-credit course called "computers for old coots."

Before dropping out, Mort was dead set on making *Guinness World Records* for having the longest computer password. Taught that passwords must have eight characters, he chose "Curly/Joe/Moe/Gabby/Daffy/Goofy/Mickey/Minnie. Later, my wife was valedictorian of a similar class, and she came up with an extremely long password. She had a distinct advantage, though, since she knew the keyboard layout going in....

SIGNS OF BIRTHDAYS AND MORE....

Mort will tackle just about any task. He's always been of a mind to zip hither and yon, starting many projects that don't get finished, at least not in the same decade they were begun. Sometimes he writes birthday messages, perhaps hoping to catch the eye of Hallmark or some other greeting card company. Once, he painted a huge sign, "Feeling Great at 98." He thought it would be a fine banner to hang above the birthday cake. "Need I remind you that the only folks needing this banner will need to have completed 97 years?" I asked.

"It's for me, nephew, and I've got lots of years left in me. My old tire of a body has lots of patches on it, but there's still room for a few more. Three figures, here I come!

We started talking about the dignity of work, and that work in itself is not believed to have ever killed anyone. I asked him about the toughest job he ever tackled. He answered that he has been "in harness with hard work since age 5." (We've joked that he's long been known for "ministerially speaking"--ramping up numbers to better enliven chamber of commerce conversations.)

"I thought you'd hit me with a hard question, nephew," he laughed. "But this one's easy. The first job I ever had was also the hardest one, requiring discipline, agility, consistency and a tolerance for early rising." Wow, I thought. His answers flowed so quickly, I wondered why I hadn't heard it before.

"It was a seven-days-a-week job during the long winter months," Mort explained. "My job was to get up at 4:30 a.m. to bring in the wood so I could get the stove heated to boil water in the tea kettle to pour through the cracks in the floor to get the hogs out from under the house."…

Clearly, that was Mort being Mort. Even at age five, I'd have guessed he would have somehow farmed out "getting up early" chores to siblings. "Speaking of work, looks to me like the New Hampshire legislature has run out of things to do," he said, mentioning a news item that the Yankees are debating whether to designate milk or cider as the "state drink." (He admitted that he probably shouldn't be critical, since the Texas legislature often bickers over less.) "It's a slam dunk that milk should be so designated," he said, talking about how such a choice would give teachers another way to introduce food groups to youngsters, and how the “juice from old Jersey” is basic to so many recipes. He pointed out that the “Got Milk” theme could be worked into skits. Somehow, “Got Cider?” has a different ring to it, and would barely be noticed when wiped away from drenched mustaches….

LIFE IS LIKE A BOX OF CHOCOLATES—SOMETIMES...

Mort’s mind is awash in theories, flopping wildly about. Most of them—if tossed into the “THROWN Room” of Great Ideas—wouldn’t be a misprint. There, they’d languish in the darkest corner, unclaimed by the rest of humanity. My uncle is accustomed to the linkage of his life rhythms to the beat of a far distant drum. His mind spins with “what ifs” during most waking moments, and often during hours of slumber as well.

He once spoke of decreased—not increased, as might be expected—charges for concession items at the Texas Ranger baseball games. When prices go down, it’s news. Granted, the decreases were modest—in the 10% to 20% range—but charge for hot chocolate went down dramatically, by two-thirds—from $3 to $1.

Okay, since the temperature usually sizzles in Arlington, hot chocolate may not be in high demand. Perhaps there can be some chocolate mustache contests, and slogans that milk “does a body good.”

There’s no bigger Ranger fan than Dr. Dan Crawford. The retired seminary professor could easily have become disenchanted with the sport a half-century ago. In 1960, the late Dr. Guy D. Newman, longtime president of Howard Payne University, offered a few young men partial scholarships in baseball. Ever the visionary, he wanted to resurrect the sport that had been dropped earlier by the Lone Star Athletic Conference. Crawford signed on, finishing his degree in the then-typical four years. Sadly, the team never materialized.

Some 30 years and four presidents later, the sport finally was reinstated at HPU on a non-scholarship basis. Dr. Crawford's tongue-in-cheek letter to the president's office detailed his baseball "scholarship misadventures." He indicated a willingness to "throw out the first pitch" for the initial game of the renewed sport.

HPU president at the time, former classmate and longtime friend of Crawford's, I took a somewhat different view about "who owed whom." Since he had enjoyed the benefits of an athletic scholarship without lifting a finger, I suggested he might want to consider "paying back" the unearned scholarship benefits. He, of course, had other thoughts.

More recently, as president of the HPU Alumni Association, Dr. Crawford shared his story. With a new season at hand, he was invited to throw out the first pitch. He thought he had two chances to participate in an HPU athletic event—slim and none. Alas, it didn't happen. The game was rained out. He was, however, offered a cup of hot chocolate for his willingness to drive more than two hours for a rain-out….

A STORY OF 9-1-1…

It has occurred that attempting participation in civil discourse with my uncle is akin to flying kites. More time is spent untangling string than actually maneuvering them skyward. Once he wanted to "fill in some of my blanks" ("blanks" I wasn't aware I had) concerning perils sometimes faced by emergency responders. "They have to laugh at themselves to keep from crying, and sometimes folks they're assisting are involved, at least in minor roles," he said. "Sometimes these guys face situations than can result in absolute belly laughs. I mean the kind calling for sitting down—maybe even rolling on the floor—as tears roll and laughter comes out in spurts, interspersed with groans."

He cited a specific experience of two of his friends—one, "Joe," the other, "Moe"—seasoned emergency medical technicians who answer 9-1-1 calls. They spend considerable time herding the rattling county ambulance toward emergency scenes. Once they got a call from a care center, where an elderly patient—her age closer to 100 than 95—had experienced a problem eating breakfast.

The care center caller—perhaps more rattled than the ambulance—said the woman "must have blacked out, then drooped forward, her face making a direct hit into the oatmeal dish." Luckily, the attendant had discovered the incident within minutes of occurrence, but his clumsy efforts to revive her were fruitless. "Come quickly, we aren't even sure she's still breathing." That's the last thing Joe and Moe heard before "floor-boarding" the ambulance toward the care center as precious seconds ticked away.

Upon arrival in her room, Joe bade his gag reflexes "go to time-out" while he got on with the business of mouth-to-mouth resuscitation. Moe, whose gag reflexes were more vigilant (Moe later said he could imagine them saying, "We got a job to do, and we ain't leavin'.") wiped away oatmeal served in an oversized dish that accommodated the pot's last big glob before serious washing made the vessel ready for the next day. Miraculously, the patient's breathing was restored, and within a short time, she was OK. Soon, she was "back at it" (according to the attendant) disliking everything in sight, hearing or "mind's eye." She shot dagger-like stares alternately toward Joe and Moe; it was evident she was anything but happy.

"Can't you guys read?" she questioned, pointing to a sign affixed to the wall above her bed. Thereupon were these words, in boldface: "Do NOT resuscitate." After absorbing what they considered to be a full volley of rants, Joe and Moe excused themselves, walking double-time back toward the ambulance, laughing so hard they risked serious smothering spells. The flabbergasted care center guy feared they might have to resuscitate each other!

There are millions of stories in care centers. This, please note, is one of them….

TERMINATOR OR EXTERMINATOR?...

During one of Mort's moments of seriousness that occur about as often as leap year, he grudgingly admits it. Yes, it would please him greatly if "boat-rocking" were declared an Olympic sport. Even though he spends much of his life flailing about, trying to stay afloat, I'm pretty sure he'd give serious thought to whatever training might be required to become a serious boat-rocker. This could lead to international attention.

A shocker to me was his confession of "using" banks for a single day. (He says this belongs among his "visionary" credits.) He says his money, "mattressed" away for more than eight decades, was once entrusted to a bank, albeit briefly. "Back in the 1970s, they were giving away toasters for new depositors. I made my deposit in the morning, got my toaster, and withdrew funds the same afternoon."

In another admission, he claimed he was "dabbling in prophecy." He claims his multiple séances on the subject led to the revelation of Arnold Schwarzenegger's plans upon exiting the governor's mansion in California. He blurted it out that all of us should expect Arnold to be a "major player in the rodent and pest control business." Asked to clarify, he explained, "For years he's been called "The Terminator. Now, he'll be the EX-terminator!"

Speaking of movies, he was all excited to accompany a great-great-grandson kindergartener to see *Yogi Bear* in a three-dimensional film. "The last time I went to a picture show must have been 60 years ago," Mort said. "They had wooden seats, evaporative cooling, but it was worth it to see James Stewart in *Harvey*. Back then, we were fortunate to get two-dimensional films, hopeful the screen didn't darken more than two or three times per showing because of film breaks."

Blown away by 3-D, he claimed to have gotten lots of exercise "shielding his kin from all the objects flying off the screen." Thinking he could relax during the cartoon, Mort was wrong yet again. It was a Roadrunner cartoon similar to the ones he'd seen in mid-20th century. "And neither the bird nor Wile E. Coyote had aged a bit," he laughed. He chirped a hearty "beep-beep" just before the roadrunner made the same sound.

With Mort's "beep-beep" that he'd have us believe was prophetic to herald the coyote's honk before he blasted off down the trail, his young partner laughed. And my old uncle cared not a whit that he was laughing AT him, not WITH him….

ON GEE-HAWING WITH PREACHERS…

Maybe one of the reasons Mort and his preacher generally "gee-haw" is that the parson often gets himself into predicaments, too. "Sometimes he paints himself into sermon corners," Mort laughed. "And about all he figures he can do then is slap on a second coat."

Once the preacher convinced the deacons to buy a two-wheeled trailer with a marquee affixed. He thought it a good idea to move it around the thicket. Further, he'd change it regularly, taking careful mind of spelling, clarity, good taste and creativity. He did pretty well for a while, usually using all four lines. His thoughts weren't quite so nimble during a Super Bowl cold spell. Conversations were dominated not only by the temperature, but also the astronomical prices for admission tickets at the BIG GAME. The preacher needed just two lines for his trailer marquee: "MAPQUEST GOT YOU HERE—GOD GETS YOU THERE."

Mort said the church folks had hoped his sermons would be as succinct as the marquee messages. They weren't. Aunt Maude said if the parson had to wear her girdle and high heels, he'd never need to watch the clock to see when to quit. Yes, he was known for what he himself called his "keen attention to detail." Many thought he included a great many details that didn't warrant attention.

He admits that in numerous ways, his church is just like most of 'em. "Our motto should be, "We ain't never done it that way before," he said. "And at our church, we expected everybody to know where they're supposed to sit. We all have favorite pews." Once, his face was beet-red when he arrived at "his pew," only to find visitors sitting there. Before Mort could gather his thoughts, he blurted, "You are occu-PEW-ing my pie!"

Once, the preacher dropped by the cemetery a couple of hours before a funeral service was to begin. He judged the grave to be no more than half dug. Two men, paid by the hour, were leaning on their shovels. "Think it'll be ready when the hearse gets here for the last rites?" the parson asked. One worker answered, "If you 'funeralize' as long as you 'sermonize,' it'll be ready with a good hour to spare."

"Boy, he could really get 'lathered up' during our summer tent revivals," Mort claimed. "Sometimes they went on for two weeks, usually winding up on a Sunday morning with baptizing down in the creek."

Saying that the population in the thicket was so sparse, they didn't even have a town drunk, Mort said that the "men took turns." One of the residents, Mort regales, followed the same pattern each week. Saturdays were particularly predictable. He partook of the grape starting at mid-afternoon, and by midnight, usually had reached a state of, uh, gentle repose. By 2 a.m. on Sundays, he began deep sleep, wherever he happened to be. Typically, he'd awaken around 10 a.m. The imbiber, unaware of the extended revival, had fallen asleep in a pasture near the "dippings." He heard the commotion, stumbled toward the creek and fell in.

Dragging the man from the deep water, the preacher asked, "Are you looking for Jesus?" Seeing all the onlookers on the banks dressed in Sunday finery, the "victim" wasn't about to answer "No!" With a hearty "amen," the parson baptized him, holding him underwater for 15 seconds. "Did you find Jesus?" he asked. "Nope." The baptism was repeated, this time for 30 seconds. Again, the guy had a "no" answer when asked if he'd found Jesus. On the third try, he was immersed for a full minute. Sputtering upon surfacing, he interrupted, "Preacher, before you say anything else, are you sure this is where he fell in?"…

NEW ENTRY FOR GUINNESS?…

The thought of mention in Guinness World Records never entered my mind—until now. My recurring fear may warrant my inclusion on the lengthening list of known phobias. (Guinness now names and defines almost 600 phobias.) I'm afraid of becoming entangled in the same dream—or nightmare—with my Uncle Mort.

Maybe the entry would fit in a sub-group under "phobophobia"—a fear of having a phobia. An apt name might be "Mortophobia."

My fear may not be as "far out" as it seems. Mort has been calling almost daily, reminding me to "keep July the fourth clear" for his 99th birthday party at his place in the thicket. Each time, he emphasizes the practicality of gift certificates and the importance of "being on time." Aunt Maude chuckles about the punctuality bit. "He's never made it anywhere on time and is from a long line of late-comers. His ancestors came to these shores on the Juneflower."

My old uncle describes himself as "the luckiest guy on the planet," beginning with his birth. "It's pretty amazing he's as normal as he is," Maude says. "He missed more classes in school than he attended, and when he did go, he was caught up in trying to win the marble games."

He has a "by gosh/by golly" record of birth, scribbled on a Big Chief tablet. His birth date was recorded as "June 34, 1912." The doctor, writing in the hurried manner of a physician, scribbled down "Mort," with the last name not discernible. "Who knows, maybe the physician was rattled—I think he interrupted a hunting trip to make the delivery," Maude said.

"It gets better," Mort laughs. "I was 23 years old when Social Security came along, so I've got a three-digit number." He said his driver's license—the one that lapsed years ago when he gave up his pickup to protest high gasoline prices—also was a "short number." He's vowed to depend on a golf cart for conveyance the rest of the way. With computer servers spewing personal information all over cyberspace for "whosoever will" to claim, my uncle could well be least affected.

I think this personal "misinformation" topic came up when Mort learned of the Texas Comptroller's Office's admission of mistakenly transferring unencrypted personal records of 3.5 million Texans, about half of whom are retired teachers. Information was accessible to the public from the Comptroller's Office's servers during most of a year; it included birthdates, as well as driver's license and social security numbers.

The office's postage budget took a big hit, what with the cost of apology letters "in the mail" to all Texans whose personal information was compromised.

"Like I said, I'm the luckiest guy around," Mort laughed. "Officially, the date of my birth is approximate, I have just one name, my Social Security number is three digits, my last driver's license expired in the last century and my address is 'way down in the thicket'." (Family lore has it that Mort was the original "007.")

He has no bank account, opting to hide his money in mattresses and syrup buckets, and he has almost no financial records, since he buys little and barters much. (He disturbed the peace at a Trader Vic's restaurant trying to trade several dozen eggs for a meal. Within a few minutes, they sent him on his way, telling him to keep his eggs.)

Mort rattled on about his indifference to the release of his "personal information." My eyes crossed and my hair hurt, partly because some of his claims made sense. I thought of an experience years ago when he and I were trapped between floors on an elevator one hot July day. "One of our deodorants is wearing thin," I joked.

"It must be yours, 'cause I ain't wearin' none," he countered. So what else is new?

It should be clear why I might fear being trapped in an Uncle Mort dream. In real life, I can blame a faulty phone, walk away or fake a coughing spell. But, shackles of dreams are hard to shake. Recently, my uncle said he dreamt of sleeping through two jobs—Vice President of the United States by day and air traffic controller by night. Wow! There's a whole 'nuther topic of fears for "fraidy cats" to be scared of!...

MUSINGS WITH MORT…

Surely he uses cue cards when he phones during bowl game intermissions, touching topics all over the conversation map in record time. Verbal responses lengthen calls, so I simply smile, nod or frown, relying on assorted expressions of bewilderment. Such was the plan when he claimed to be "awash in holiday excitement akin to a ten-year-old on Christmas morning." Like horses released from barn confines, his words fairly galloped. Committed to a vow of silence, I listened….

First off, he spoke of the year's final meeting of the Lions Club. (No, he's not a member, but he hastily accepts when friends invite him. Sure enough, they had turkey, dressing and pecan pie—two pieces, since Mort sat next to a guy on the front end of a diet dare.)

At meal's end, a usually-timid Lion—for whom joining in the Pledge of Allegiance was problematic and voicing a holiday prayer was unthinkable—approached the lectern. He wasn't scheduled to speak, but requested a "point of personal privilege." Members stopped at mid-bite, moved that the mild-mannered, "milquetoast-y" man might muster the mettle to make meaningful microphone mentions....

Gripping the lectern, the Wizard-of-Oz-like Lion admitted his fondness for juice of the grape and occasional indulgence to excess. "Sometimes I reach a state of loving everybody," he said. "But this time, good judgment prevailed." At a holiday party, he was warmed by "too many trips to the eggnog bowl." When hours wound down to wee, a sunny thought broke through his cloudy mind. "I decided to take a bus home," he said proudly....

Members applauded him silently, thinking better of breaking out with real hand-claps and/or back-pats, but making mental notes—albeit back burner items—to drop him congratulatory notes.

"I'm sure some of you have imbibed to excess, and that my decision to take a bus home comes as a surprise to you," the speaker said. "It shocked me, too, since I don't know how to drive a bus, don't know where I found it and have no clue where I parked it."

Stone-faced, the speaker walked slowly back to his table to finish his pie...

Switching topics, Mort mentioned feeling sorry for football coaches. "For the few who run championship flags up the pole, there are hundreds of others who feel run over at worst, or run down at best," he said.

He cited a recent high school state championship game at Cowboys Stadium.

"The losing coach probably felt like he'd been run over by a truck—figuratively—and the winner's response hit dead center of the truth button," my uncle opined. "He likely felt as if he'd been run over by a golf cart—literally."...

Sometimes Mort reaches "way back" comparing current notables to historical figures. He asked what Dallas Cowboys defensive Coach Rob Ryan has in common with the late Gorgeous George—whose showmanship did for TV wrestling what Elvis Presley's did for rock-n'-roll music.

I kidded that since both showed partiality to long locks, maybe they had the same hairdresser. Mort agreed, adding that both of them seem better known for their bravado than for "delivering the goods."

Gorgeous George warrants Googling. A showman and well-above-average wrestler, his flamboyance propelled him to stardom. Wearing garish capes and sparkling jewelry, he sprayed the ring with what he called "Chanel No. 10." (Why be half safe?)

His entry to the ring, set to music with assorted folderol, often took more time than the matches. Oft-quoted, his admonitions usually ended with zingers, such as "Win if you can, lose if you must, but always cheat!" With that, Mort signed off, I dozed off and the second half kicked off....

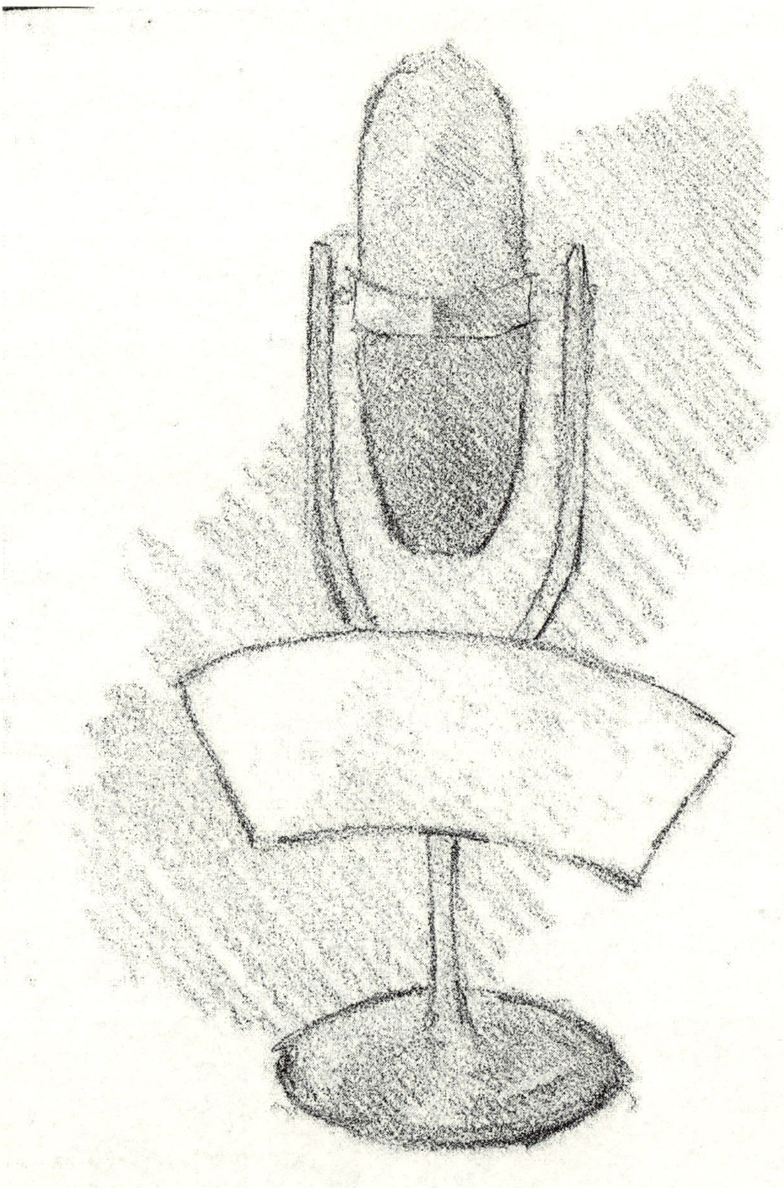

LECTERNS AND RADIO GUYS

Speak right into the microphone...

TRAVAILS IN TRAVEL...

Dallas radio sports guru, Norm Hitzges, now in his fifth decade at Metroplex microphones, belabored worldwide airports, citing Chicago's "O'Hare" as "the very worst."

My uncle is well-known for telling train story after train story back in the day. A common theme, of course, is that they were painfully slow, and sometimes never showed up at all. He told of a conductor helping a woman give birth to a baby, then urging her "never again to board a train in such a condition." Her answer: "Before I boarded the train, I wasn't in such a condition."

Quite content to hang out mostly on the middle rung of life's ladder, Mort has enjoyed all the brouhaha about the Fort Hood gunman who refused to cut his beard. He says if they'd turned him over to Maude, he'd be happy to become clean shaven, if only to get her off his case. "She'd have him shaved slick as a whistle if she harped on him like she does me," Mort said. "She won't stand for it if my ear and nose hair dangles for a day or two." Mort was actually happy to talk about the issue, pulling out all the stops to avoid conversation about his wife's 100th birthday a few days earlier that Mort **"plumb forgot about."** He'd already smarted off about her new diet, claiming she was "going to great lengths to avoid great widths."

Actually, Mort said if he had time, he'd like to study Lance Armstrong's star-crossed life. Truth to tell, he has time in abundance. Recently, his only physical activity occurred during what he calls "recliner duty." It came when Maude asked him to lift up his feet so she could sweep under 'em. He believes Lance's spotlight once was bright enough for a midnight plane landing, and now is "snuffed out" by the cyclist's lousy judgment. Mort spoke of a dream about a bicycle built for two. "It was really sad," Mort mourned. "Lance was on the front seat, and the back one was empty."

As to sadness, Mort joined other Texans in lamenting the fire that took "Big Tex," leaving a substantial void at the Texas State Fair. The 52-foot icon went up in flames some years back (later was rebuilt, bigger and better). "We love Big Tex because he is one of us," Mort says.

We spoke of the $750 spent for delivery of Big Tex from his previous home in Kerens 60 years ago, and how it might require that much just for the buttonholes when he was re-clad. Mort—noting that Big Tex "went down talking"—might include a recipe contest for "twice-baked denim" at upcoming fairs….

BEST/WORST OF TIMES...

Timing isn't everything. The Lone Star State's two flagship universities—The University of Texas and Texas A&M University—are once again at extremes. The Longhorns picked a year when football was "down" to begin its own cable network. (I mean, UT faithful simply aren't accustomed to being on the losing ends of games with foes like Brigham Young and Ol' Miss.) Texas A&M, however, perhaps couldn't have chosen a better time to acquire its own law school.

"Acquire" is the right word. The Aggies bought one that was "up and running" at Texas Wesleyan University. Uncle Mort thinks this was a brilliant move on the part of A&M brain trusts. "With the Aggies adapting to membership in the Southeast Conference and trying to keep football star Johnny Manziel on the straight and narrow, the law school can perhaps stay busy with two shifts and maybe three," Mort laughed.

He thinks Danny Snyder, owner of the Washington Redskins, might be a client, too, with his ongoing "hot potato." Many Native Americans insist the team take on a name other than "Redskins." And a group opposed to the move says if a name is removed, erasing the word "Washington" could ease embarrassment. Snyder has dug in his heels, and the arrows of many quivers will fly before this issue is settled. (Watching from the sidelines are the Kansas City Chiefs; they're holding their breath that their mascots continue to blaze a trail under the radar.)

The NCAA has pressed the issue of Native American names with numerous smaller colleges and universities, including two in Texas. McMurry U. in Abilene and Midwestern U. in Wichita Falls both have yielded; both formerly were called "Indians." Bigger universities with stronger alumni bases—such as Florida State University—seem untouchable. Yep, the A&M Law School could stay right busy with athletic issues.

Speaking of Indians, one tribe built a big new airport, a project finished up early and under budget. "How in the world did you manage it?" a senator asked the chief. His answer: "We didn't get bogged down in *white* tape."...

Mort thinks A&M's Law School will be compatible with its long-respected School of Veterinary Medicine. He says the way pets are being pampered these days, it soon may be common for angry pet owners to sue veterinarians. "The Aggie fleet of attorneys should be most helpful defending malpractice suits against vets if Fido don't make it," Mort chuckled. (I heard of one Aggie visionary who insisted on extending graduate school to include doctorates in both Veterinary Medicine and Taxidermy. His business cards had this message: "Either way you get your dog back.")

Known more for the "money-losing" reality hatched by "money-making" schemes, Mort can't quite decide whether he wants to make a Johnny Football bobble-head doll or perhaps a "block-head" doll. He's leaning toward making a doll with interchangeable heads. "His play on the field for the Aggies deserves a bobble-head for sure, but once he's out on the streets, block-head 'fits' too much of the time."

Hey, this time Mort may be using his head....

MORT AND MYRTLE BELL—REALLY 'OLD SCHOOL'...

Okay, so some editors think calling my work "commentary" feel they are "top-heavy generous," but this column reduced some of 'em to "re-thinking." Probably I won't hold out for "satire" any time in the near future. Maybe the only safe course is to hope that my writing, year after year, can be abided by bottom-feeding, comment-seekers—the kind usually thought to be readers from “kivver to kivver.”

Frequently, my writing includes the goings-on of relatives—some blood kin, others imagined, the latter living in mythical places. This one concerns Mort’s participation at Poverty Squat School’s “Bi-Decade” Homecoming Reunion. A 1928 graduate, he and Myrtle Bell Southern are the only two alumni left from a senior class of 16 members. (I know, morbidity is not a topic I deal with often, at least, not yet….)

In recent years, their classmates have been “falling faster’n flies,” Mort says. He and Myrtle Bell decided to proceed with the “reunion,” despite their being the only two alumni remaining “on the top side of the grass.” It commenced at the smallest table—a “two-seater”—in a tiny eating joint located so far back in the thicket, Watkins’ products were available by mail order only.

Retired in Granbury, Myrtle Bell—two months younger than Mort—rode the bus to East Texas. He waited at the bus station, his golf cart at the ready. She hopped on, and off they went to “The Squeeze-In,” a “chili joint” aptly named since one “squeezes” into the café. He ordered a cheeseburger “all the way,” and she took one dry, well done, no onions. Relieved at her insistence to “get the check,” he decided to let her do most of the talking—or at least allow her an equal share of the discourse. Five years earlier, with six alumni gathered ‘round the largest table, he’d “led the gab.” In most settings, this is a given.

She was in a "tell-all" kind of mood, admitting to "extreme insecurity" as she "bumbled" through school. She blamed much of it on her parents. "My mother, with the maiden name of 'Bell,' wanted to have a hyphenated married name," she said. "You know, Hattie May Bell-Southern. Daddy wouldn't hear to it, but agreed that if they had a daughter, Mom could have 'Bell' in the name, but with an 'e' at the end, of course."

In first grade, her face reddened when the teacher called out alphabetized students' last names. Just imagine: "Southern, Bell." Snickers always erupted. "There've been lots of reasons for others to laugh," she said. "Later, they called me 'Ma Bell.' I was ready just to try my MSB initials, but that sound too much like a broadcasting network. So there we were, with one wall telephone, and it on a party line. I guess the only other 'technology' in the house was one battery-powered radio."

She asked Uncle Mort if he remembered her excellence in playground volleyball. "It's the only thing I ever did at school I was any good at." Though quite small in those salad days, she was "lightning quick," soon earning a nickname—"The Hummer"—for her dipping, setting, bumping, blocking, spiking and, well, whatever other volleyball terms I may be leaving out.

Mort asked if anyone still calls her "Hummer." She countered, "Heavens, no. "Way too much has changed in 85 years. 'Humdrum' would fit now."

That prompted a topic change. "Do you recall that I was the first East Texas girl to sport a tattoo?" Yep, Mort remembered; could anyone forget? Since volleyball had brought her out of her shell, she made a "sophomoric" decision to get a tattoo atop her left shoulder. Inscribed were two tiny figures—a humming bird and a volleyball. She was forever pushing back her sleeve when classmates wanted to take a "look-see." Mort asked if he could "get a gander" at it, but he got a not-in-a-million-years response. "I was happy to show it off in high school," Myrtle Bell said. "But that was then—four score and five years ago, for those keeping score."

She said for the full effect now, she'd have to be "flattened out, since the artwork has, uh, expanded, like the rest of my body has. Now, it looks like Big Bird and a beach ball."

How time flies! Their high noon meeting was about to crowd supper time. The diner operator cleared his throat several times, asking them if "there'd be anything else." They paid no attention, too busy laughing about what classmates might have called her had her initials been "AT&T." Finally, they hurriedly left, headed for the bus station on his golf cart, it leaning to Myrtle Bell's side. They "good-byed," vowing to meet up there again in 2019….

FOR THE BIRDS...

Personal experiences racked up across three-quarters of a century—including yips and yaps at lecterns spanning more than five decades—offer positive proof that many times, utter silence is preferable to spoken words. I was reminded of this age-old truth the other day when Mort called. Upon his mention of a new-found interest in ornithology, the call—during the morning hours of April 1—likely meant he was up to his old tricks—"spoofing it up" on April Fools' Day.

Interrupting him was as tempting as a clearance sale on banana splits, a promise of bonus airline miles, or biggest-ever senior citizen discounts. Assuming this was his annual BIG JOKE for the holiday, it was little short of miraculous that I remained silent.

Maybe I was stunned to hear Uncle Mort take on pronunciation of a word like "ornithology." He did so with clarity, confidence and unbridled excitement. What sparked this new-found interest in birds? It couldn't have involved "tweeting," since he stated that if God had intended us to "tweet," we'd all look like "Tweety Bird."

Perhaps his mind was jarred with the long-ago memory of Mr. Wallace Wimple, the little mush-mouthed guy on the radio show, *Fibber McGee and Molly*. (Wimple, always the patient listener, worked in mentions of his ever-present "bird book," no matter how conversations began.) A standard line on every episode—Fibber saying: "That ain't the way I heerd it, Johnny."

Or, maybe Mort was prepping me for the old story of two buzzards, flying lazily aloft on a hot summer day. One of the buzzards said, "Patience, heck, let's kill sumthin'." Another possibility involved the two feisty magpies in "Heckle and Jeckle" cartoons seen in olden days at the picture show. Or, maybe Sesame Street's popular "Big Bird" in the children's morning TV show was in play.

Okay, I admit it—my mind was largely in neutral when Uncle Mort said his interest centers specifically on crows, and how they've developed New England accents. I was hooked, eager for him to fill in several additional blanks. Pray tell, what was Uncle Mort talking about? Since his prejudices have been stacking up for decades, I figured crows with New England accents would rile him from the git-go.

Mort has little use for Yankees—a name mentioned regularly in his diatribes against the government. He's long been opposed to southern migration of northerners, and is on record supporting efforts to turn 'em back when they attempted to enter Texas from Oklahoma. "Dangers in Texas will multiply if our government doesn't start 'getting it right.' They've got troops on our southern border, keeping illegal folks out, yet Yankees are pouring in through Oklahoma, crossing freely over the Red River. The Feds are guarding the wrong river."

Mort said his study of birds began one winter day when he saw a flock of crows pecking away at road kill. (What with insects—as well as vegetation—provided by Mother Earth in short supply, they "made do" with this sustenance.)

Mort claims he was mystified by several crows taken out by speeding trucks, but flew to safety when autos approached. Why, he wondered, weren't they "spooked" by the 18-wheelers, but flew quickly away from the four-wheelers? He returned to the scene several days in a row. "Finally, the mystery was solved," he bragged.

Balderdash, thought I. There had to be an April Fool's joke in there somewhere, but if so, it was well-hidden. "It all came into focus when I realized the crows had a plan. They stationed a 'look-out' in the tall oak tree alongside the road," he said. "The 'look-out' provided ample warning when cars approached, and his buddies took flight."

"Why didn't he warn them when he saw trucks coming?" I asked. "That's a reasonable question, nephew, and logical as well," he answered. "The same thought occurred to me, and I'm glad it did, 'cause if it hadn't, I might never have realized crows have a New England accent." Okay, so I was "bumfuzzled" to the max.

"When four-wheelers approached, the 'look-out' crow cut loose with loud 'caw, caw, caws'," Mort said. "Too bad the 'look-out' couldn't say 'truck, truck, truck'."

It could have been worse, I thought. At least he didn't ask if I had been second in line for breakfast. "Remember," he warned, "The early bird gets the worm, but the second mouse gets the cheese." Again, I felt like a 14-carat bird-brain, falling for one of Uncle Mort's favorite pastimes—fooling me….

IT DOESN'T LOOK LIKE A BUICK
But nobody knows for sure, it could Mort's golf cart with Lincoln add-ons underneath the leaf piles. Maude told him to rake 'em, but he'd rather "shake-'em" at the general store domino table...

WHAT'S IN A NAME?...

It was a central question in Shakespeare's play. Romeo and Juliet were from warring families, so their romance was star-crossed from the git-go. She downplayed their plight, cooing, "What's in a name?" Then there was something about a rose by any other name smelling just as sweet.

The same question posed today begs several "sub-questions" before it can be meaningfully answered. Who's asking? What's the purpose? Have popularity surveys been checked? Is it likely to trigger an IRS audit? Is there an "app" for that?

Space limitations shorten this treatise on naming human offspring, never mind there also are plenty of resources for persons pondering pet names. Across the pond, they're scratching heads by the millions—as well as betting considerable "tonnage" of pounds—concerning the name to be given to Prince William and Kate Middleton's offspring, who will be fourth in line for the crown.

Mort was in town recently to visit wrecking yards. As usual, he was searching for an obscure--yet "just right"--body of the smallest ever Lincoln automobile. He didn't need the "innards," since he planned to configure the body shell somehow over his golf cart—ongoing proof, really, that one of his strongest desires in life—upon arising each day, every day—is to be noticed. And he prefers it if he is—in the words I've heard from his lips many times—viewed as someone he ain't!

With Matt McConaughey's ads that Lincolns are "all right, all right, all right," maybe Aunt Maude would be willing to ride on the cart if passers-by think they're in a "little Lincoln." Mort also had a word for the little old lady in another ad—the one who says, "It doesn't look like a Buick." To her, he says, "If you are looking in my direction, lady, that's because it ain't a Buick. We're just trying to pass a golf cart off as a miniature 'alright' Lincoln!"

Mort said he wanted to talk about the excitement in naming Great Britain's new royal baby. "When I came along, most babies were given biblical names, whether or not they ever darkened church doors," he said. "Of course, we shortened the names later—'Abraham' became 'Abe,' Solomon was shortened to 'Sol' and 'Ezekiel' later was 'Zeke'." He claimed it "saved on ink later when signatures on official documents required such." (Idle thought: I don't think I've ever heard of anyone named for "Hezekiah," or, in today's text-flooded world, "Hez.") He finds it interesting that most feminine names from the "Good Book" more nearly remain intact—mainly, he thinks, because they're "shorter to start with—like Martha, Mary and Ruth." (He told me not to throw a wrench into his theory by mentioning names like "Bathsheba.")

Mort asked me if I realized many girls' given names now are chosen from plants, and the list is long. "I'm plenty glad my folks didn't name me after a plant," Mort chuckled. "I'd have a hard time living down 'Kudzu'." He figures if the royal couple's second baby had been a male, it would be a "slam dunk" to call him "Kong." Then, if he ascended to the throne, he'd be "King Kong."

Such thinking caused him to go further on down his verbal side trail. He recalled the name of an Italian priest many years ago many followers thought had a good chance one day to be named Pope. "I knew he didn't have a chance in the world," Mort said. "His name was Zicola. And 'Pope Zicola' sounds way too much like a soft drink."

After he left, I couldn't get my mind off the "baby-naming" thing. And, I thought of his name having no biblical origin. Yet, he's proud of the name "Mortimer." This was clear to me during a conversation exhausted years ago. "How many other 'Mortimers' do you know with a dummy named for them?" he questioned. (Late ventriloquist Edgar Bergen allegedly named "Mortimer Snerd" after my uncle.) I couldn't think of a response worth making, but I was interested in learning whether lots of girl babies these days indeed are named after plants.

Sure enough, the *Chicago Tribune* confirmed that plant-based baby names are increasing. Examples include Lily, Violet, Willow, Hazel, Ivy, Iris, Olive, Dahlia, Juniper and Azalea. Violet is at its highest rank since 1924. Further, Laura Wattenberg's namewizard.com is a popular resource for name choices. "Lily" is now America's top botanical name. In general, parents want fresh, original names that stand out—but don't seem "made up."

So, I must straighten you out, Juliet. There's quite a lot in names, and admittedly, Rose is a popular one. There are those by many other names, though, who sniff at the thought of being "just as sweet." They might contend they're even sweeter....

A HOT TIME IN THE THICKET...

Friends who have known Mort for decades say he's a walking contradiction and as stubborn as a billygoat. And his brain churns out—as Aunt Maude puts it—"more ideas in a day than some men in a lifetime, and some of 'em are good."

He cornered me to detail an upcoming event in the thicket he's calling "The East Texas World-Championship Lick-Off." Winner of the hot pepper-licking contest will be awarded a tow sack full of the world's hottest peppers. "The winner may not know how many peppers have been won, because most folks don't know a tow sack from a trolling motor," Mort laughed.

Actually, it's not causing too much of a stir, since most Texans complain rarely finding Mexican food hot enough. "And in other states, it's even harder," they contend. He's hoping there'll be braggarts who'll "put their kissers where his peppers are," and, most importantly, fill his "Mort-marked coffers" with entry fees. He's been steadily building toward this moment for years, cross-breeding peppers so many times that some of 'em now glow in the dark.

It is envisioned to be something akin to another East Texas contest a few years ago called "three hands on a hard body." Contestants had to keep at least one hand in contact with a shiny new pick-up truck. The winner—the last one "in touch" with the vehicle after others had fallen out—drove it home.

"The peppers have hundreds of pin holes, and we'll see who can lick continuously the longest," he explained. "When one pepper is licked bone dry, another one pops up, and so on. I imagine the contest will last a good three hours." He's going to enter himself, going at it with both hands, licking two peppers at once. By the time the others figure out his technique, he'll be too far ahead for it to matter. At least that's what he thinks.

"I've got a thick, flat tongue to start with," he bragged, emphasizing that he's "practiced up," with fingers on each hand twirling peppers with equal dexterity. "I knew I was 'amphibious,' but maybe I'm a multi-tasker, too," he cackled.

Maude has learned to tolerate his hare-brain, off-the-wall, get-rich-quick schemes which—so far—have never panned out. He forges on, though, in the manner that Wile E. Coyote pursues the cartoon Roadrunner, often getting close, but never capturing the prize.

"I'm happy for him to be out in the workshop," she explained. "I'm sure he is blabbering away out there, too," but if I shut the kitchen door, I can't hear him. I just hope I never catch whatever 'itch' he has that causes him to enjoy talking to himself when there's no one else around to listen."

Early in their marriage, she said she kept a close eye on the workshop. Over the years, she remembers many times when it was ground zero for Mort's malfunctions. "When I've seen smoke curling from the window, water running in or out, windows and/or doors blown off, walls bulging or sparks flying, I know Mort's right in the middle of something he ought never have been close to, but now faces an urgency to run out as fast as he can."

She said other telltale evidence that her hubby is up to no good is in the barnyard. "When hens cluck something that sounds like *Standing in the Need of Prayer,* hogs stop eating to watch Mort, and buzzards are poised to swoop in and get what's left, I know I'm about to hear something loud or see something cratering," she laughed.

Believe it or not, Mort's licking peppers with both hands isn't the first multi-tasking in their home. Actually, Maude introduced it many years ago when she and Mort became great-grandparents of identical triplets—beautiful baby girls. "It wasn't easy, and it involved some contortion, but after a little practice, I learned how to kiss all three of those precious babies at the same time," Maude claims.

Mort has heard that some leather-lunged Texans want something really hot, complaining that too many peppers "go down like candy." He swears his will go down like fire balls, and predicts contestants will scream for water. "I'll have it available, stadium-priced at $6 a bottle," he said.

Maude is a little worried that one of Mort's best friends who used to come around regularly is rarely seen now. It is said the man now prefers the fruit of the vine over friendships. Maude saw him in town the other day, asking him point blank why he never comes around anymore. "Well it's not 'rocket surgery'," he said. "Mort don't like to be around me when I'm drunk, and I don't like to be around him when I'm sober."

Mort can handle being alone. Always looking toward his next challenge, he's drawing up diagrams now for a new app. No, not for computers—it's for aerosol cans. "It's an app to help shavers get out just a 'smidgen' when that's all they need. Right now, all the cans release blobs only."…

TURKEYS IN THE NEWS...

Turkeys, I suppose, are unaware that their "jobs" in life are to gobble down granular foodstuff in a timely manner that will render them prime menu targets for us to gobble down—particularly at

Thanksgiving and Christmas dinners. They do so with little fanfare—save the one that is "spared" by presidential decree.

Chicken—the meat Chick-fil-A's advertising cows urge us to eat more of—make far more "news" if only in billboard, TV and stadium ads. (Oh, I should also mention the ones stationed to wave at us when we drive past Chick-fil-A stores. I'm still waiting for "breaking news" of some kid suffocating while wearing a cow suit on a really hot Texas day.)

But turkeys? Not so much. Mostly, we use their name in derisive manners. When we label others as "turkeys," we are verbally lowering them several rungs below the place on the ladder of life they think themselves to be.

The "we-give-it-all" birds are at the center of platters, artistically depicted on school bulletin boards, included in plays and central to conversations during the two biggest holidays observed by Christians in the fading weeks of each year.

Mort admitted he "made a plumb fool of himself" at last year's Thanksgiving table. "I ate three servings of turkey, two of everything else and four slices of assorted pies," he groaned.

I can imagine a rotund Sumo wrestler putting away this much food, but Uncle Mort? His soaking-wet weight is usually around 145 pounds. "I stared at the last four bites of mincemeat pie, afraid I was already 100% full," he explained. "But, I wasn't about to let it go to waste. Luckily, by flossing my teeth between each bite, I licked the saucer clean," he bragged….

Sometimes, unexpected memories are made by children well-drilled in school trappings associated with the holidays. Kyra, six-year-old granddaughter of Dr. Harry and Marsha Krenek, remembers last year's kindergarten class had a "Thanksgiving Feast." They dressed as Pilgrims and Indians, dining on traditional holiday fare—the kind purportedly served at the very first observance.

During the Kreneks' summer vacation trip to the mountains of Mesa Verde, CO, it was mentioned to Kyra and her nine-year-old brother Colin that they might get to see some "real Indians" there. Kyra's response was quick and emphatic; she didn't care to see any Indians. "They might want to have a feast with me," she explained. (Turns out, the Indians were busy selling fry bread and jewelry, so Kyra's fear didn't materialize.)

Christmas came early for the Ohio State University football team when it was chosen over Texas Christian University and Baylor University for the coveted fourth slot for the play-offs leading to a national championship. Talk about having a Thanksgiving spirit, but talk about it with someone other than the football players, coaches and fans at BU and TCU, who felt shunned by the play-off selection committee. They are as upset as the parents of daughters who finish runner-up in pageants, festivals and assorted other competitions. Ah, yes, school colors of beholders are the very brightest of all!

Uncle Mort has his own ideas about the NCAA playoff game selections. "I'm not sure there's two cents worth of difference in the top six teams," he claimed. "Maybe the lucky four schools were named so there'd be a wide representation of nicknames—Crimson

Tide, Seminoles, Ducks and Buckeyes. And perhaps BU and TCU were left out to avoid religious wars."

Undoubtedly, Google will get a good workout. Outside of Ohio, not too many folks know what a Buckeye is. And, the name "Seminoles"—long associated with Florida State—will remind smaller institutions whose mascots formerly were Indians that the NCAA is consistent mostly in its inconsistencies. It is, and perhaps always will be, the organization that chooses its battles carefully.

My criticism of the NCAA is longstanding. Mentioning it again is likely both tiring and pointless. Mostly, it is a lapdog for TV; the mega-millions generated by Division I football dictate far too much. Sportsmanship is "out the window" as teams roll up "style points." And too many coaches' salaries are beyond ridiculous.

OK, I'll make my exit here, already having made a turkey of myself—again. . . .

STUCK IN REVERSE...

I guess it's a good thing that OSHA introduced horn-blowing safety signals for vehicles in "back-up" mode earlier. Otherwise, Uncle Mort might not yet be reduced to driving his gas-saving golf cart. Had he been in the workforce a half-century earlier, he'd have hired out to drive trucks if only to stay in reverse gear. He would have delighted in counting the number of people, pets and other creatures scurrying to get out of the way.

Clearly, he's an "other side of the news" kind of guy, drawn to items most Americans classify as minutia. For them, they'd be at the bottom of radar screens—if seen at all—or victimized by slick ads used to "put the fine print chill" on unbelievable advertised specials splashed in the bold headlines above. He calls some ads "muffled mentions," whispered by scalawags peddling fraudulent telephone offers to senior citizens. Whatever. Taking multiple salt grains is warranted before considering Mort's dissection of Super Bowl XLIX. As usual, he has more questions than answers.

"How long will the Disney people cling to the 'we're-going-to-Disneyland' campaigns?" Mort asks. He says the ad has become tiring after two decades of such advertising. He didn't hear much "Disney talk" at the Super Bowl this year. He thinks it may be because they're speculating that the California measles outbreak may have started at the Disney park, or at least been a prime "spreading area" for the outbreak. "Old Walt would be spinning in his grave if his beloved park turned out to be connected to the disease," Mort said. "Disney has one of the most inspiring Hollywood stories, having shown up there with just a 'mouse and a dream'."

Mort sent a sympathy card to ESPN, which scrapped its NBA game from national TV broadcast opposite the Super Bowl. He claims ESPN waved a white flag of surrender in the TV rating wars.

"Can you believe ESPN chose to run a celebrity bowling tournament that occurred nearly a month ago against SB XLIX?" he asked. He thinks a blank screen might have attracted as many viewers. Further, he chided ESPN for its broadcaster crediting the winning bowler for his "astounding ability to knock down multiple pins at once." Huh, or maybe duh?

Whatever, Mort said, "If bowling tournaments catch on, the NBA may be the league most damaged," Mort believes. "Up the way, ESPN may be 'basketballing' for dollars instead of bowling for 'em."…

Several decades ago, my ever-frugal uncle hoped his doctor had made a mistake. Holding up X-rays to prove the accuracy of his diagnosis, the physician said Mort needed surgery. Mort's response, of course, was to determine the estimated cost. The doc figured it would be "roughly" $2,000. Rather than ask what the charge would be "smoothly," Mort instead wanted to know what the charge would be to re-touch the X-rays.

Bowling pin knock-downs bring to mind light moments and heavy "brunching" that precede the "get serious" part of our weekly Sunday school class. Members are allowed to "say their piece," even when such verbosity invites—as Uncle Mort would say—"bona fide heckling." (It's true that Wayne West, for whom the class is named, is "steady and studied" as teacher. His wife Betty handles a myriad of schedules and details, and Wayne's cousin Ray West coaxes the musical best from a class with few members who'd ever enter singing competitions.)

Until discussion of hospital lists and prayer concerns, our gathering's early going often is a bit "Lions Club-esque." One wag joked that our class is "about as far as one can get from the cradle roll and still have a pulse." Member A. L. Teaff risked one of those "sock-it-to-me" moments when he recounted a recent visit to the doctor's office. "Took a new test," he said. "Doctor called me in to discuss results, indicating 'normal-normal-normal' on items all the way down the list." Then he claimed the doctor's signature on the report means it's a lead pipe cinch he's "certifiably normal."

Uh oh. His last shot meant "open season." Hecklers fired away, without bothering to line up. One said, "You need to get a second opinion." And wife Earlene—whose subtle wit matches anyone's in the class—countered that "even doctors make mistakes." ...

ABOUT THOSE COLOR WHEELS…

Uncle Mort has blown the old "once an adult/twice a child" saying to smithereens. Having seen the snow of many winters and blown out candles of many birthday cakes, Mort is a man of strong opinions, many of them forever child-like. Often clueless on many topics, somehow he manages to re-group, usually making good on promises, mistakes and foibles from here to yon.

He's a live example of the axiom that a "little knowledge is a dangerous thing." This is what we can blame his recent pratfall on. They're still laughing about it in the paint department down at the hardware store.

My uncle dismounted his golf cart, grumbling that he wasn't saving as much money on gasoline as he was a couple of months earlier. I pointed out that price per gallon has dropped by almost 50%, so really, he's saving even more money. However, logic is usually wasted on him. He said he didn't have time to discuss the economy, and he left without mentioning anything about a painting project. However, he said he needed to pick up one of those new "favorite color wheels before they were gone." He headed for the hardware store, eager to learn more about the color wheel people are talking so much about.

The paint sales force was taken aback by his request. After all, for decades on end, color wheels have been, uh, color wheels. "There are no 'favorites'," one of the sales people responded. "It has to be the favorite," my uncle protested, insisting that everyone is "talking grey"—the color he thinks to be the choice of millions of Americans this year. As if orchestrated, the hardware people's heads pivoted 180 degrees, now cocked in the other direction.

"It's hard to imagine they could come up with 50 different grey hues," Mort said. Then, it dawned on the manager. Mort thought *Fifty Shades of Grey* to be a color wheel. The wonder of it all is that their side-splitting laughter didn't erupt until Mort took off down the street in his golf cart.

Friends of Mort and Maude agree with her longstanding contention: "I can't do a thing with him." A few years back—while he was attending an auction for freight cars loaded with new hula hoops and croquet sets—Maude's succinct comment made sense. It still does. "Just let him be."

Truly, there is much about today's world Mort simply doesn't understand—or even try very hard to figure out. Maude is right on almost all legitimate topics. Ideally, Mort should be granted "let him be" status.

So, if he chooses to believe—or wants others to think he believes—*Fifty Shades of Grey* is a color wheel instead of a sordid movie, why not let him? The world will continue on its axis, and it will be business as usual for millions of Americans who yawn upon hearing Uncle Mort's take on the much-discussed movie....

MORT'S THEORY OF EVERYTHING...

Hearing my Uncle Mort screeching to a stop on his golf cart seems to occur seasonally. This time, though, he left the motor running. I thought this might suggest his visit would be brief. It was "briefer," but several minutes short of "briefest." He brags, "I'm the luckiest guy in the thicket. The two-hours-only shoe sale coincided with Maude's kick-off of spring cleaning. I volunteered to fetch her some new sandals, and that's how I kicked off the day." The sales guy asked me her shoe size, and I told him Maude always says she wears a size 9, but a 10 feels so good, she usually buys 11s." He then claimed good fortune followed him to the thrift store, where he found a virtually new pair of brogans for $3. "And I talked 'em into a buck trade-in for the ones I've been wearing for 20 years."

Mort said he wanted to tell about his analysis of our country's defense system, as well as reveal the gist of a recent dream. "Can you believe a man could land a gyrocopter on the White House lawn, even after announcing he was coming?" he questioned. Yes, I'd read and heard plenty on the subject, and am still eye-rolling after the 61-year-old Floridian flew the contraption at an altitude of 150 feet at a speed of 45 miles per hour. My uncle said this postal employee is taking special delivery to a new level, predicting further that since he made the landing so easily, airlines will be clamoring to begin scheduled passenger service to the White House lawn.

"My historical perspective helps to understand how such a thing could happen," my uncle said. "More than 50 years ago, during what was called the "Cuban missile crisis," our military leaders assured us that we had missiles that could be fired with great accuracy toward many major cities of the world." I asked him why we didn't flex our muscles more against Cuba?

"That's precisely the point," he fired back. "Cuba is less than a 100 miles from Miami, and we don't have any missiles that will shoot that close."

What, pray tell, does the Cuban missile crisis have to do with a guy who builds a gyrocopter, announces it to the media and then flies to Washington? "I don't claim to be a fortune teller," Mort laughed, "But I can read your mind." Again, he was correct.

"Well, just as we didn't have any missile that would shoot that close, it's clear that we don't have any radar that detects aircraft flying that low." Whatever, there has to be considerable squirming by members of 32 different agencies, all of which—to varying degrees—have Capitol security jurisdiction. Little wonder they're going postal.

I'm not suggesting Mort was on a high; clearly, though, he was on a roll. Wink-quick, he changed the subject, switching from our country's defensive flaws to Jordan Spieth's offensive assault on the world's golf courses. What's not to admire about this young man who appears to be "hound's tooth" clean from every angle who is ahead of schedule in becoming a national hero? Mort admitted his golfing efforts have been way south of miserable. "If my golf game was a prize fight, they'd stop it," he lamented.

"You won't believe the dream I had about Jordan," Mort said. "He was on the tee at a major PGA event. As the 21-year-old approached the tee, all the other entrants flanked him in a horseshoe configuration. The other guys provided a choral rendition with new lyrics for the tune of a wonderful old Christian hymn. The hymn, you might ask? '*I won't have to cross Jordan alone*'," Mort joked. "It had different lyrics, of course, but if golfers do cross Jordan, they'd better gang up on him and bring their biggest guns."

Before he puttered off toward the thicket, I asked him the secret to a happy marriage, acknowledging his 81-year marriage to 102-year-old Maude. "An easy answer, nephew," Mort said.

"I wrote the Constitution for our marriage," he explained. "But I accept all of her amendments." As he drove away, I smiled at the recollection of Maude's gift to Mort for Christmas—shaving lotion called "Old Spouse." I was surprised that he didn't end our visit by waxing poetic, perhaps with a poem by Ogden Nash: "To keep your marriage brimming—with love in the loving cup—whenever you're wrong, admit it. And whenever you're right, shut up."…

UNCLE MORT ON AGING...

On a night when sleep was fitful, I caught the tail-end of a TV talk show. A guy quoted my Uncle Mort, who believes drinking buttermilk daily is the secret of his longevity. Of all the claims I've heard Mort make—and there are many—none I recalled involved buttermilk. First thing the next morning, I called my uncle to share what I'd heard on TV.

"The guy quoted me correctly, nephew," he answered. "Actually, I've drunk a pint of buttermilk daily for more than 40 years." Scrambling, I told him I'd never heard of his drinking buttermilk, daily or otherwise. "Maybe you should have asked," he said sharply.

"I did hear of a guy who believed drinking buttermilk extended life," I said. "But he died at 85." Mort countered, "See what I mean?" He failed to drink it long enough."

He reminded me of his upcoming birthday on July 4, and was emphatic—for the first time ever—he wanted no one to bring gifts. "I won't need 'em, 'cause I should be rolling in enough dough soon to buy whatever I want." Oh, my. I'd heard this a few hundred times before, and to date, none of his "get-rich-quick" schemes has worked out.

He's long been convinced that he'll get a surprise inheritance, find stacks of gold right over the next hill or benefit from oil discovered smack dab in the middle of his spread down in the thicket. Knowing I'd best drag up a chair and get comfortable for a "lengthy listen", I asked him what he's up to this time.

“We live in a world abuzz with social media, and we’re plunging headlong into entanglements that are inevitable when too many people believe in the laws of the land as long as they’re applied only to others,” Mort began. It was hard to argue with his beginning premise.

“Way too many shots are being fired today,” he moaned. “When I was a kid, we were much into western movies, plunking down our dimes at the picture show every Saturday. We called the movies ‘shoot-‘em-ups’. Nowadays, there are shots up, down, angled and sideways, with social media at the ready with pictures and sound. Now, too many shootings are real, and some theaters say they are examining purses and backpacks for weapons. I think it’s also a failsafe way to keep us from smuggling in candy and gum.”

Then, my uncle played the “stay with me” card. “You’ll see in a minute why my invention is going to revolutionize motorcycles.” Though his invention has nothing to do with the basic operation of motorcycles, he claims to have revolutionized three-wheelers—the ones with side cars. “Lots of cyclists are bound to opt for three-wheelers when they learn about my invention,” he bragged.

With a second wind, he rattled off what he says will make the new side car immediately popular. He said that with the press of a button, direction of the sidecar can be reversed. Immediately, passengers see where they’ve been rather than where they’re going. “At the center of a pop-up shield is a gun rest for weapon of choice for the tail-gunner to fire off accurate shots.”

Mort said a sign holder is attached to the side of the car. "That way, others won't have to guess about his or her chosen gang affiliation." (He claims this will be particularly helpful on hot days when leather jackets aren't worn.) As an aside, he said he's planning to attach a sidecar to his golf cart, hoping this will entice Aunt Maude to ride along more often. "She's adamant about firearms, though," Mort said. "Maude says she's not about to fire anything with more pop to it than a single-shot 22."

Eager to change the subject, I asked him if he thinks there should be governors on motorcycles. "I've felt for a long time this would be a smart thing to do," he stated. He added it might be a good idea to put quite a few other elected officials on 'em, too.

Since it's just a few days until Mort's birthday, I seriously doubt all of his projected riches will come to pass, so we'll take along a gift, just in case. I'm planning to give him a t-shirt reading, "I Don't Believe Everything I Think."…

NON-PROFIT FOR 103 YEARS…

Predicting my uncle will ever succeed with his zany, "off-the-wall" ideas is the rough equivalent of believing that the day will come when Wile E. Coyote will outsmart the Roadrunner. It's simply not going to happen even in dreams—wildest or tamest. On the cusp of his 103rd birthday, he phoned feverishly, hoping I'd have a "straight line" to Southwest Airlines. "You know—the kind of line a big bass stretches tight trying to get rid of a lure." He claimed he had few hours until unveiling his latest project at his birthday party in the thicket. "Don't bring a present, but be sure to bring your handgun and iPhone," he advised.

I didn't tell him the only gun I own is a gag gift that has a yellow flag with "BANG!" written thereon, falling limply from the barrel's end when triggered. Or that I've drawn the line on the new cell phones, doggedly clinging to my old flip-top. (Further, I want to learn a few more of its features before my bucket list is replaced by my bucket kick.)

Excitedly, he told me how he could "help out" Southwest—the airline that lightened its load and saved $100 grand annually five years ago with the elimination of lemon wedges formerly served with drinks. Now, it is making charitable use of leather taken from 80,000 plane seats—some 500 planes—donating the 43 acres of leather to non-profit and social enterprise organizations for conversion to handbags, soccer balls and such.

"I didn't plan it that way, but I've managed to remain 'non-profit' my entire life," Mort joked. He wanted to see if SWA has any remnants left; he's "heck-bent" for leather needed to make his "six-in-one" handgun holsters.

"It's a 'one-size-fits all' concept," he said. "It has side pockets where cell phones of all sizes slide right in. Another pocket holds fingernail and toenail clippers. Still another has fold-out mesquite limbs with iPhone attachment for making 'selfies'." As usual, I made the mistake of offering a correction. "If my count is correct, that's a 'five-in-one' item."

"I plumb forgot," he explained. "I'm going to use mesquite limbs with mistletoe on 'em--that should pump up pre-Christmas sales. I'm gonna give AT&T a shot at 'em first; they're always looking for other things to sell."

As he droned on—he does so quite easily without a plane—it dawned on me why guests were asked to bring their handguns and cellphones. "When we serve ice cream, cake and punch, they won't know what to do with their side arms and phones," he said. "That's when I'll roll out the sales pitch urging them to be the first to own six-in-one handgun holsters," he laughed. He claims they'll never become obsolete, but forever practical, since size/shape changes in iPhones will still fit in the spacious pocket.

Mort hopes to "makes good" on a seventh feature that might be worth touting. He's working on a toggle switch with dual use—turned one way, it silences the gun, and the other, the phone. "If I can figure out how to attach it, I'll throw it in at no extra charge," Mort promised.

Somewhere in the background, Aunt Maude shakes her head. Whatever keeps him busy without harming himself or others is OK, she always claims.

She's been at his side for more than 80 years, watching his "inventions" fail—one after the other. "I've seen so many 'plosions'," she said. "Plosions?," I questioned.

"Yep, both implosions and explosions," she cackled, comparing his enthusiasm to an "Amway salesman on steroids." Maude claimed to be ready for the party, the giant cake still warm from the oven.

She's going to serve Blue Bell ice cream she's been saving, and lemonade won't take long to prepare. "I've still got to paint a sign Mort wants nailed on the gate," she said.

The sign reads. "Open carry is permitted here. If you don't have a gun, I'll rent you one." It'll be nailed next to the sign with this wordage: "When crossbows are outlawed, only outlaws will have crossbows."....

ANOTHER NEW YEAR...

From time to time, readers send email or call to pose similar questions: "Is your Uncle Mort real?" My unvarying rhetorical response is: "Do you want him to be?" I sense their sinking feelings, let down by my failure to provide the answer they are hoping for. Finally, I have to admit that he is a figment of my imagination, as was explained in some detail on earlier pages.

Perhaps I should be grateful for the queries. In an ever-darkening world, I believe there should be pauses in the action, with a bit of time taken daily to take deep breaths, to think and to even read of the make-believe escapades of Uncle Mort. (I should confess that the picture on the cover of this book looks mighty close to the uncle of my mind's eye.) For years now, celebration of July 4 each year reminds me that Uncle Mort—in make believe, perhaps like some of the figures in Mr. Roger's neighborhood or maybe even Sesame Street—somehow is related to all of us. (Or maybe everyone has an uncle or two similarly outlandish!)

Someone asked what I consider the most unbelievable statement he ever made, question he ever posed or description he ever verbalized. I think I'll choose "door number two," the one about a "bumfuzzling" question. It didn't take a lot of deliberation, but I'll need to set it up for you. It was a typical "just wanted to drop in to say 'hi'" sort of visit just a year or so ago. Mort and Maude had come into town to buy a few groceries, and located next door is a pet store. They often visit it, not to buy, but to look, listen and of course, question.

"The pet store had a parrot in there today, but I'm pretty puzzled. I'm not sure if it is a parrot," he said, mentioning that he'd asked Maude to stay on the golf cart. "I wasn't about to ask the high school kid working at the pet store, and I'm afraid the question I'm posing to you would be confounding to her." (I couldn't imagine her being "confounded," and became intensely interested in the upcoming question.) I interrupted, asking why he doubted if the parrot is a parrot. Did he think it might be a cockatiel, or some other exotic bird resembling a parrot?

"On, nothing like that," Mort snapped back. "I mean there's some question what kind of creature is under those feathers, or what it—or he or she—used to be. The conversation already was way beyond weird. This time, though, I did not wish to be someplace else. I was eager to hear his question.

"Nephew, Maude and I heard that parrot, plain as day. I mean the words were broadcast quality. They'd fit well on a network telecast in prime time." I could hardly wait. "What did the bird say," I insisted, vexed to be led on in such an extended manner.

"That's just what I'm trying to explain, nephew," Mort said, letting me know that vexation can go both ways. "It may NOT have been a parrot. When we were even with the cage, and feathers seemed fluffed as they often are before birds want crackers, and we weren't more than two feet from its beak."

Fretful now, I raised my voice, "WHAT DID THE PARROT SAY?"

"He, she or it said this plainly: "Help me. Somebody turned me into a parrot."

This was as dumbfounding as the grandkids asking, "Why is a cow?" And maybe closely akin to the analysis that it couldn't be a bicycle, because a vest has no sleeves."

What to do? I walked Mort out to the golf cart, and you guessed it. Maude backed him up. "That's exactly what was said," Maude remarked, "And we don't know what to do. I advised them to say nothing more about the matter, and to head back toward the thicket before the ice cream was melted, ready to be salvaged by straws. I then went back in the house, calling the pet store to see what time it closed....

With a sharp eye constantly out for the quick buck, Mort is usually about as successful as a fisherman with a bare hook. But, like the golfer who keeps swinging—hoping to finally hit that perfect shot—he keeps right on truckin" An incurable optimist, he's as hopeful as

California gold rush pioneers, believing that one day, a scheme, invention or half-baked gadget idea will pan out.

We visited on New Year's Day. I wasn't surprised to learn he was hard at work on a new "can't miss" exercise program. I was taken aback, however, that he had aborted his latest invention project. Since these are distinctively different initiatives, each will be considered separately….

"They're pushing the Daniel Plan at the church house to lose weight," Mort said. "I don't think many seniors are going to buy into it, since most of us get our exercise serving as pallbearers for our friends who exercise." This set him to thinking about an exercise plan for seniors—one he said is "economical and as effective as participants want it to be." He said he was going to market his plan for $1.99, and if he delivers the bags, he'd clear $1.87 on each sale.

Figuring the "whole load" was unavoidable, I requested details.

He said that during the first week, participants hang five-pound potato bags from each outstretched hand for five minutes daily. The second week calls for hanging 10-pound bags for three minutes, followed by a final week of 25-pound bags for one minute.

"If folks don't feel like this is quite enough exercise, they can toss a potato into each bag the third week," he laughed, emphasizing they have to furnish their own potatoes….

As to his aborted "invention," he claimed to be well along on a meticulous formula that, once perfected, would cause bodily sweat to accumulate on our feet. Deodorant manufacturers, he believes, will seize the opportunity to aim their products specifically at the feet, where Mort thinks sweat will accumulate in puddles.

He admitted, though, that a "for-real" invention announced recently for drivers' GPS units may thwart his plans. The new device sends electrical tingles in the proper foot—left or right—depending on which direction drivers are turning. "That sounds like an electrocution waiting to happen," Mort said. "But I'm afraid I'd face lawsuits from here to kingdom come. Sure as shootin', those GPS electric signals hitting sweat puddles in shoes might cause shocks that go way beyond tingles," he opined.

Before our visit ended, he asked, "Got milkweed?" He expressed delight that monarch butterflies are expected to migrate in larger numbers this spring, mostly because folks have planted milkweed to attract them. I told him that so far, zinnias have given them pause in our backyard.

He left, mumbling about the feasibility of crossing monarchs with lightning bugs. "There'd be the chance for 24/7 popularity," he maintained, beautiful creatures flying in sunlight by day and bodily lighted at night. Mort said that such hybrids might have a clever name, such as "butter-bugs." He projected the possibility of a contest to name the new creatures.

This was a better "winder-upper" than the ending of our first 2014 visit. I asked what he planned to give up for New Year's. His answer? "Resolutions."...

Go ahead and admit it—you probably have some uncles much like him. Mort is a piece of work, sometimes thinking way ahead. I almost chose one of his cockamamie plans in front of his "parrot story". He figures before too long, he may be a candidate for hip surgery. "Before I go under the knife, though, I'm going by the court house to see if I can get my open carry gun permit for half price, since I'll only be able to shoot from one hip."...

He has a serious side, though—really he does. Quizzing me, he confirmed that I underwent successful quadruple bypass surgery in 1998, along with repair of my heart's mitral valve during the same operation. He also reviewed Brenda's breast cancer surgery in 2009 when she underwent a double mastectomy. I confirmed both dates. "And you both are in good health now?" I answered affirmatively—failing to mention what our doctors say after examinations we undergo these days—"for your age."

I told him we're both optimistic, thankful to God for rich, full lives and the prospect of a 50th wedding anniversary soon. "Yep, you've got thousands of reasons to be thankful," Mort said.

Then, as if to tie a ribbon on this book, Mort told me he had "polled the delegation" at the general store during heated "42" games. They tried to reach consensus on what they consider my best columns from my first dozen years in syndication. "Now we didn't say they're any good, we just said we'd vote on the ones we think are the best." He reminded me of what one editor asked back in 2003, when six newspapers started carrying my columns. "What do you plan to write about?, one editor asked. "Columns about what I know, and see, and hear, and do," I answered.

"How did he respond?" Mort asked, as I knew he would. Sheepishly, I provided the editor's reply, verbatim: "Sounds good, Don. But what about for the fourth week?" Well, it's still fun, I'm still writing and soon will hit the mark of 650 weeks.

With Mort and his bunch, it was—had it been a used car transaction—tire-kicking time. At the risk of rambling, I reminded him that he and his cohorts no doubt had missed reading some of the columns; indeed, some of the guys may have nodded "yes" simply to feel included. Some of them had never seen it, but all were looking for excuses to justify showing up at home several hours later than spouses anticipated. We were back and forth on the proposal for a half-hour; finally, it was "acceptable" to the guys if I included columns and excerpts I feel best about. So, responding to Mort and his domino buddies, I'll try to pick some columns, hopeful for more decorum than one of Mort's colleagues seemed to have in his admonition, "Don, just let her rip!"...

JUST TRYING TO HELP OUT…

The water of 38 years has flowed under the bridge since I "stole" a hearse. Surely the statute of limitations has kicked in by now, thus this confession.

I am NOT, however, admitting guilt. Instead, I was the "victim" of yet another Groner Pitts prank. Friends who knew this merriest of morticians—who reigned in Brownwood for a half-century—also were "victimized" from time to time.

Yet, I never had a better friend, and Brownwood (TX) never had a greater ambassador. And thousands who followed his antics for three decades through the late George Dolan's daily columns in the *Fort Worth Star-Telegram* never lacked for laughs. Many were often ensnared in his web of tomfoolery. I'm probably the only "victim," however, to "steal" a hearse—one partially owned by Pitts himself….

The "pro's pro" among morticians, he had fitting first and last names (Groner? Pitts?). Even his initials (GAP) pointed to the grave. The Cleburne, TX, native conducted funerals with utmost dignity. To the Brownwood community, he was "Uncle Groner," the "go-to" guy counted on by several hundred grieving families annually.

During slack time, however, he was helping college students…or assisting others who'd reached rope's end (maybe striking out in Austin or Washington, DC)…or co-signing bank notes…or—maybe this should head the list—plotting his next shenanigan.

He befriended me from my first enrollment at Howard Payne University. Though 15 years my senior, he was a fellow "trooper" in the Texas National Guard, and best man when Brenda and I married in Alpine. I was privileged to speak at his funeral in 2004. Upon his death, thousands of "Groner Pitts stories" were shared, locally and beyond….

Admittedly, I was an accomplice during many of his escapades. Yet, many times when pies were thrown toward him, they coated my face instead.

That's the way I choose to remember the day I "stole" the hearse. Had it happened today, I might have gone down in a hail of bullets, or, short of that, endured the indignity of arrest, the messiness of fingerprinting, the ordeal of a trial, etc.

I might never have been a university president, but likely could have remained the "PR flack" at Tarrant County College, because my boss, Dr. Joe B. Rushing—a classmate of Groner's at Howard Payne—might have ruled in my favor. He KNEW Pitts well, and sometimes was a co-conspirator. It was indeed an era not unlike "Mayberry, RFD."…

Here's what happened. On that long ago day, Pitts was bored. He decided to charter a plane to fetch some press people to Brownwood, ostensibly to "cover" a reception for new Filipino nurses at Brownwood Regional Hospital. As requested, I contacted a half-dozen press folks, promising them chicken and biscuits on the way down and a "surprise" on the flight back. I was blissfully ignorant, NOT privy to what the "surprise" would be….

On the returning flight over Granbury, Pitts feigned boredom, ordering the pilot to land. (He'd arranged a special act for the press at the Opera House.) One of the writers, Roger Summers, groaned, fearing he'd miss a deadline.

I spotted a hearse near the theater, presuming the late George Martin, Groner's Granbury partner, was "in" on the deal. The key was in the ignition, so, when lights darkened, Roger and I slipped out of the theater. We took the hearse—okay, I took the hearse—dropping Roger off 40 miles later in downtown Fort Worth at the *Star-Telegram*. Then, I was off to DFW where I'd leave the hearse and retrieve my car. (I didn't realize Martin was not privy to the goings on, and was merely stopping off for a cup of coffee near the Opera House.)...

When Martin discovered his hearse missing, things got tacky. Another hearse had been stolen a few days earlier, so the local mortician was somewhat edgy. He notified authorities. They gave chase. We missed several road blocks by minutes. No arrests were made. All—or most, anyway—was forgiven. Summers made his deadline. I was spared....

COACHING BEYOND THE GAME...

The stillest water at greatest depth has much in common with a recent retiree at Sul Ross State University in Alpine. Dr. Chet Sample also runs deep, having provided exemplary leadership that encouraged scholarship ahead of intercollegiate athletics.

That said, he's as rare as a spotless leopard, helping students focus first on the goal of college graduation, then on athletics. Along the way, he earned the respect of EVERYONE—student athletes, parents, colleagues, alumni and the rest—even opponents on the basketball floor.

On the big canvas of life, he painted potential in vivid colors, with scoreboards and statistics relegated to the background....

His 42 years in education included almost 40 at SRSU—20 as both Chair of the Physical Education Department and Athletics Director. He was men's basketball coach for five years and women's mentor for 15, winning or tying for conference championships six times.

Sample's skills were called into play early when he directed the transition from scholarship to non-scholarship sports two years after arrival. The Lobos were among the first in Texas to compete without athletic scholarships.

The university's remote location complicates travel. The closest opponent is more than 300 miles away; some are almost a thousand. Merely arriving at some destinations should count for something….

Traveling a million miles or so provides many memories, and some cause Sample to redden on the retelling. Arriving in Stephenville with his women's team well after the midnight hour, he distributed motel room keys, wearily urging them to retire immediately, hoping they could be as fresh as possible for tournament play a few hours later.

He hastened to his room, first removing contact lenses from tired eyes. Feminine voices, laughter and general revelry in the adjoining room made sleeping impossible. Rapping on the wall didn't help, so he slipped on his clothes and knocked on their door. Explaining the cow's methodology in cabbage-eating, he made it clear that the girls should begin the quiet game immediately, and they did.

Hours later at breakfast, the same girls were seated at the next table. Their voices were familiar, but their faces weren't. Oh, how he wished his contacts had been in place when he'd threatened them earlier. Turns out they were members of another team from another university….

Proof positive of his commitment to academic excellence came with his recommendation that grade point minimums be INCREASED for athletes. It was so ordered, much to the delight of the faculty.

The requirement that players take their classes seriously worked. Thus, SRSU student athletes earn the right to play sports. Some 40 graduates of his programs now have doctoral degrees. Hundreds more are teaching and coaching. Several years ago, he underwent a medical procedure performed by a surgeon who was one of his former students.

Born in Athens and a graduate of Seminole, TX, High School, the 6-3 Sample was an all-state selection in basketball. At Wayland Baptist University, he made NAIA All-District three years—once was named an NAIA All-American—and set a school career scoring record of 1,726 points.

Following graduation there, he served two years in the US Army before becoming a men's basketball graduate assistant while completing his master's degree at SRSU. He received his doctorate at East Texas State University in 1975. No one in Alpine is more respected than this man whose values, goals, integrity and character are beyond reproach.

Sample has received a ton of honors, and with his wife, Belinda, has initiated a number of endowments throughout the university.

He's served as scoutmaster and as a board member of both AISD and the Wesley Foundation, and has been a Lions Club member for more than 30 years. Dr. and Mrs. Sample are members of Alpine

United Methodist Church. She is a former SRSU student and was payroll supervisor there for 25 years. Their children, Michael of Austin and Denise Dusek of Wall, are SRSU graduates, and grandchildren Jake, 14, and Melanie, 9, say they're SRSU bound…. He's been my friend for 30 years; I admire no one more.

The Samples plan to remain in Alpine, helping as they can as volunteers. Students won't find Sample's name among active personnel in the SRSU catalog in the future. He's listed in the phone book, however. He'll help students "do life" if asked, and wise ones will. Dr. Chet Sample is as good as it gets….

GRADUATION SHAKIN'

"A Whole *Lotta Shaking Going On"* covers much ground from rock-and-roller Jerry Lee Lewis to descriptions of earthquakes and end-time prophecies. It also describes chapter-closing handshakes for some 300,000 youngsters crossing Texas stages this month to accept diplomas and degrees….New "officiants" extending the sheepskins forgetting to remove rings and/or victims of bone-crushing handshakes in return will learn much.

Educators give impetus to the National Day of Prayer in May—teachers are ready for a stop-out, seniors want to get out and parents are willing to "shell out" for events/gifts/memorabilia associated with these annual rituals. (Actually, there may be more prayers of educators prior to the next school year, when they fulfill promises made back in May: "Oh, God, if you'll just get me through this year, I'll give it another try in the fall.")

Prospective graduates are rehearsed, graduation speakers engaged, diplomas ordered, pronunciations checked and arenas booked (sometimes years in advance) so the predictable hassles can be eliminated. Programs are proofed and re-proofed; woe unto that person who misspells a graduate's name in the program—the one guests can't know participants without. Yep, even weeks before the event, there's shakin', planning and praying going on.

For the majority of participants, a common desire is that the big event progresses without hitches and with zero embarrassment. Sometimes they do. And sometimes they don't. "I am grateful for those full sleeves in the robe," said Dr. Russell Dilday, longtime president of Southwestern Baptist Theological Seminary. He said that one graduate, during a handshake, palmed off a banana on the good doctor. "I had the good sense to let it slide down my sleeve," he admitted. Next time you attend a graduation ceremony, watch for the billowy sleeve covering the presenter's right arm. It may be weighed down by bananas, marbles and other items.

Other prayers for indoor ceremonies include petitions for microphones and air-conditioning to function properly, and that diplomas and recipients will come out even. Never you mind crying babies, loosed mice and air horns. (The more often officials plea for decorum, the less likely it is to prevail.)

Many eventualities, of course, are unpredictable. At Howard Payne University, during the first commencement exercises held following my retirement, Brownwood Coliseum was filled to the rafters by some 4,000 people. Somehow, fore-and-aft doors were opened simultaneously at the same time a strong wind blew through. Sadly, it occurred at the very beginning of the program as platform participants crawled out from under a 15-foot tall backdrop that shrouded the bunch. ("Such as this never happened during my presidency," I kidded my successor.) Only egos were hurt; the audience laughed; the day was saved.

A teacher once said, "There is no such thing as a bad short speech." Obviously, the inimitable Dr. Theodore S. Geisel, better known as Dr. Seuss, agreed. He made his admonishments to one class in about one minute, speaking about his "Uncle Terwilliger on the Art of Eating Popovers":

"My uncle ordered popovers from the restaurant's bill of fare. And when they were served he regarded them with a penetrating stare. Then he spoke great words of wisdom as he sat there in that chair. 'To eat these things,' said my uncle, 'You must exercise great care. You may swallow down what's solid...but first spit out the air! And as you partake of the word's bill of fare, that's darned good advice to follow. Do a lot of spitting out of hot air. And be careful what you swallow.' "

Whatever happens at your ceremony, try to relax. This, too, will pass. In Pascagoula, Mississippi, the "First Self Righteous Church" still functions, despite having some straightening up to do after order was restored. Maybe Ray Stevens will write a song about your graduation when he learns of antics there that might make the Mississippi squirrel seem plumb tame.

Graduates, we trust, have learned to deal positively with the future—no matter what. I heard of one such person the other day who insisted on living "sunny side up." Despite an illness calling for chemotherapy, he forges on. "I've developed a friendship with my therapist," he said. "I call her 'Chemo-sabi'."...(05-2003)

A WHISTLER FOR THE AGES...

The only real "superstar" I've known up close was Fred Lowery (1909-1984), arguably the finest whistler in the world for a half-century. A mainstay on the Horace Heidt network radio show after appearing regularly for years on Dallas radio station WFAA's Early Birds, he whistled in more than 10,000 "live" concerts.

Fred was on the same stages with Bing Crosby and Bob Hope; the former called him "king of the whistlers." Blind since a toddler, he wanted no pity, no advantage and no "superstar" status. He once challenged Bob Hope to a golf match—at 12 midnight.

I was privileged to know him during the final two decades of his life. Without pretense, he went about doing good, amazing royalty, presidents, fans at Yankee Stadium, you name it. He was most at home, though, at schools, churches, civic clubs, hospitals, retirement centers and yes, jails.

Gracie, his wife of 45 years who outlived him by a dozen years, was "behind the wheel" (mostly motor homes, six of them covering some two million miles) without so much as a dented fender. They even survived a fire in one vehicle and another was heavily damaged when an Illinois tornado leveled buildings all around them. Talk about guardian angels.

Once in Nashville for a recording session, their first order of business was helping a young man to relax. He'd been there for hours, doing take after take. "He was the 24-year-old son of an Arkansas farmer," Gracie said. "His name was Johnny Cash, and his *Walk the Line*, was soon to be #1 on the country charts, and he was off and running."

In 1964, an inauguration was held for the late Dr. Norman L. McNeil, president of Sul Ross State University. We had $75 for "special entertainment from out of town." Fred and Gracie were in Fort Stockton the night before, an hour's drive away. They accepted our invitation, and our friendship began. During the next two decades, he and Gracie were guests in our homes in Fort Worth and Snyder. Making hamburgers one night, I asked her, "Does he prefer mayonnaise or mustard?" Fred answered: "Ask me—I'm blind, not deaf!"...

BACK ROADS BY CHOICE...

There's much to be said for back roads. I choose them often, yielding to slowdowns that include curves in the road, tractors on the road and chickens crossing to the other side. The rewards? Relaxed moments to "drink in" beautiful sunrises and the sound of mournful hounds whose prey is treed. There is much to remind of gentler times.

Outside Dallas on a side road, I spotted an old farmhouse, and I geared to reverse to get a closer look. Nearby, no longer standing straight was a lever-operated gasoline pump with "Onyx" printed on it. Nearby was a pygmy-sized drink bottle with the faded word "Grapette." Old cafe humor came to mind about the outcry rising when soft drinks—long priced at a nickel—went up by one penny. "Our drinks are all sick scents," one sign read. Another touted Garrett Snuff….(The snuff that seemed most fittin', good for dippin' but better for spittin'.)

I watched a farmer painting an old Burma-Shave sign. This medium started in 1925, the $200 brainchild of two sons whose dad owned Burma-Shave—the shaving cream of choice before electric razors—when the surgeon general was but a surgeon lieutenant—and when drugstores still stocked Absorbine Sr.

The clever signs soon appeared on fence posts throughout the nation; at one time, 7,000 were in place. Usually, they were in clusters of a half-dozen, maybe 20 yards apart—just two or three words, white in red backgrounds. I appreciated the old farmer updating his sign: "The USofA/can now relax/the terminator's sworn in/and Limbaugh's back. BURMA-SHAVE."

They were no match, however, for the ad assaults we all endure, many kinds unknown until recent years. I remembered some childhood favorites: "When in school zones/drive real slow/let our little/shavers grow.... The bearded devil's/forced to dwell/in the only place/they don't sell....Cattle crossings/mean go slow/that old bull/is some cow's beau....On curves ahead/remember, sonny/that rabbit's foot, didn't save the bunny....My job's keeping/faces clean/nobody knows/de stubble I've seen....Her chariot raced/80 per/they hauled away/what had "Ben" her....Burma-Shave/was such a boon/they passed the bride/and kissed the groom."...Sadly, a lone sign remained, spotted in Oregon in 1986: "Farewell O verse/along the road/how sad to see/you're out of mode." Now, 78 years after the first sign was posted, the farmer I spotted insisted on having a new Burma-Shave sign!

Guess who wrote a lot of those ditties? Some student at the University of Omaha around 1950. He had a great sense of humor, and the Oracle of Omaha has an abundance of business acumen to boot. His net worth is estimated to be more than $40 billion; his name is Warren Buffett....(11-2003)

WHEN THE CARNIVAL CAME TO TOWN...

Cruising arrived in Texas "big time" when Carnival risked a vessel there for a season in 2001. It has been a storybook ride, now with four ships in place, and Galveston in 2015 was the third-busiest cruise port in North America.

We've taken to the sea many times; each cruise holds unique stories, waiting to be told. Rich friendships begin on board. People talk, listen, share and care. One of the best aboard the *Elation* involved members of its crew. Tears well up upon remembrance of the crew's re-telling of Christmas, 2003. Such accounts aren't available in travel brochures. Here 'tis:

The ship's crew wanted to do something for some children in Belize City, the port of call that Christmas Day. Some of them visited an orphanage, and their hearts were touched. They decided to invite all 72 youngsters to visit the ship, since most guests were in port. The children rode tenders to the vessel; many of them had never been more than a few yards from the shore, and never, of course, on a modern cruise ship. They had the run of the place, and enjoyed a sumptuous Christmas repast.

Oh, and they got presents. Carnival folks noticed that the children were sleeping on one-inch thick mats. They "visited" the mattress storage room on the ship, and each child returned to the orphanage with a new mattress! The crew's subsequent trips to Belize City found them visiting the orphanage, taking food and other gifts to the children.

"On that first trip to the orphanage, we learned a new meaning of Christmas—it is about giving," a crew member said….(02-2004)

A GREAT CLOUD OF WITNESSES…

Just before Thanksgiving, death claimed Darren Nix, who, at age 36, seemed "just out of college" to me. Just eight years earlier, I handed him his Howard Payne University diploma.

Death also claimed legendary football Coach Gordon Wood during the week before Christmas; then, just before St. Valentine's Day this year, Groner Pitts—"Mr. Brownwood," and perhaps the merriest mortician ever—died after several years of failing health. He was best man at our wedding in 1966, and a friend since my college years.

Winner of nine state championships in high school football, Wood averaged 9.3 wins annually during his 43 seasons of head coaching. He retired at age 70, but was alert, enthusiastic and active until hours before his death 19 years later. He drove to the coffee session with his friends daily. There, problems of the world, nation, state and their own community were chewed on, and sometimes solved.

Wood's service was held in Mims Auditorium at Howard Payne. When it ended, a majority of the crowd—mostly coaches, former athletes and retirees—gathered in the student center where coaching icon Grant Teaff held forth. Tributes and stories were shared, and there were many. The session, begun in the brightness of an afternoon sun, ended more than two hours later, after darkness had set in.

Pitts, 79, was a decade Wood's junior, but friends said his odometer was "beyond 120." Ever defying convention, he was a founder of the "Brownwood Mafia," a civic group dedicated to promoting the community. His funeral service, seven Sundays after Wood's, was held on a snowy Valentine weekend of leap year….

First Baptist Church overflowed, so his service—like Wood's—was carried on local television. Ever eager to promote his church, community, Howard Payne, Texas National Guard and the Democratic Party, Pitts was arguably the most colorful funeral director ever. "That great cloud of witnesses in Heaven has been sequestered this day," one speaker said, "To decide who breaks the news to Groner they don't have Democratic precincts in glory."...

Nix, a seminary student after college graduation, was active in youth work at Sherwood Park Baptist Church in Irving. A veteran of the Gulf War, he was 28 when he finished at HPU, and in so many ways, older than his years. His specialty was serving others—regardless of cost or sacrifice. In military service, he smuggled Bibles by the hundreds into a country where such was forbidden and where Christianity was embraced by a smattering. For Darren, life was beyond an adventure. He, like Pitts, had a high odometer reading.

Friends and loved ones crammed into the church, where there was seating for 350. Several dozen stood. Testimonials, music and a comforting message filled the better part of an hour. It was—to that point—a traditional service. The final moments, however, were "uniquely Darren." Following the prayer, the preacher said, "Darren loved Moon Pies and The Big Bopper." With this announcement, funeral directors flooded the aisles, handing our Moon Pies as we passed Darren's casket. Bursting through the sound system were the unmistakable lyrics of *Chantilly Lace*....(You remember it: "Chantilly lace and a pretty face and a pony tail hanging down....") We left the service, smiling through tears.

On the drive home, it occurred to me that in but two months, we had buried three unique friends. This trio sniffed out every hint of roses along the way. Their rich lives provided lessons worth learning. And so did their memorial services. (02-2004)

CHICK-FIL-A FOUNDER COMES TO CAMPUS…

In 1994, the late S. Truett Cathey, founder of Chick-Fil-A, was guest speaker at chapel. Upon his arrival, I invited him to our home for breakfast, promising him a treat of my mom's made-from-scratch biscuits, a daily repast I'd enjoyed daily growing up.

My wife, in panic mode, straightened the house for the arrival of the man whose chicken empire is world-renowned. Mom moved briskly around the kitchen, right at home around the oven.

Mr. Cathey put away three biscuits (but who's counting), commenting they were the best he'd ever tasted. Pushing back from the table, he insisted that Mom take some coupons for free sandwiches. She demurred, but finally gave in. "Now I want to be sure I see you when I get my sandwiches out at the mall," she said, "What shift do you work?"

He smiled, I changed the subject and Mom went on with her day. I never told her about Mr. Cathey's status. On the way to chapel, I said, "Mr. Cathey, we need that every day, don't we?" He answered, "We need it every minute of every hour of every day."...(3-2004)

WHEN A PRESIDENT GOES HOME…

It had a quiet week in the Reagan home, like most of them had been for almost a decade. It was as if a fine clock—its hands long still—had morphed into a sundial. A dark cloud snuffed out the shadow at 3:08 p.m. (CST) on June 5 when the remnant of our nation's 40th president took leave to join mind and spirit that had taken flight several years earlier.

What irony that when the 93-year-old signed off, National Public Radio's Prairie Home Companion was on the road in tiny Gilford, NH, ready to sign on for its weekly broadcast. Minutes before, host Garrison Keillor had learned of President Reagan's death. It was a somber opening as he made the announcement to 6,000 people crammed into the music hall and to some 4.5 million radio listeners throughout the nation.

But how fitting! Radio was President Reagan's first love, unless you count lifeguarding. He spent a couple of teen-year summers rescuing—by actual count—77 swimmers. He was an Iowa sports announcer who loved radio so much he was reluctant to move to Hollywood in 1937; there, he made 53 movies during a 20-year career.

A big slice of America was to learn of Reagan's death from Keillor, another national treasurer long revered for his spoken and written words. Keillor seemed totally unruffled by a couple of people—just two—who cheered the news. He described Reagan as "a great man who befuddled us old liberals, mainly by his great, shining charm which never failed him." Then, he offered touching solos: *Lighthouse* and *Where Could I Go.*

Reagan, a tension-easier, might have said of the hecklers, "Relax, Garrison. Those two guys bought their tickets and are exercising free speech."

When seriously injured by a would-be assassin just a couple of months into his first term, he joked with doctors. "I hope they were Republicans. If so, I should have ducked."

As the sun set in the west on his burial day, I imagined President Reagan might be urging Ray Charles to hasten his pace. Perhaps Reagan slowed down a bit, scribbling a note to Garrison as he waited for Charles to come alongside. He so loved writing notes. "Hey, Garrison, let me know if you ever have a noisy week in Lake Wobegone. And what do you think of going national with traits of Wobegoners? It would be great to have a nation where the women are strong, the men are good-looking and the children are above average."...

An aside: My wife and I visited St. Paul last fall to "see" the NPR broadcast. After microphones were put away, Dr. Keillor held forth in the lobby of the historic Fitzgerald Theater, chatting as guests lingered. "Where are you from?" he asked one. "Scotts Bluff, NE," she answered, mentioning that her hometown newspaper was the *Star-Herald.* "What a coincidence," Garrison responded. "In Lake Wobegone, we've got Harold Star. Harold has owned the paper for 30-40 years, I guess."…. (06-2004)

'EAR BOBS' AND SECOND CHANCES…

This was a generational thing. The young undertaker had been trained to cope with all situations that could reasonably be anticipated, like teachers, doctors, lawyers and others must likewise do. The young man smiled confidently when the woman dropped off a pair of brooches. Her mom, whose body was soon lie in state at the funeral home, had loved them so. When dressed "Sunday best", the brooches were always in place.

"These are really heavy," he said, assuring her that the brooches would be included as adornment was finalized. The search engine of his mind was already purring. "What in the world are brooches?" he asked himself, remembering the emphasis in mortuary school to "get it right". He also recalled that some older women might want adornment with their favorite "ear bobs".

"Aha," he thought. Wheels turned; his mind raced. Maybe "ear bobs" are clip-ons and brooches are for pierced ears, he reasoned. He remembered the woman was glancing at her mom's ears, so that was a clue, too. A few hours later, she was back to make sure her mom looked "just right" for visitation viewing. "I think the brooches would look better on her dress than her ears," she said, sighing as if instantly realizing it was an error to be charged to generational differences. He resolved that in the future, when he didn't know, he'd simply ask. And that's a good thing….(11-2004)

DENTISTS AND JUDGES KNOW FOR SURE…

Until now, it's been a teapot-sized tempest, merely bubbling. Now that two corporate behemoths have squared off and a federal judge has stepped in, we're nearing full boil.

Dentists across the fruited plane are smiling, and most may even decide to renew their professional oaths.

In the blue corner is dental floss (Johnson & Johnson) and in the red, Listerine (Pfizer). After swishing for a while, flossing hourly and considering briefs from dueling attorneys, the "ref"—Manhattan Federal District Judge Denny Chin—has ruled.

It is a mouthful. Contrary to claims on its labels, websites and TV ads, Listerine CANNOT claim to be "as effective as flossing". Thus ruleth the judge….

For decades, dentists have recommended regular flossing, even though most of us answer with "yeah/yeah, sure/sure" assurances that we're turning over new flossing leaves. Out of sight, however, and likewise out of mind. Only 13% of Americans heed these dental sermons. (Most preachers would settle for this percentage, of course.)

One patient, bragging that he flosses regularly, says he does so seasonally—every third month. Pfizer contends that half of the populace has periodic bouts with bad breath. Dentists, on the receiving end of exhales daily, think the figure is way too low.

Oral hygiene deserves this new spotlight. For too long, we've simply joked about it, saying, "Halitosis is better than no breath at all." Dentists seem to be auditioning for comedy night as well, defending a $100 charge for a tooth extraction that takes 20 seconds. "I can pull it slower," one joked.

A half-century ago, when all-female and all-male colleges dotted American landscape, a joke trickled down from New York state. There, Vassar College admitted only females, and nearby Colgate enrolled only males. NY dentists claimed Vassar women preferred Colgate men to tooth decay, four to one.

I digress—again. Perhaps the smart-mouth took his cue from the FCC that recently levied stiff fines with its "you can't say that" edicts. The judge maintains that Listerine advertising poses a "public health risk" that could "undermine the message of dental professionals." Pfizer heard him loud and clear, springing for $2 million to hire 4,000 workers who'll crisscross the United States. Their jobs will be to paste over the "as effective as flossing" label claims on products in all stores. Labor Department personnel are smiling; for a few weeks, US employment is bound to be "up."

Wording on the replacement stickers wasn't mentioned. How about: The judge owns stock in Scope. Our claims remain true for denture wearers or the toothless. For heaven's sake, use one or the other. First job I've had since working as a seasonal Santa. Or maybe this: Don't federal judges have anything better to do?

Don't expect the ultra-liberal who believes in killing nothing with hopes for all living things to have continuance: "Don't use. Help rehabilitate the germs that cause bad breath." You get the drift—the ruling is from the government, the one that claims is here to help us.

Whatever, let's keep oral hygiene conversations going—over backyard fences, down the block and over coffee. It could help reduce bad breath, improve oral hygiene and encourage dentists, who'd probably stage parades if serious flossers increase their numbers to 15%. During meals on "hug your dentist day," we could vow to chew each bite 28 times, swish with mouthwash, floss like we believe it matters, and—for good measure, stop biting off more than we can chew…. (1-2005)

ANOTHER MAMIE IN FLAMES…

Mamie McCullough, who in many ways is a clone of *Mame*—-played by Rosalind Russell on stage and in the delightful movie—has spoken in many venues, covering millions of miles with her "pump-'em-up" encouragement to educators and the masses. Her talks and books undergird her claim to being an "incurable optimist" whose ongoing message is, *I Can—You Can, Too.*

She dresses, jokes and cavorts to whatever the extreme is beyond flamboyant, and has never seen a dress with too much red, earrings with too much dangle or outfits with too much glitz. (If they can't see her earrings on the back row, she won't wear 'em.)

Gripped more and more by, uh, maturity, for the longest time, she's intent on giving honest answers. "I just stop after the blank asking my name," she joked. In the age blank, she used to write "atomic"; now, it's "digital". Yes, she's had fun with the age thing.

Here lately, despite her "mid-60s" looming around the next corner, she's been writing "59.95" on the age line.

When she underwent foot surgery, she accepted wearing a cast for several months, as long as she could choose pastel colors for each replacement cast—and red, of course, for her February Valentines. With her "show must go on" pluck, she rolled to her engagements with her foot elevated on a rolling contraption. Recently, attendants rolled her wheelchair toward a commuter plane where boarding stairs were more than she could handle. "How much do you weigh?" one asked. "250 pounds," she insisted. They decided they were up to making the lift—Mamie, chair and all—to the passenger door.

"You don't feel like 250 pounds," one said. "I'm not even close to that," Mamie laughed. "But I wanted to make sure you didn't drop me and I didn't want to challenge the plane's weight limit for lift-off."

My road experiences fade in compared to Mamie's. Still, the best night's sleep I got once—albeit in daylight—is worth recalling. Following an engagement one evening, I decided to ride the train to my next one in Topeka, KS. It was my first time to get a ticket for the Pullman car, and I was afraid I'd sleep through the train's brief stop in Topeka.

"Sir, you ain't got no problems," the porter said. "You're the only person in the sleeping car tonight, and we cut it loose on the side tracks when we get to Topeka, so you can sleep here all weekend if you want to." It took hours to fall asleep, but when I did, slumber was deep. By mid-afternoon, I was fully rested. I got dressed, walked across the rail yard and hailed a cab to my evening engagement….(2-2005)

IT TAKES A HEAP OF LIVING…

This lady with five names—Gertrude Edna Lee Kirkwood Tapscott—was like no one my wife and I had ever met. We were mesmerized during our visit to her home in Prairie View. At age 105, she was Texas' oldest annuitant in the Teacher Retirement System. Her life had spanned parts of three centuries.

En route to Texas Retired Teachers' Association's annual convention in Houston, we called to make sure it was okay to stop by. We visited in her "house by the side of the road," adjacent to the railroad tracks. It has stood there for nearly a century, a scant mile from her beloved Prairie View A&M University, where she earned two degrees and served in numerous roles for more than three decades. The darling of a quarter-million retired teachers, she "joined up" with TRTA some 40 years ago, and is now, of course, their matriarch. Still, she brightens meetings with her wit and recitations.

When we arrived, she was munching on pork skins, her daily treat. Her phone was at hand for calls—outgoing and incoming—and she never mentioned being bedfast. Life took a southward turn the previous December. On the way to a retired teachers' meeting, she was injured when her wheelchair lift into a van went afoul. It was always "first things first" with Gertrude, who insisted on proceeding to the meeting. The next day, a broken hip was diagnosed at the hospital.

Walls and shelves in her home were covered with citations, trophies and certificates—"whereases and wherefores" noting her 40-plus years of teaching and countless good deeds rolling all the way to eternity's shores. To her colleagues, her church, community, family and race, she was a shining star—a life always giving. Her conversations were sprinkled with words like blessings, faith and mercy.

She never nodded off that day; sakes alive, I'm not sure she even blinked. Her eyes, though, looked tired, like lingering embers of a campfire near trail's end. Recitations began, complete with pauses and telling smiles between selections. She ticked off all 32 lines of Edgar Guest's *Home*, and next was a 55-line poem including names of all books in the Bible. Then she spoke of Dr. Red Duke, who "saved her life" back in '95….

Gangrene set in, and Dr. Duke was called in. It was necessary to remove a leg. He called her "tougher than wet leather," predicting she would bounce back. She did. After all, her life was one of ongoing "make do's," most of them against a backdrop of sacrifice. Her watchword was insisting on seeking the possible, with upward and outward thoughts of what might be.

Widowed 32 years ago, she and her late husband, James, were married 47 years. He was a chef at the Prairie View dining hall for 33 years. They had no children of their own, but their home became "one away from home" for almost 100 youngsters across three decades. The "guests" were, after all, mostly Prairie View A&M students. Some stints were short, others were for four years. When they needed room for a dozen folks at a time, the Tapscotts found it, sometimes forfeiting their own bedroom. (One of the students was the late E. V. Hill, a renowned minister.)

She had so wanted to attend more TRTA meetings, but kidney problems set in about a week after our visit. Friends swarmed to her hospital room for memory-dredging. One former student, now 87, was a student in Gertrude's first-grade class. Another recalled being bare of foot, until Gertrude learned about it. She bought him his first new pair of shoes. They spoke of her learning to swim after she was 80, and her dreams of riding in a space ship. But late on April 12, 2005, after reciting poems and scriptures an hour earlier, she slipped away.

Her casket was borne to the church on a horse-drawn wagon. Some 50 relatives walked behind, and 300 mourners met the entourage outside the Hempstead, TX, church. Her memorial program noted that she "came over a way—sunrise, May 23, 1899; sunset, April 12, 2005."

(After thoughts: We left Gertrude a signed book. Her niece, Amy Boykin, called to say it was a bother to Gertrude that she never had the chance to open it. I kidded her that many thousands of others in good health never opened it, either. Neither did she see the column, excerpted here, since it was released about a month after our visit.

I am pleased—and most grateful—that Dallas' WFAA-TV sent a team to her home for an interview, a heart-warming piece shown a couple of times on the Dallas newscasts. I am told they sent a DVD of the interview to Gertrude. I pray that it arrived in time for her to see it before she went His way. (05-2005)

COLUMNISTS/OPTOMETRISTS SEE EYE TO EYE...

It was an odd mix—optometrists, the sublime, and columnists, the ridiculous—landing at the same hotel on the same weekend for annual meetings. Without claiming "20-20 hindsight," I'll admit what I remember two weeks later is fuzzy at best. For most folks—including all of advanced age—sight in either direction falls far short of 20/20.

American Optometric Association reps outnumbered the National Society of Newspaper Columnists by about 10-1. The former was 2,000 strong; ours fell one zero short of that. For both groups, it was mostly participants talking to each other; but for the eye docs, continuing education credit was trumpeted. Some writers—school drop-outs, beating chests and drums about being "self-educated"—worried not about credit, except maybe for paying hotel bills. Shared intent included the letting down of hair, said "letting down" as in the eyes (or over the eyes) of beholders.

Most optometrists didn't stray far from their daily attire, but men removed ties and women wore sensible shoes. Though proceedings of both groups seemed largely uneventful, one writer did fall into the moat, an accident that went unreported in the press. Oh, several wore "goofy glasses" plucked from convention packets. Slinkies sprang from the frames, with eyeballs of bloodshot plastic bobbing at springs' ends.

Hotel personnel quickly noted affiliations, with or without lapel IDs or slinky glasses. The optometrists left actual tips; "the writers promised to put our names in the paper if we served them well," a waitperson said, eyes rolling. Another staffer, accustomed to checking pay phones' coin return slots, had to hustle. Some columnists were arriving there first for "quarter-claiming."

Columnist session leader Keith Woods of the Poynter Institute was terrific—until his final point was augmented by a large visual reading, "Purse accuracy aggressively." He meant "pursue," of course. Muttering about the dangers of trusting spell check, he made a bold admission: he'd prepared the visual himself.

Also refreshing was Wil Haygood, *Washington Post* writer and Pulitzer finalist who later was to become a renowned author, one whose book became a grand motion picture, *The Butler.* Warning against errors of assumption, he spoke of decade-ago research efforts for his book about Sammy Davis, Jr. Wil found reams of information about Sammy Jr. and Sammy Sr., but he was chagrined that he could find no obituaries of the star's mother. He shared his puzzlement with a colleague who commented, "Well, for starters, she's not dead."

Truth to tell, we should have bowed at the optometrists' feet. Without them, there'd be fewer readers. Many newspaper aficionados have corrected vision, and they have markedly different "druthers" than counterparts with impaired hearing. "I hear as much now as I want to hear," some hearing aid holdouts contend. However, I've never heard similar expressions concerning sight....(7-2005)

WHERE BAGPIPES ARE KING...

The little college is an oasis near life's busy freeways, a throwback to a gentler era. A few blocks from Interstate 35 in St. Paul, MN, it feels light years removed from reality.

Maddening paces now are the norm. The beauty and serenity of Macalester College seem straight from the easel of artist Norman Rockwell. And, if there'd been a campus in mythical *Brigadoon*, it would have been Macalester.

A place that refuses to forget its past, the 120-year-old institution is forever plaid, proud of its Scottish origin, Presbyterian heritage and dogged determination to be first-rate. Dancers in Scottish plaid prancing across campus would not have seemed out of place on the September Friday of our visit, when the sun dipped toward the western horizon. A breeze gently reminded that cold winds and snow soon would come.

From the second floor room in the music building wafted mournful sounds of the lone bagpiper, teacher Michael Breidenbach's final student of the week. Taking steps two at a time, I was eager to meet the man who spends most of his time blowing bagpipes and teaching the art to others.

A North Dakotan arriving at Macalester as a freshman in 1992, Breidenbach has a bass guitar and jazz trombone background. He was introduced to piping by a part-time teacher who spent 15 years as director of the program. Ultimately, Michael was "hooked," and in 1999, eager to succeed his teacher in the part-time role.

He learned the job requires inflation in at least two ways. First, it is necessary to inflate male egos to abide wearing kilts—and other foreign accoutrements. Plus, he must push fitness and lung development if players are to conquer the physically-demanding 'pipes that were popular in Scotland as early as the 1400s. (This is the only place I know where being "full of hot air" is a good thing!)

I feel like the guy who first saw bagpipes without the piper attached. "I didn't know whether you're supposed to blow it, quarantine it or use it in battle," Michael prattled, wondering if it had a front or back end, and was animal, vegetable or mineral. He says piping remains prominent in Scotland to this day because the conquering English told the Scots that piping, kilts and the whole caboodle would no longer be tolerated. Scots "piped, kilted and caboodled" anyway.

The director's groups (along with the drum corps) play at a dozen or so special campus events annually. Highlights include an opening convocation, founder's day, graduation and homecoming—the latter called, of course, the "gathering of the clan." The other half of his time is spent independently, playing for weddings and funerals.

He'll not forget one of the first funerals. When it was time for the casket to be taken from the church, he walked slowly to the front, playing *Amazing Grace*. He realized too late that he'd forgotten to dispose of his chewing gum. Wouldn't you know it? It almost lodged in his windpipe. If it had, there might have been an additional pall on the whole occasion.

Breidenbach will be married soon. Maybe he'll provide the music. In the meantime, he might want to work on a bagpipe fight song for the Fighting Scots' football team. The current one is not working; the team was winless this season….(11-2005)

IN SEARCH OF SMALL BLESSINGS…

Blessings, even small ones, are hard to come by. At gas pumps, tears flow. We should be thankful we aren't topping off a 747. Gasoline tab for a flight to Asia, for example, is $100,000.

Topic-skipping: For some people, "cutting to the chase" is an art form. But Amarillo's Victor Leal, CEO of a Mexican restaurant chain and a member of the 24-member Texas Tax Reform Commission, thinks Chairman John Sharp is doing his best to explain proposed reforms. On the house floor to introduce a bill, Sharp was asked by a representative to "explain it one more time, just for me." Finally, Sharp said, "I'll be happy to explain it to you, but I can't *understand* it for you."...

I had "asked around" about Mexican food places, and that's where I met Leal, who served up the best avocado enchiladas I'd ever lapped lips over. He was brimful of optimism, telling me how pleased he was that his parents decided to "plunge into business" with a Muleshoe, TX restaurant in 1957. Their options were to open the business or pay down on a home. "Life is pretty much what you make it," he said. "We can choose to be victors or victims. You can guess the CEO's choice. He insisted, by the way, that the letters stand for Chief Enchilada Officer….

At the "top of Texas" to commit a speech, I flew to Amarillo, sawing many logs at a hotel there, ending a long day. Arising at the "crack of 10:30 a.m.," I proceeded to the car rental place for the short drive to Pampa. In front of me, a woman tearfully begged for a car—any car. Kirk, the rental car guy, repeatedly gave the "no more cars" spiel, no matter how critically important it was for her to get to Lubbock.

"Give her my car," I interrupted. "But then you'll have no car," Kirk said. I could tell we were "lengthening to the chase," so I repeated the offer, slowly and firmly. Done deal, and she was on her way, showering me with thanks as she exited. Now, I was next in line. "What types of conveyances do you have today?" I asked. "Sir, surely you heard me say that we have no more cars. All we have is a cargo van." I said this vehicle would do nicely, if I could afford the rate. He gave me the very best: a compact car rate.

Grabbing the steering wheel, I catapulted into the driver's seat, considering the possibility of hiring out for floral delivery. Pampa folks said I was their only speaker in memory arriving there in a cargo van, decked out in a tuxedo. As I drove back to Amarillo, I was grateful for small blessings, and wondered if the woman made it to Lubbock on time….(5-2006)

BISCUITS, FLEAS AND PUMP HANDLES…

Zig Ziglar would be one of the few people on the planet who could get by with such a title, but he did, and it later turned into a tidal wave of success for the late king of encouragers. That's what he called his first book, self-published 30+ years ago.

It didn't make a ripple in the big publishing pond, however, until it was picked up by Pelican Publishing. Re-titled *See You at the Top*, it—and Zig Ziglar—were on their way. It became the bible in motivational literature, perhaps second only to THE BIBLE. He credits the latter for making the former possible. Queried about his pilgrimage to the top of the motivational-speaking world, he credited his salvation experience in 1972 as the starting point. *See You at the Top* is now in its 61st printing, with 1,600,000 copies in print. It is the credo for the Ziglar organization. In the meantime, he wrote 25 more books. Arguably the most effective communicator in history, this Yazoo City, MS native is likewise recognized for his thousands of motivational programs throughout the world.

They had a birthday party for him the other night at a fancy hotel. It was a two-meat, three-fork affair, where the wait staff wore tuxes and valet drivers parked the cars. Dessert was birthday cake for an audience of 600 Ziglar faithful, some who traveled from Canada and England to attend Zig's 80th birthday, or, as the banners proclaimed, "The 59th Anniversary of Zig's 21st Birthday." Son Tom emceed, and testimonials from all walks of life credited the honoree for new-found sunshine. Hearts were warmed.

Zig, a high school graduate with a couple of years of college, has a bucketful of honorary doctorates. More importantly, he's an honor graduate of the University of Life. No doubt, he was itching to step forward for the blowing out of candles long before he was presented to an adoring audience.

"People periodically ask me why I don't retire," Zig said. "They say, 'You've now been working for over 50 years, speaking most of that time. Why don't you quit?' One friend heard Zig had retired. "My response to him was, 'I said *refired!'* I'm not going to ease up, let up, shut up or give up until I'm taken up! As a matter of fact, I'm just getting warmed up! And that's the truth." Sounds like he and Paul Harvey drank from the same dipper, or maybe the saucers old ranchers drank their coffee from, 'cause their cups had overflowed.....(11-2006)

MR. PRESIDENT, DO YOU HAVE THE TIME?

My friend, Jean David, sat up in her chair when she heard the news of President Gerald Ford's death at age 93. Her thoughts retreated to that spring day in 1976 when she, her husband, Bill, daughter Lisa and several hundred others had lunch with President Ford in Fort Worth. She remembered just three days later, a tornado swept away the 120-year-old barn at their ranch. And her late husband's comforting admonition: "Relax, Jingo. It was just a barn. The house wasn't touched, and you weren't hurt. Relax." Her husband, a grand jurist, was masterful in seeing the "big picture." So, she relaxed.

Smiling, she didn't dwell on "ill wind" aspects of the day, happily recalling April 28, 1976, and the Fort Worth/Tarrant County Bar Association's Law Day luncheon. She and Lisa—a high school senior—hurried to their places. They felt the warmth of eyes and smiles—from Bill, and from the man next to him, the President of the United States!

"Those two men really hit it off," Jean remembers. "Both played college football, served in the Navy, went to law school and loved the land. And both were lifted to the offices they held. It seemed as though they'd been friends for years."

David, who vowed never to wear a wristwatch or carry a timepiece after WWII service, was aware of the meticulous schedule calling for President Ford to speak at 1:29 p.m. Bill asked the President to nudge him when it was 1:29. President Ford smiled, and, as requested, nudged him at the precise moment. Then, Bill would say, "Ladies and gentlemen, the President of the United States."

A few minutes earlier, a Secret Service member quickly switched plates between these two principals at the head table. Thus, the Tarrant County Bar President became the "official taster" for the President. He did so happily, chuckling, "There are plenty of lawyers should the taste test take me out."

I've never met a sitting President, but once sat where a sitting President sat many times, and it was President Ford. In Grand Rapids to address Michigan grain growers on a bitterly cold January morning some 30 years ago, I ordered a cinnamon roll and coffee at the hotel coffee shop. "You are sitting in the very booth President Ford chooses when he visits, and he orders cinnamon rolls I've heard him call 'the best in the world.' Many's the time I've served him," the waitress beamed.

I've thought of the moment many times when I would, perchance, sit at "his" table, eating his favorite cinnamon rolls! Recently, though, I heard more about his culinary choices, and one took luster from the memory. They said his typical White House luncheon fare called for cottage cheese, topped with a liberal dollop of catsup. Ugh!

I join others in remembrances of President Ford. Though there was much coverage about his death, we know only smatterings of his acts of kindness and steering the nation when it was difficult to steer.

One such act was noted within days of his appearance in Fort Worth. The David's' daughter, Lisa, planning to participate in high school graduation days later, was killed in an automobile accident. President Ford penned a letter of sympathy to the Davids.

Our friend Jean and Mrs. Ford never met. They have much in common, too, including long marriages—the Fords, 58 years, and the Davids, almost 60.

Of the wonderful tributes to President Ford, none, I believe, was more profound than that of CBS newsman Bob Schieffer: "He's the nicest man I ever met in public life."

Bill warrants such "top shelf" accolades, as does his wife. They both have expressed their love for Howard Payne University, and during several of my years as president, Bill was Chairman of the

Board of Trustees, and a valued confidant and friend. He's been gone for almost five years, and is greatly missed….(1-2007)

AS THE WORLD SPINS…

Dr. Richard Jackson is a preacher who joins me, and others of a certain age, in admitting a long tenure of watching our planet spin. While we were classmates at Howard Payne in the 1950s, he was pastor of small area churches, where plastic flowers adorned the altar except on special Sundays—really special ones, like Easter and the Sunday nearest Christmas. In his churches, a few dozen people gathered for worship each week, most of them calling the others by name.

His final pastorate spanned a quarter of a century. The church grew from a few hundred members to upwards of 25,000, almost all of whom he baptized. He was in the glare of TV cameras each week; thousands of parishioners worshiped; multiple services were required in the sprawling church. North Phoenix Baptist Church became "huge" during most of the years he spent in ministry there. (And, yep, real flowers all the time.)

I know something of his schedule and demands of such a pastorate. He illustrated. "Life's work is a lot like a spinning ball," he said. "If we are passionate and growing, the ball seems to get bigger and bigger, gradually becoming more difficult to spin. We feel we have to keep it spinning, so we continue to do so. If the ball were square, we could put it down, like a suitcase, thus resting from time to time. But instead, it is round, and has no handles. Eventually, we don't feel we can maintain the spin," Richard added. He spoke of the difficulty in letting it go; he prays that successors will take care of the ball, putting their unique spin on it.

He's in Brownwood, now, far from retired and much committed to gear-changing. He's writing, preaching most Sundays and serving as Chairman of the Board of B. H. Carroll Theological Institute in Irving. Much of his passion is committed to his Jackson Center of Evangelism, located within one block of Howard Payne. With wife Wanda at his side and a Savior to share, one day he'll wear out, but never rust out….(1-2007)

RIGHT SIDE UP…

Kenneth Ashworth, Ph.D, scaled great heights in the world of higher education. And, his diplomatic bent is serving him well as he changes gears from administration to academia. Who else, pray tell, could hold teaching posts for the University of Texas and Texas A&M University AT THE SAME TIME?

Dr. Ashworth is doing just that. The longest-tenured Texas Commissioner of Higher Education (1976-1997) is presently teaching courses in public policy development and public administration and management at UT's LBJ School of Public Affairs and at Texas A&M's George Bush School of Government and Public Service.

"You've got to be kidding," the printer laughed when Dr. Ashworth ordered a two-sided card, each side with different information—and drastically different colors. You're way ahead of me, aren't you? Yes, he wanted an orange background on one side, and maroon on the other....

For more than two decades, the veteran educator's task was to coordinate and "make better" all public colleges and universities in Texas. To say that his chair wasn't warm most of the time is akin to TV weather people trying to hedge Texas' frying pan temperatures in Texas by sometimes calling it "less hot." I doubt very much that he ever sat in a really cool one, nor sought to.

He represented all institutions, large and small, with the same fairness, logic and fervor. His legacy is the respect, admiration and confidence from constituents throughout the state. Now in his sixth decade of public service, he says he's "still trying to retire." My guess is he's having too much fun teaching graduate students the "how" of administration in theoretical settings before they sign contracts to serve where real bullets await. He's also having fun writing, churning out numerous scholarly articles and four books to date. One book is entitled, *Caught Between the Dog and the Fireplug or How to Survive Public Service.*

Dr. Ashworth is delightful at lecterns. A favorite admonition is included in most speeches for administrators. He says, "Despite all your many good works for the people, do not expect sainthood and beatification. You will never experience the ecstasy of Saint Teresa. Learn to think of yourself as a martyr, specifically Saint Sebastian. The model public servant—the one with his hands tied behind his back and shot full of arrows."

Now does this sound like someone who's trying very hard to retire? Oh, he may retreat to play his clarinet or violin for a few minutes, but stick around. He'll be right back….(06-2007)

A DESIGNATED DRIVER...

Another guy who loves his work is Dr. David Green, a minister whose undergraduate study was at Carson-Newman University in Tennessee. There, his dormitory friends promoted him to "designated driver." Oh, it's not what you're thinking. It has to do with food, not drink. Mention food to dorm guys late at night and there's salivation. Mention free food and you've got the making of a riot. His "designated driver" remembrance is connected to the "free food" topic.

Late one night, he and some buddies were in Knoxville's first Krispy Kreme store, where they put away doughnuts with abandon. As the midnight closing hour approached, they watched employees trekking to the dumpster in back. There, they tossed the day's unsold delicacies. That's when the "designated driver" idea hatched. On many subsequent occasions, Dr. Green made nocturnal drives to Knoxville, some 30 minutes away. He'd leave campus around 11:25 p.m., reaching the store just before the pastries hit the dumpster. Upon arrival back on campus around 12:30 a.m., he was roundly cheered.

Between doughnut consumption, they shared jokes, stories and philosophies. You decide the category for this one: "Vegetarians don't choose meatless diets because they love animals. It's more likely that they hate plants." That said, they grabbed more doughnuts—before they got stale….(06-2007)

WHEN FLOWERS SAY IT BEST…

"**And who** knoweth whether thou art come to the kingdom for such a time as this?"

These are the final 16 words of the 14th verse, fourth chapter, Book of Esther, King James version of the Holy Bible. The scripture has been fleshed out to full sermon proportions countless times. It speaks to God's impeccable timing and rarely has been so fitting for nature as well. God's flowers, nodding by the millions in silent salute across the 60-mile stretch from Austin to Stonewall, beautified the good-bye trail for Lady Bird Johnson.

A passion of this sweet-spirited former First Lady was promotion of wildflowers for Texas' roadsides. The blossoms hung around extra-long this year, extending one of their best-ever seasons, perhaps for "such a time as this."

We can't script growing seasons, or, for that matter, blow-outs. A bus carrying mourners blew a tire en route to the burial, and several cars in the cortege stopped to offer rides. My guess is that plenty of folks pitched in to retrieve the tire remnants. "Helping out" is a Texas tradition, particularly when folks need a ride and when smoking hot rubber mars a patch of beautiful flowers.

Press coverage of Mrs. Johnson's death was gentle, detailed and dignified. One account included her years-ago conversation about possible epitaphs. She opined that it would be fine if they stated: "Lyndon built four dams, and Lady Bird planted three trees."

The radio and TV guys failed to do their homework—or maybe they forgot—how Texans pronounce some words, regardless of their spelling. Most Texans know that we call it the "PERD-inales River," even though it is spelled "P-e-d-e-r-n-a-l-e-s." Some national news folks repeatedly called it "PEDDER-nal-less."

The Johnsons loved this river and the home place nearby. Soon after LBJ declared in 1968 that he would not be a candidate for re-election, it was clear that he wanted to retreat to the ranch. "The first year back home, I'm going to sit in a rocking chair on the front porch," he declared. "And if I enjoy it, the second year, I may rock." Alas, he didn't get to sit or rock very long. He died at age 64 in 1973, just four years after leaving the presidency, and a month after the death of Harry S. Truman.

Renowned journalist Bill Moyers is remembered as the President's press secretary. Once he was asked about dealing with news people day after day, from early morning until late night. It was, of course, a "can 'till can't" meat-grinder, like most Washington assignments. He claimed a mantra that served him well. His was to "tell the truth whenever possible—but never lie."

Moyers came to mind when my wife and I stood in line at a popular new burger joint in Fort Worth. It wasn't the hamburgers that made me think of him. I was reflecting on Lady Bird's death. (I thought of the coincidence that both she and Bill attended Marshall High School, albeit in different eras. She walked the stage in 1928; he in 1952.)

Upon entering the café, my wife nudged me, whispering, "That man behind us is a minister." I asked, "Do you know something I don't?" This time, she was particularly adamant about her usual reliance on intuition. I finally asked the man, "Are you a minister?"

He gave a "sorta/kinda" answer. His name is Benjamin Roy Chamness. I'd call Dr. Chamness a "preacher's preacher." He's been pastor of numerous Texas churches, but now they call him "Bishop Chamness." The Central Texas Conference he serves includes more than 300 churches in one of Methodism's largest geographical areas. I give my wife an "A+" again. There are only four other Methodist bishops in Texas, but he was the only one in the hamburger line Saturday night.

Bishop Chamness, having served in virtually every ministerial role, re-defines humility. He'd prefer being called a "good ole' boy" from Carthage. He married the former Joye Stokes, a Henderson gal, 47 years ago. With sparkling eyes and a ready smile, she looks like a preacher's wife. They have two sons, six grandchildren, and love Kincaid's hamburgers.... (07-2007)

A LIFE OF FULL MEASURE...

Let's "fess" up! Who among us has not attended memorial services that stretched toward eternity? Given advance warning of lengthy services, we might opt to be absent.

Or concoct an exit strategy triggered by a coughing spell. A tribute held in Fort Worth was to memorial services what *Lawrence of Arabia* was to movies: long, but worth every second.

The service was for Kyle Ogle of Texas, a real-life hero to the thousand-plus mourners who crowded into McKinney Memorial Bible Church to honor the life of this 38-year-old hero. A bold Christian who battled cancer for a dozen years, Kyle met the disease head-on with dogged determination, deep faith and a trademark smile. Honoring Kyle's detailed directives for the service, eulogist Tommy Saxon set the tone: "Keep it light. Keep it fun. Keep it real." Saxon and fellow eulogist Jeff Turner were "thick and thin" buddies who forged friendships from their youth. Their bonds began in childhood days of neighborhood scrapes, bicycles and BB guns.

Reflections ran the gamut, with laughter and tears in equal measure. "Kyle died young but lived old," observed minister friend Dr. Tommy Nelson. Powerful words, videos and music stirred mourners. More than two hours passed, really unnoticeably. "More," collective souls seemed to beg, "more." Wanting to glean additional lessons from this magnificent life, fully half of the crowd lingered in the foyer for the better part of another hour. "Kyle stories" abounded. And there are many.

Though cancer was a backdrop for a dozen of his 14 years of marriage to the former Darla Ward, Kyle and his bride refused to let his disease dominate their lives—until recent days. They "lived large," building their dream home overlooking a lake on acreage near Weatherford. They worked hard, her at home with son Turner, 9, and daughter Katherine, 7, while Kyle earned #1 sales status for a world-wide medical equipment firm. The family was the picture of perseverance.

He rarely flinched in his slugfest with synovial cell sarcoma. Known far and wide for his self-effacing humor, he "laughed off" much of the grimness that typically is "part and parcel" of cancer.

Intimate friends gathered for his 2002 "Farewell to Arm" party that preceded the surgery that took his shoulder and right arm.

It was one of many surgeries. Immediately "left-handed," he soon was driving again. To the sporting world so important in his life, he introduced a new bow hunting technique. Pulling back arrows with his teeth, he claimed deer, wild hogs, bear, elk and turkeys.

Kyle was always "at the ready" to share his testimony. And he was featured on TV hunting shows. He reached the hearts of tens of thousands with his Christian message just as certainly as his arrows felled prey on Texas ranches, the mountains of Colorado and the wilds of Canada. His witness never wavered. He "leaned into life's struggles," friend Jeff said, "never asking 'why me?' Instead, he asked 'why not me?'"

He was loving, giving, selling and joking, even during those final 10 days at Baylor Hospital in Dallas. He closed deals on medical equipment from his hospital bed, all the while greeting loved ones and friends who visited. During some lucid moments on Sunday, three days before his death, he led son Turner to Christ. Fighting kidney poison that was having its way, he struggled to utter a prayer for his son. Darla finished it.

Though not a mystic, Kyle hearkened back to a vision that seemed so real to him eight months earlier when he had neurotoxicity from chemo poisoning. He told Darla about a black coat, a train, a bright figure and a voice requesting his coat. He told her how the bright figure took his coat, telling him, "it's not your time yet," as the train pulled away.

A dozen hours before his death, Kyle said, "The train's coming and I'm getting on it."

At 1 a.m. on October 29, he was restrained when he tried to get out of bed. Who knows? Maybe he heard a train whistle. And maybe he was determined to get on board. Perhaps a bright figure handed him a coat as white as snow, in case of a chill in the morning air.

His one-way ticket punched, Kyle leaves a legacy of a man who squeezed life to extract the very last drop. His stories will be re-told across the years. Hearers will smile, weep and marvel.

Sounds of the service will echo for a long time. Still resonating are Dr. Nelson's reminder: "We can dry our tears on the memory of this man's life." And Saxon's summation: "Kyle could do everything well except quit."

(I was in Kyle's presence just twice. I took him parasailing at Lake Brownwood just prior to his initial diagnosis. Soon after the radical surgery that took his arm, I enjoyed a two-hour lunch with him. He spoke of God's powerful words: "I am." There are more accounts and pictures at: (http://caringbridge.org/visit/kyleogle, 11-2006).

ON FLYING AND FEEDING THOSE WHO DO…

Motel Six "leaves the light on for us," and Southwest Airlines reminds regularly of our freedom to move about the country. When I call Southwest, the wait to talk to a "real" person is worth it. The sensible music soothes, and occasional "factoids" make me laugh. During one such recent call, I broke into full-blown laughter with this pronouncement: "You are now free to move your phone around to the other ear."…

A dozen years ago, our men's basketball team at Howard Payne University qualified for a national small-college tournament in Nampa, ID. As HPU president, I was always yammering about the need to be ever vigilant to put the squeeze on every dollar, including travel. We took sack lunches as we hopped, skipped and jumped across the map from Dallas to Boise. There were four stops and a plane change, but hey, we had more time than money.

Alas, our team was eliminated in the first game. So, we began the circuitous flight home, this time with peanuts only. Noting a 30-minute layover at Houston Hobby Airport before the final leg to Dallas, I hatched a plan for the team to enjoy giant pizzas there between planes. No, not airport pizza, but the good stuff—and the kind deeply discounted by coupons. I called Jeremy Denning, an honor graduate who was in medical school there at the time. I asked him to bring a dozen giant pizzas to the airport. And he did. If this scenario were repeated today, I wouldn't hesitate a second to ask Dr. Denning for the same favor, though I imagine he'd send a stand-in.

He has always been as humble and gentle as anyone I've ever known. At age 36, he's now a leading neurosurgeon in Dallas, cited recently as one of *D Magazine's* "top docs"….

We laugh later about travel experiences that whiten knuckles at the time. Once, en route from DFW to Washington, DC, our plane began a sudden descent about 20 minutes into the flight. The plane was 100% full, and ashen stares were exchanged when the pilot announced a possible emergency before releasing oxygen masks. They all fell—and I realize this may be considered a selfish position—except mine. I glanced toward my wife, who quickly got her mask in place, albeit without the "continuation to breathe normally" as routinely instructed by the flight attendants during pre-flight drills.

I asked if she would share her oxygen with me. Not about to lose one breath of oxygen by answering me verbally, she shook her head vigorously, left to right, NOT up and down.

During the descent for an unscheduled landing in Oklahoma City, a flight attendant took a screwdriver to my oxygen mask compartment, so I lived to tell about it. (Not one of the attendants, it turned out, had ever experienced real-time mask use.)

Soon we were on our way again on a back-up plane. At lunch time, my wife was served first. "You don't mind if I go ahead and eat, do you?" she asked. "I didn't mind if you went ahead and breathed, why would I mind if you went ahead and ate?" I answered.... (02-2009)

(Addendum: Dr. Denning continues to distinguish himself as a neurosurgeon. He has won numerous honors, and remains the same humble, sincere, thoughtful, engaging and genuine person he has always been.)

GOOD-BYE TO A NATIONAL TREASURE...

Writing a tribute to Paul Harvey, a hero to millions, is akin to firing an air rifle at the sun—both will fall miserably short. He was without peers in his field. We are grateful for that unique "voice with a smile in it" that graced radio airwaves for more than 75 years.

Fascinated by the medium of radio since boyhood, he built his own crystal set receiver as a lad. Later in high school, he started hanging around the KVOO studios in his hometown, Tulsa, OK. He swept the floors there before landing mike-side assignments in 1933….

Bob Greene, noted Chicago columnist/author and longtime personal friend of the 90-year-old Harvey, captured the essence of the man who for decades had more radio news listeners than anyone else on the planet. He compared Harvey's newscasts to symphonies, underscoring not only the news maestro's unique delivery, but also his careful choice of words. Greene believes that Harvey was every bit as good a writer as broadcaster.

Harvey made hash of punctuation marks, particularly periods that were as puppets on his string. Listeners never knew when he was going to glide right over them like a thoroughbred horse on a simple jump, or perhaps stop completely, as if waiting for a 100-car freight train to lumber by. Often Harvey's long pauses were more profound than spoken words on either side of the caverns of nothingness….

A champion of the work ethic who rose for work at 3:30 each day, he had 25 million listeners over more than 1,500 radio stations worldwide. He was everyman's American. If he said it, you could take it to the bank….

Forever committed to his beloved medium, Harvey gave TV a try for a while, but it wasn't for him. Maybe he preferred stirring lazy minds to paint their own pictures from the words he presented. He joked that he hoped that television would one day be found to cause cancer….

Successor to the late Lowell Thomas as king of radio news, Harvey also eventually exceeded him in longevity. They had much in common, both relying on subtle humor.

Complimented for his strong listenership, Thomas always demurred when praised for having more listeners—in his era—than any other newsman. "Oh, there's a reason," he laughed. "My newscasts precede *Amos n' Andy*. Many listeners hear me because they tune in early, making sure to not miss a single word of *Amos n' Andy*…. Harvey was even more modest than Thomas.

I was privileged to meet Mr. Harvey just once, more than four decades ago. We were backstage, prior to his Fort Worth address. His warm, generous spirit is warmly remembered. His speech, like his broadcasts, mesmerized. He was a man to be "tuned in", and never "tuned out"….

Radio loyalists are like that. The late Grady Nutt, preacher/comedian killed in a plane crash nearly 30 years ago, told a story about his dad who loved to hear the Stamps Quartet on the radio every day at noon. "He set the dial squarely on the frequency, and he set the volume exactly where he wanted it," Nutt said. "Then, he sawed off the knobs." The elder Nutt didn't want anyone fouling up the radio knobs for the only show he cared about….

One of the Harvey tributes reads: "All candles burn out eventually, but this candle was special. It gave us hope that we might find our way through the thick darkness of life. It kept us warm when we felt cold. It made us feel safe when the cold winds blew. Good-bye Mr. Harvey. We'll all miss you."…

This radio giant believed in and worked toward better days for Americans. His home-going leaves an irreplaceable void. He always entreated us to "stand by…for NEWS!" But it will be impossible to stand by with the same sense of anticipation for his successors...(3-2009)

KNOWLEDGE BY THE STACK...

My parents bought some books in 1943, signing on for their first-ever purchase strung out with monthly payments. But Dad defended straying from his usual "cash on the barrel head" practice because he was intrigued by advertising promoting the books. The Compton Encyclopaedias, ads claimed they contained "all the information known in the world." And Dad was sure that's all we'd ever need to know. For me, it was love at first stack.

Mom may have voted "yes" to the purchase out of enlightened self-interest. Hair-cutting was one of her many talents, and with three encyclopedias stacked on a chair, no longer did she have to bend over to "whack away" with her hand shears. As a six-year-old who learned the importance of "sitting right still" during hair-cutting sessions, I knew that there'd also be drills about "Compton book-learnin'." Within months, questions about names of states and capitals—all of them—were fair game….

I didn't get a "store-bought" haircut until college years. Mom bought electric shears a few years earlier, but she drew the line on cutting burrs and flat-tops, both of which I favored. I don't remember her being openly critical of the then popular cuts, but the "standard cut"—mastered by trial and error—was as much as she cared to attempt.

Many's the time relatives showed up for dinner, and before dishes were washed and dried, a granddad, uncle or cousin would trot out well-worn barbershop humor to ease into not-so-subtle requests for free haircuts. Recollections include: "Reckon I could get my ears lowered? Could you remove this growth from my head? Is the 'clip joint' open?" Perhaps the most memorable came from an uncle who invariably asked her for a "hair-yank," avowing that the hand clippers yanked out as much hair as they cut….

Her barbering really got crackin' at holiday time. Names were drawn first for gifts, and then for the men's hair-cutting order. She'd call a name, and a relative would ask someone to "play his hand" at the "42" table while he got his hair cut. Sometimes a dozen relatives were sheared in a single session.

Occasionally, requests were for "a simple trimming, just a little off around the ears". (Typically, "cute" remarks came from relatives a couple of months late for haircuts.) Mom would protest, saying that if she didn't give full cuts, "they'd do just as well wearing dog collars."

She took no money, always doing what she could for loved ones, saving them 50 or 75 cents, then maybe $2 before she put the clippers away. A sincere "much obliged" from 30 or so kinfolks and neighbors was pay enough. (If they had 50 cents, they'd go to a "real" barber, she often laughed, and that if she took a dime, it would ruin her amateur status!)

Dad was particularly grateful. His death at age 83 in 1992 ended a marriage of more than 61 years, and I don't think he ever visited a barber shop. She passed in 2000 at age 88, but some six decades of hair-cutting ended with Dad's death….

Lots of styles have come and gone over the years. Mom had no use for what she called "extreme cuts," whether shaved heads or unshorn locks. She was forever asking me to "tell that joke about the long-haired boy." I always did so, even though she knew it, word for word.

The story goes that a youngster, a high school senior, refused to get a haircut. His dad told him that if he would do so and read the Bible in its entirety, he would buy him a car for graduation. A few weeks later, the senior, his hair still long, told his dad that he'd read the entire Bible, and was ready for the car.

"Son, you forgot to get your haircut," his dad responded. "Dad, I'm glad you mentioned my hair. Jesus, the central figure of the Bible, wore long hair." Then came his dad's big moment: "You're correct, son," he said. "And Jesus walked everywhere he went."…

After Sunday school the other day, I chanced to see Larry Smith, a young man who distinguished himself as a student and football player during my presidential years at Howard Payne University. He's continued the same pattern as a football coach and teacher at Everman High School.

I asked about his haircut, noting a two-inch square of hair in front that was spiked skyward. He said something about meeting the high school guys half way. "Some of them have Mohawks," he explained, "And mine is a "faux-hawk."

Mom would have laughed, and she would have loved Larry Smith. She, too, believed life is about far more than hair—yes, even more than all that learnin' in Compton Encyclopaedias.... (04-2009)

A COUPLE BLESSED
Married in 1966. Don, open heart surgery, 1998; Brenda, breast cancer surgery, 2009...

You remember the sign on the bookstore door when the business went south: "Words Failed Us." That pretty much describes our reflection on the blurry weeks involving diagnosis/surgery/convalescence faced recently. By way of short review, my wife, Brenda, is ahead of schedule as she works back toward driving a car, lifting more than 20 pounds and resuming everyday life following a bilateral mastectomy.

She was undergirded by a deep faith, many prayers and innumerable acts of kindness. I would wax poetic theologically, but don't want to tax my limited repository of theology. Like the guy who doesn't know art but knows what he likes, I join my wife in being thankful and overwhelmed by gracious acts of friends.

Her prognosis is excellent. Comforted by doctors' findings, we now are free to sort out dream-like moments in the surgery waiting room. Some comments that lightened hearts at the time, in retrospect, provide wider grins as time from her surgery now is weeks instead of days.

For example: Dominating the bunch of three dozen or so in our corner of the large waiting area were members of our Sunday school class, mostly 70-somethings. Some wore "we've had it" looks on furrowed brows, fitting cowboys' descriptions of "rode hard and put up wet". A majority had seen the snows of many winters, these friends with heads topped with graying hair, or, in some cases, nary a strand….

One was Raymond West. He surveyed the crowd, then, with one sentence, reduced tensions. "From the looks of the crowd, it seems to me that if a feller set up a Metamucil stand up here, he'd make a killing." Point taken….

Our caring daughters were faced with the need to disrupt their daily schedules in deference to their mom's surgery. Included were last-minute calls for child-sitters, etc.

Jeanie, about to dash out the door to the hospital, detected a sheepish look on the face of four-year-old Jonah. Dick Tracy-types aren't needed to get the truth from preschoolers, a truism Jeanie now knows.

"I've been splashing on Dad's cologne," he admitted. "Carly's coming over, and I want to smell good for her so she'll follow me around." Carly is the four-year-old daughter of a family friend coming over to "kid-sit."…

Jana, our Tyler daughter who has made numerous trips to the Metroplex of late to see her mom, was flustered the other day upon hearing an unfamiliar cell phone ring in her home. She traced it to her luggage. (Now quit filling in the blanks, and let me finish!)

Yes, it was MY cell phone that had fallen into her suitcase, and yes, she sent it back with overnight delivery. She even recorded a temporary message, explaining to callers that the phone might be on a FedEx truck somewhere between Tyler and the Metroplex. Yes, I reimbursed her for the cost of shipping the phone. The figure was considerably more than the value of my archaic cell phone which is heavy enough to weigh down whatever side of my clothes in which it rests….

Grandparents, by the trainloads, wince when their kids' kids say or do something to jump the tracks. This in mind, it should be trumpeted when they "do good".

Brittin, our granddaughter who just turned five, took her mom's instructions seriously as they entered the Harris Hospital parking garage. "I have much on my mind," said Julie, her mom. "It is your job to remember where to find our car."

The garage has numbered levels, each of which is named for animals, perhaps so preschoolers can help befuddled parents find their cars. Later, when they returned to the garage, Brittin confidently pushed the correct elevator button. They exited the elevator and she hopped, bunny-like, toward their car. "It was easy to remember, Mom," she said. "You parked exactly nine hops from the elevator on the jackrabbit floor."... (06-2009)

CERTAIN OTHER DUTIES AT THE SCHOOL HOUSE...

I'm convinced that when unsung heroes get their due, most school personnel will warrant an ongoing, well-deserved chorus of thanks from the rest of us. The good ones—and most of them are—log service "off the clock," working into the night, and sometimes into the next day. There are deeds we don't hear about, usually because they don't tell us. Many prefer not to risk misunderstanding, charges of grand-standing or seeking attention. In these days, our downtrodden society needs detailed information of stories that warm the heart.

I want to share a true account of utter compassion from earlier this year. The parties, as well as the school, will remain nameless. If you happen to be a school employee, I thank you, and if folks close to you are, please thank them for me.

It was on a cold Friday afternoon. The elementary school vice-principal was churning through the final hours of a challenging week, looking forward to a dinner engagement. The phone rang, and after a few words from the anxious fifth-grade girl, she thought briefly of her contract, the last words of which pretty much say it all: "and certain other duties as may be assigned by the superintendent". This phone call, though, triggered her sacred Christian obligation to help the hurting, whoever they are, wherever they are with whatever is most needed….

The youngster spoke through tears, phrases coming out in chunks. "My mom's awful sick," she said. "Would you be able to go by to see her? She's in hospice." Well aware of the youngster's "life story" and cognizant of what hospice care typically means, the administrator put the week's wind-up duties on hold. She knew that the youngster was being reared by a grandmother who had been granted custody several years ago. (The youngster had learned just months earlier that the woman she thought to be her mom was, in fact, her grandmother, but she kept calling her "mom," anyway.) The educator knew also that the cancer, diagnosed three years ago, was gaining the upper hand….

"Could you please come by after school?" the youngster begged. Of course she could, and she would. The vice-principal made calls to delay dinner, then hurriedly drove to the hospice facility in the city nearby.

When she arrived, the student was crying, standing vigil at her grandmother's bedside. Already unconscious, the precious patient, just 50 years of age, passed from this life within a minute of the comforter's arrival….

The educator sat down, her arms engulfing a 10-year-old who perhaps was already wondering where she'd live next. Yes, dinner—and a weekend "must do list"—seemed unimportant and far away. The student needed her desperately, and she was there.

A couple of days later, the educator drove to visitation at a funeral home in an adjoining county. The youngster ran to meet her, proudly introducing her to family and friends gathered for the funeral. She wanted everyone to know her friend who happens also to be a school official….

Multiply this vignette by several hundred thousand, maybe millions. Know that situations just like this, or closely akin thereto, will occur multiple times in the coming school year in communities across the land. School bells will be sounding soon, and the new school year will begin.

A slogan coined for the Association of Texas Professional Educators rings in my memory. It says much: "Supporting your freedom to teach." I'm sure the Association of Texas Professional Educators would be tickled beyond words if the public at large showed similar resolve. For many students, educators are their only advocate.

Make a genuine effort to thank someone at your school, extending warmest wishes for a great year. Better yet, thank several of them.

Offer your prayers and support. Maybe you can compose a fresh bumper sticker to support educators. If you can't, the old, well-worn sticker will work fine: "If you can read this, thank a teacher". Remember, when students need them, for more reasons than can be listed, they'll be there…. (07-2009)

(Addendum: If identifying the educator now suggests I am using my "bully pulpit," so be it. The vice-principal was not identified when the column ran in newspapers—at her request. I didn't ask her for permission to include the vignette in this book; her name is Julie Anna Newbury Choate, our oldest daughter. She continues to serve as vice-principal at McCall Elementary School in Aledo, TX.)

'BUCKET-KICKING' IN 21ST CENTURY...

It seemed risky, as kids, to mimic what full-grown adults said or did. More boundaries were known then, when lines in the dirt could have passed for deep-plowed fields.

"I see here in the newspaper where old so-and-so kicked the bucket," a spouse might say to a mate. As a rule, the expression wasn't used for close kin, but adults tossed the expression regularly for deceased folks on the outer edge of their social circles. On hearing it, even youngsters knew that someone had died. "Passed away" was a more delicate phrase, the one usually chosen by ministers, next-of-kin or candidates running for political office. (One long-time Tarrant County politico always "signed in" at the funeral home, hopeful to lead family members to believe links had been broken in a strong friendship.)…

My first journalism professor, Joe Swan—as well as all his colleagues in the English-speaking world—jarred our impressionable psyches with stern instruction about writing obituaries. Among threats was forfeiture of two letter grades for misspelling the name of the deceased, with something close to the full "death penalty" meted out for committing another definite "no-no"—the "flowering up" of the event. "The deceased don't 'go to their eternal reward, fade into the sunset, cross that mighty river or enter into heavenly rest,' they die," Swan insisted….

New ways for handling obits are foreign to those of us still driving our fathers' Oldsmobiles. Today's obits are written much differently. Now, it is the rule rather than the exception for charges to be made for newspaper obituaries. And the rules for writing same have changed--have they ever!

Now, submissions usually are printed as submitted—within the generous bounds of accuracy and common decency. Otherwise, editors look the other way, and if the obit says the deceased has "entered those heavenly gates, graduated to that land beyond the clouds, or claimed a room in that mansion in the sky," so be it….

Somewhere between the austere preparation of obituaries "back then" and the "almost anything goes" approach today suits me fine. In fact, some obits today bring smiles, perhaps capturing the "puckish" personality of the deceased.

Certain people—realizing their demise is at hand—may write their own obituaries, leaving only a few blanks to be filled in, such as date of death and time/place of service. How else would you explain one that appeared in a major Texas newspaper? Listed among the woman's survivors were "her favorite ex-husband, and his favorite new wife."...

One of my most delightful friends was the late George Dolan, whose daily column in the *Fort Worth Star-Telegram* brightened days of thousands of loyal readers for some three decades. Though he never thought so, he was as funny at the lectern as in print. He could casually face a one-hour column deadline with little in mind, and spend three sleepless nights before—as he put it—"committing a speech".

He was amused when his editor asked employees to provide their own obituary information, "in the event of need". So, he did. "Pallbearers were credit managers of Fort Worth's eight leading department stores," he wrote. "They carried me when I was alive, so they might as well finish the job." Dolan added that "guitarists strummed 'Aloha' on Hawaiian guitars." His running buddy, legendary columnist Blackie Sherrod (who also hailed from Temple) summed up his friend in one sentence: "Just *before* they made Dolan, they broke the mold."

Cancer claimed Dolan in 1983 at age 60. They crowded into Fort Worth's First United Methodist Church to honor the life of this brilliant writer who had no use for formality; this may explain his burial attire. He had on red striped pajamas and the worn-out robe he'd puttered around the house in until noon or later most days. He had a pipe in one hand and a newspaper in the other. As the organist played *Sentimental Journey*, a man, 30-something, remembered Dolan's "stern" instructions concerning delivery of his newspaper, a couple of decades earlier. "Throw it on the roof, son, and that's where I'll leave your payment each month." Then, I am sure, Dolan cackled in a way that only he could….(12-2009)

OLD-TIMERS WORTH REMEMBERING…

Two longtime friends, Dr. Robert Smith and businessman Al Lock, come to mind.

Dr. Smith, 85, was in pastoral ministry for 35 years before a 26-year stint teaching Bible at the collegiate level. "He flunked retirement three times," laughed Ethelyn, his wife of 62 years.

He's been teaching an Old Testament class in retirement for several years, and this was the plan for the current spring semester at Howard Payne University. However, his current teaching assignment has doubled. A class load of students signed up for "The Smiths and New Testament," even though it wasn't on the printed schedule. What to do? The Smiths are pulling a "double shift." (My wife and our three daughters were in Dr. Smith's classes, and all of them gave him an "A+.") For the past several years, the Smiths have "team-taught" a Sunday school class where 50 or so adults show up each week….

A Fort Worth entrepreneur, Lock, 82, continues to work full time at his office furniture business. He and Druena, his wife of 56 years, also have farming and ranching interests.

The Lock family has loved skiing for some 40 years. The couple still makes multiple ski trips annually. Next month they'll be in Park City, UT for their 27th consecutive year. For many years, Al was a familiar figure on the black diamond runs. (Druena put away her ski gear five years ago and now favors shopping. A while back, Lock underwent a thorough physical examination, laughing that he "had every test except water-boarding.")…

Such long, vibrant lives bring to mind the inimitable Dr. May Owen, who practiced pathology for some 70 years and was the first woman president of the Texas Medical Association in 1960.

She never took time to learn to drive a car, never married and lived some 60 years as a permanent guest in Fort Worth hotels. In later years, she lodged in the "honeymoon suite" of a neighborhood hotel, often joking she "finally had two rooms". She practiced medicine throughout life, and was working in the lab on the day before her death at age 96 in 1988. Though Dr. Owen never sought fame, it found its way to her. She inspired thousands of people, showing them how to serve and how to live….(01-2010)

(Addendum: In 2015, Al Lock still works daily. Dr. Smith, however, died in September, 2014, almost reaching age 90. The final column in this book addresses lives of his widow Ethelyn and son Robert Jr., both now residents of Redstone Park in Brownwood, TX)

PRAYERS THAT DON'T LET GO...

The importance of prayer is at, or very near, the center of all things Christian. Most of us could recite the "God is great" mealtime prayer—as well as the "Now I lay me down to sleep" beddy-bye petition—before we could count to 10 or say the "A-B-Cs".

We've pondered the "pray without ceasing" admonition and Jesus' teaching. His followers to spend much time in prayerful communion. The Lord's Prayer, a model for Christians, has been repeated by millions across the centuries.

Many prayers surpass, or at least equal, the world's most beautiful literature. Hebrews 11:1 is a classic example: "Now faith is the substance of things hoped for, the evidence of things not seen." It is admitted, however, that mortals' words do not always come out neatly packaged. Recalled are preachers—and others with microphones in hand—who entangle their tongues or fail brain engagement before speaking. We trust God has a sense of humor. "Goofs" from church bulletins feed on preachers' prayerful pratfalls, and my fear subsists that "there but by the Grace of God go I"....

Two legends are Texas A&M's R. C. Slocum, head coach of the Aggies for 14 seasons, and Baylor's Grant Teaff, football boss there for 21 years. They still chuckle about pre-game invocations voiced a few years apart at Baylor Stadium. Teaff remembers the 1975 season opener that followed Baylor's 1974 Southwest Conference championship season, the Bears' second in a half-century of trying. That miracle-on-the-Brazos season was still much on the minds of the Green and Gold when the next season rolled around. A well-known Texas pastor, groaning for years when the Bears' won only the coin toss, enthusiastically prayed for the Almighty to "make us humble."…

Humble? Baylor? During 57 years of Baylor football prior to Teaff's arrival, maintaining humility was a slam dunk. For the record, in 32 of those seasons, BU finished in the half of the conference that made the top half possible. Teaff wasn't sure that he heard the exact wording of the prayer, but he is sure the Bears turned the ball over via fumbles six times that day.

At the post-game interview, Teaff lightened the moment with reference to the prayer. "God's getting' on up there in years and maybe not hearing quite as well," Teaff teased. "He obviously thought the preacher said, "Make us fumble instead of humble."…

The prayer Slocum most remembers was during the Aggies' visit to Waco a few years later. Himself a churchman, he found himself nodding in affirmation of petitions voiced in the pre-game prayer. He wilted a bit, though, when he realized the preacher across the field with the Baylor warriors was HIS pastor from Bryan!...

The men were model coaching gentlemen, passionate mentors first committed to building lives, then football teams. Teaff brought respectability to Baylor football, and Slocum remains the winningest coach in A&M history. Both hold highest professional awards and have come great distances from their places of birth—Teaff in Hermleigh, TX, and Slocum in Oakdale, LA.

They are "as good as it gets," and they "keep on keeping on." Teaff is now Executive Director of the American Football Coaches Association, and Slocum is Special Advisor to the A&M President and works with the A&M Foundation. He also is the current President of the AFCA Foundation. In the words of the old cowboy trail riders, "they'll do to ride the river with"....(02-2010)

THE RED BRICK ROAD...

For about 750,000 Oncor customers whose kilowatts now are measured by "smart meters," add another front-burner concern. Howls are becoming choruses as sharp billing spikes seemingly coincide with installation of the new meters. PR people probably yearn for the "good old days," when their efforts kept the company in the news, but off the front page....

My daddy was in the energy business around 1940. He was a front-line PR person who also looked after the gas wells, fixed leaks and fetched pipe with a truck that couldn't have been as big as I remember. He also collected monthly bill payments customers left at grocery store collection points in May and Blanket, two Brown County towns with populations of a few hundred. (The monthly charge was $2 for residences and $4 for businesses, with the rate doubled during four winter months.)

Each grocer had a cigar box, with cash and checks stacked high. A four-year-old, I was "bug-eyed" at the sight of so much loot. Some paid with coins, knotted carefully in handkerchiefs. Others wrote notes about payment shortages, with promises to "catch up next month." Some left mournful pleas to avoid termination of gas service.

That's when Dad did his "PR-ing." He'd huddle with the grocer to learn what financial hurdles some folks faced. Gas service was rarely denied in the "good old days" before, as my Uncle Mort put it, "they started metering us to death."...

The current allegations that the "smart meters" are running short on accuracy reminded my old uncle of a post-World War II story. Meters of all kinds were popping up, including for utility services. "Oncor customers are howling now, but folks back then were many times more upset," Mort laughed. "They squealed like a thousand pigs stuck under gates." Meter-readers were easy targets of customers' wrath. One of Mort's friends, however, took on the job for the electric company, and even boosted the economy....

A veteran of World War II, the friend had dodged death many times. What irony, he thought, to risk death by boredom in his monotonous peacetime job. He vowed to be "on the lookout" for ways to introduce fun to his daily meter-reading routes.

He carefully recorded kilowatt usage, but was chafed when "close personal friends" (by their estimation, not his) begged him to "share the secret" to lowering electric bills. His mind spinning nearly as fast as the meters, he concocted a two-pronged fib—one to get them off track and the other to get his laughs on track....

One customer, a bona fide major league gossip, hammered daily for a share of the "secret." The meter reader finally admitted, "There is a way, but if I tell you, you'll spill the beans to the whole community, and that'll ruin it for sure." The customer did the "cross my heart with hopes to die" pledge if he ever shared the secret with "any other human being."…

As serious as a funeral, the company guy insisted on a hand-on-the-Bible vow before whispering the "meter fix." He insisted, "You must buy a new red brick. "Don't try to get by with a used one, or one that is chipped, or of another color. Place it on top of the meter in a vertical position. If you lay it horizontally, it won't work. Within three months, your bills should start going down. Remember, you must not tell a single soul." The customer claimed he hoped to be struck down by lightning if such occurred….

Sure enough, when the next reading was taken, a new red brick, centered vertically, topped the confidant's meter. As he proceeded down the block—and on all other blocks on the route—new red bricks topped all meters.

Brick sales spiked, clearly a stimulus for the economy. Some three months later, the meter reader resigned his position, deciding to further his education on the GI Bill. He chose to study sociology, believing that he had a head start on understanding human nature.

Smiling about profits from investment in the local brick company, he thought about the magical world of secrets—the ones "hushed" around town…and others that were either not worth keeping or were too good to keep. He remembered Charlie Chan's old line, probably heard at a long-ago Saturday movie matinee: "Necessity, the mother of invention…also, it's the stepmother of deception."…(03-2010)

THROUGH THREE-YEAR-OLD EYES...

In the years between birthdays two and three, youngsters make great cognitive strides, often risking information overload. At age three, they want to feed zoo animals that will scare the "bejeebers" out of them at age two. They're likely to cozy up to the same mall Santa Claus who reduced them to tears a year earlier. At birthday time, they feel more than equal to handling honoree chores without parental guidance.

Before party time, they're well-drilled on ritual sequences. "First, we light the candles," mom says. "And while we're singing 'Happy Birthday', you may blow them out." (It goes without saying that the honoree's next order of business is to grab the slice with the most frosting and the most letters from the cake-top greeting.)...

Our Addison, who blew out most of the candles at her recent party celebrating three years of life, is a world-class granddaughter who has joined contemporaries in voicing choruses of "whys" numerous times daily. Her curiosity never takes a holiday. At mid-party, she noticed our puppy munching grass on the lawn. "Why?" she asked....

I explained that sometimes dogs eat grass to make them feel better. That would have been a good place to stop, but I added, "unlike horses, dogs don't include grass in their daily diet." Addison corrected me. "Horses eat hay, and Baby Jesus ate hay, too."

Recently-deceased Art Linkletter, confidant for the children of the world, would have "made hay" with this story....

I met Mr. Linkletter just once. He was a guest on our campus for a few hours in the early 90s. He was every bit as gracious as he seemed to be on national radio and TV. Whatever ego he may once have had was long since checked at the door. His smile was disarming and his cheerful countenance comforted like furry house shoes on a cold winter morning. He spoke of his love for snow skiing, even late in life. "In fact, if I had my 'druthers,' I'd depart this life airborne on skis, in those seconds between sailing off the slope and touching down on the snow run below."...

A long-time friend, though not an entertainer, has a similar countenance. Oh, in a way he entertains, often injecting puns at unexpected times to keep students in his theology classes on their toes. His name is Dr. Gary Gramling, longtime faculty member at Howard Payne University. He is deeply revered by peers and students alike.

During a recent phone visit, he spoke of conducting graveside services for a couple, one for the husband three years ago, the other for the man's widow earlier this spring. (It should be noted that the hubby's memorial service was held on a hot July day.)

Dr. Gramling mentioned his commitment to brevity at such services, particularly in extreme weather. "I never speak for more than 10 minutes," he said. "For this couple, remarks likely were 6-7 minutes each, the lengths varying by no more than a few seconds," he emphasized....

On the day of the man's burial, a mourner fainted near the grave (though soon revived by wet cloths applied to his forehead). Following the widow's service this spring, a relative of the deceased couple offered what she considered to be a genuine compliment.

"I'm so glad you conducted this service; your words were wonderful," she said to Dr. Gramling. "Thankfully, they didn't get the guy who conducted her husband's service. He spoke so long that a man fainted."...(06-2010)

A GRANDDAUGHTER IN STITCHES...

It's an "old shoe kind of common" for grandparents, their doting in overdrive, to be proud of their grandchildren. With the fervor of Super Bowl combatants, they stretch moments into hours, plunging into overtime with painful details about their grands. Or at least until the senior center director tells them it's time to go.

One granddad spoke about his rough-and-tumble quadruplet grandsons as often as he took pills for what ailed him, and much did. "You name the sport, and they excel in it," he wheezes. "And any one of them can whip the other three."

Our six grands were all singularly born, now ages three to nine, who amuse us often and amaze us occasionally. We will, however, pit all six against Garrison Keillor's "above average" Lake Wobegone children at the time and place of his choosing.

I realize columnists run considerable risk when writing about their kin, and some write of little else. The topic can become repulsive to readers in short order. I write of ours rarely, except when their pronouncements are such that I know Art Linkletter would smile and Erma Bombeck would burst out with a full-blast cackle.

This is such a time. We have a seven-year-old granddaughter who may be on the cusp of qualifying for *Guinness World Records*! The cusp seems only a hair short of reality, comparable to a horseshoe teetering against the stake, ready to plunk down to ringer status with the very next breeze.

She brought first grade to its knees, and now is ready for second grade, and maybe some elective college classes. On top of that, she's well-behaved in Sunday school. Further, she's got a bulletin board filling up with ribbons for her considerable grace at the gymnastics place. Why should I be surprised she wants to develop still another talent?

"I want to learn to crochet," Mom," she to our daughter, Jana. Trouble is, Jana doesn't know squat about anything related to yarn, thread, needles, hooks, etc. She did, however, provide basic instruction for the "simple" chain stitch—after she *Googled* to learn how…

Resigned to reading, or otherwise staying quiet in her room while little brother Kedren naps in the afternoon, Juliana was gung-ho about her new hobby. While mom and brother snoozed, she quietly chain-stitched, her hook flying on the "straight and narrow." And she didn't cut any corners, either.

After Mom awakened, she resumed household chores, then decided to check on Juliana's progress. She was taken aback. Her zealous daughter's chain-stitched creation stretched 21 feet—straight with no corners. "Mom, I've made an afghan for a really long earthworm," she laughed. Now shouldn't that be noted by Guinness for longest earthworm garment?...(08-2010)

AN APPOINTMENT KEPT...

Perhaps still a few degrees shy of "going postal", but with temperature rising, teeth gritting and a "mail must go through" mentality, I skidded to a stop on the parking lot scant seconds before my noon dental appointment. Who could have guessed that a mouse glue trap could cause such a messy scene? I'm sure they've affixed a "doofus" label on my file at the dental clinic, where a missed appointment would have assured a tearful plea to re-schedule—in the same year, if possible—and an excuse they'd never heard before.

When funny guy Dave Barry waxed humorous in his columns, he usually tried to prop up his credibility with claims of "not making this up." Well, neither am I....

Upon leaving for the appointment, much was right with the world. Thirty minutes seemed like a generous time allotment for the short drive. However, my disposition changed quickly when a "floppity" noise grew louder. Afraid a tire was about to blow, I made three stops for visual checks. Finding nothing amiss, I still continued mental finger-pointing toward the tires.

"My tires are nearly new," I muttered to myself. Frustration mounting, I toyed with the thought of dropping by Discount Tire

Store, offering to toss the "faulty" tire through the plate glass window if they'd like to "freshen up" their long-running ad….

But wait! On the third stop, I spotted what I thought was a well-worn plastic trash bag lodged above the left rear tire in the wheel well. Surely I had found the source of the offending noise. Alas, my tires were doing what tires are supposed to do, and I was sad to have thought ill of them. Flushed with a sense of superiority for diagnosing the problem without professional help, I grabbed the "bag" with a vengeance, a death grip, if you will.

But it wasn't a "bag"; it was a mouse glue trap, and I was stuck, big-time, in the muck of industrial-strength adhesive. In a flash, I felt like Lou Costello, a Keystone Kop or the dumbest of the Three Stooges.

What to do? There was no time to rid myself of the messy glue trap. So, I resumed my trip to the dental office, driving with one hand while hoisting my "glue trap hand" aloft. I knew that my wife would have my hide if any glue came in contact with the leather upholstery.….

And my tires didn't help any. In four-part harmony, the quartet of rubbery road-meeters sang a musty old ditty, with special lyrics just for me, or so I imagined. The tune was *Shame, Shame on You.* Again, I regretted presuming their guilt until proven innocent, afraid that their memory might be as long as their tread life.

Upon arrival, I hurried into the clinic, tearing away the glue trap en route. With both hands now "icky," I kicked the door to announce my arrival. Ushered straight to a dental chair, I "blubbered out" the details of my misadventure, one hand still "fisted", glued completely shut. My dental hygienist nodded knowingly as she reached for a small spray bottle. "Usually we only have adhesive problems with stubborn dentures," she laughed. Seconds later, I was "free at last"....

When Dr. Marshall Brown approached my chair, I gave him the full dose of my harrowing half-hour of horror on the highway. He listened patiently before launching "one-upmanship" with vivid details of his travails just one day earlier.

Upon arrival that morning at his clinic, he had waded through ankle-deep water. A plumbing seal had failed during the night, and the place was a mess. I was accustomed to seeing Dr. Brown moving from chair to chair in his orange "UT scrubs", but the thought of his sloshing about in wading boots painted a comedic picture.

One who chuckles at everything except Longhorn sports losses, my dentist has a wonderful sense of humor, and he's quick. How quick? He paraphrased Julius Caesar's quote to describe my predicament: "Veni, Vidi, Velcro," he enunciated with the enthusiasm of a freshman drama major. "You came, you saw, you stuck around."...

Back home, my wife filled in details. The previous night as she swept the garage, a frog hopped in. She gave chase, eager to "swoosh" the uninvited guest back to the flower bed. "In my eagerness to sweep out the frog, I guess I accidentally knocked the trap from the trash bin corner, uh, maybe it came to a stop under the rear car tire."...

Composure somewhat regained, we headed for a Waco speaking engagement.

En route, a sobering thought occurred about unusual billing I would face on my next dental bill, something about "getting Newbury unglued." I also had grim thoughts about what my obligation would be to help him with a four-figure plumbing bill…(09-2010).

PHUNNY PHYSICIAN LEAVES 'EM IN STITCHES...

Brad Nieder, MD, faced directional decisions for his life when this century was still in diapers. He'd completed 21 years of formal education, including degrees from Stanford and the University of Colorado Medical School, then an emergency medicine internship in Virginia.

Immersed in emergency room medicine, he somehow couldn't stay "dunked". He pondered baseballer Yogi Berra's mind-bending advice about forks in the road, as well as poet Robert Frost's views about the road not taken. After all, he'd straddled two career paths—medicine and humor—for about a decade. He made a big decision in 2002. Berra would say that he "took the fork"; Frost would offer him congratulations for following his heart….

Now then. What would loved ones think of his decision to pursue a career in, uh, "alternative medicine"? Six eyes—in sockets of his fianceé, Sara, and his parents, anesthesiologist and Mrs. Bob Nieder—rolled. After all, his folks had invested much in him, and

Sara admitted thoughts of her soon-to-be hubby becoming a neurosurgeon. He thinks he and his wife are "coming out even" on expectations. "She told me she could cook."….

The healthy humorist is what Nieder yearned to be. After all, that's alternative medicine, isn't it? Whatever, he wanted to induce laughter instead of labor, dreaming of making "auditorium calls" instead of house calls and prescribing laughter through stand-up comedy to "cure" much of what ails us. At first, his decision seemed about as feasible as pregnant pole-vaulting.

He hammered away, emphasizing freedom from traditional entanglements with malpractice insurance, burgeoning alphabet-taxing medical abbreviations and weary hours logged in futile attempts to keep pace, never mind getting ahead….

Now, almost a decade after his pronouncement, he's doing well by all measures. Speaking to dozens of audiences annually (largely to health care professionals across the land) Dr. Nieder offers original humor—and delivery—equal to Jerry Seinfeld's.

He finds new humor topics in life's everyday wrinkles. With the verbal precision of a surgeon, he flashes engaging smiles, throws in leg kicks as needed and gestures with animation during remarks that flow steadily, like an unhurried river.

He has Paul Harvey kind of timing, with humor twists like the late radio personality's "rest of the story". His verbal vignettes feature clever why-didn't-we-think-of-that twists….

Dr. Nieder's healthy humor pitch is indeed timely, what with heightening problems of widening bodies, not to mention such unexpected disruptions as wildfires, tsunamis, airliners that become convertibles in midflight and budgets at all levels in red ink. His banter is balm-like in a world cluttered with sharp-edged adjectives like "beleaguered, besmirched, bemoaned, belittled and, yes, even befuddled".

I was emcee for one of his "gigs", and relished the chance to watch his work up close. My contribution was like the guy in charge of the stage curtain—we both get things going. A majority of the audience laughed off a pound or two, except, as Nieder explained, a few stone-faced guys in the back "who were only hurting themselves".

Back in Denver, he has no bigger fans than his wife and parents. That this third generation Nieder became a physician didn't surprise his folks. They never dreamed, however, that his "medicine" might be more akin to Dr. Seuss than Dr. Oz. One audience at a time, he prescribes practical pointers, buoyed by research, that laughter is good medicine.

Opening remarks included his title—*Laughter is the Best Medicine*—should be revised. He recommended that it be followed by "unless" provisos, such as "unless you have an infection. Or you're having a heart attack, or you're recovering from surgery, or you have 'giggle incontinence'. So, laughter is about the fifth or sixth best medicine." One fan, impressed with Nieder's recitation of his lengthy fitness poem, credited him with a *photogenic* memory. Avoiding the temptation to ask if she might have meant "photographic," he said maybe it won't be necessary for him to get his MRI's retouched.

His healthy humor regimen trumps an apple a day. And around 2040, if son Isaac, 3, or daughter Molly, 1, decides to work in the circus, join an aquatic team to perform with whales or to sell sea shells, their dad should smile and pray as they follow their dreams….(04-2011)

VERSATILITY REDEFINED…

He was the most unique student I met during a 40-year career in higher education. Upon completing high school in Toronto, he was off on his bike to "seek his fortune". This sounds like a nursery rhyme beginning; for Dan Murray, though, it was the real deal. First, he flew to Vancouver, the starting point of his 3,400-mile biking adventure that ended in Texas 36 days later. (The only "break" was a stop to run in the San Francisco marathon.)

He was a freshman at Howard Payne for the 1991 spring semester. Like most other first-year students, he was unsure of his academic path. Dan seemed certain, though, that while at the undergraduate fountain, he would take on collegiate experiences in big gulps. My family and I—as well as colleagues and his fellow students—quickly realized he didn't march to drummer beats. A sharper picture would show him strapped to a laser beam—perhaps multiple beams—hanging on….

This is not to say I always understood his judgment. Sometimes when I heard "can-you-believe-what-Dan-did" stories, I cringed, thankful he survived. I'll cite just a couple. One Thanksgiving, he headed for Sacramento on a rag-tag motorcycle one would expect to buy for a three-digit figure at Sanford and Son's place. Never mind it was sleeting, with the temperature in the teens. He fell asleep near Las Cruces, struck a road sign, sustained a deep gash on a big toe and knocked a foot peg off the 'cycle. He bought a needle, thread and alcohol, sewed up the toe and proceeded to Sacramento.

I also would have recommended that he leave it to others for challenges of a country road's "thrill hill". It was near the campus, and its 75-foot drop on a thousand-foot descent lured students for assorted races. Dan, though, was the first to make the descent on roller blades, sometimes at speeds exceeding 50 MPH. Clad in leather clothing, he came to sudden stops by falling down before smacking into a foreboding cable-topped fence....

Thankfully, his list of accomplishments is far longer than his "freshman follies", some in which he was engaged through all four years. A graduate of the university's prestigious Douglas MacArthur Academy of Freedom, Dan's interests were many and varied. He was a member of three honor societies, played trumpet in the marching and concert bands and appeared in a college drama. A cheerleader all four years, he was a three-time All-American and "top-gun stunter". As head cheerleader for two years, he led the school's first-ever team in national competition.

He also was a member of HPU's championship track teams in 1993-94, running in the 800-meter, 1,500-meter and 5,000-meter events. In '94, the conference track meet was held in Abilene, where he was to take the MCAT exam on the same day. I urged him to forego the 5,000-meter race. Undeterred, he ran the race in the a.m., then sat for the MCAT in the afternoon. And he did well in both....

He won numerous academic honors, and later was the alumni association's "outstanding young graduate" during 2004 homecoming activities. In 1995, he was off to medical school at Texas A&M University. In an initial class, his studies included a textbook written by his father, Dr. Robert Murray, a longtime member of the faculty at the University of Toronto Medical School. Dan received his M.D. diploma in 1999 before completing his residency in family medicine in 2002. Specialty honors included his being named chief resident and "resident of the year."

Next came duties as a flight surgeon in the U. S. Air Force. Yet another degree was forthcoming. He received the Master of Public Health degree as part of the residency in Aerospace Medicine from UTMB-Galveston. Awards continued to multiply....

He was one of eight officers graduating from the residency in Aerospace Medicine. At the San Antonio ceremony, my wife and I "teared up," noting how Dan has continued to not only distinguish himself, but also to gain endearment of others. He was host for the commencement speaker, Lt. Gen. Bruce Green, Surgeon General of the Air Force. It was a weepy occasion for everyone; it was the final event for a facility providing medical training for nearly a century.

Now, Lt. Col./Dr. Murray—or just "Dan, the guy who conquered 'thrill hill'"—is Chief of Aerospace medicine at Vandenberg AFB in California. When astronauts come back into play, his name is on the candidacy list. Any parents would be proud to call him "son". (08-2011)

GRADUATION DAY AT HOWARD PAYNE
Board President, the late William B. David, left; Chancellor Newbury, center, and graduate Lt. Col./Dr. Dan Murray.

THIS LITTLE LIGHT OF HERS...

There's much to appreciate about friendly competition. This said, an addendum is in order—all's fair not only in love and war, but in Christmas decorating as well. In the latter category, however, we should forgive otherwise normal people who, at Yuletide, cast judgment and common sense aside.

Mild-mannered folks who never keep score on eggs or tomatoes borrowed over backyard fences during other months of the years sometimes grow fangs in December. Peace on earth and goodwill toward neighbors take back seats to frenzied quests for the best in annual outdoor Christmas decorations.

Feverish decorators—some creative, some klutzy—strive greatly to create the most talked-about neighborhood decorations. Their hero is Clark Griswold in the movie *Christmas Vacation*….

Until this year, my wife has been in the major leagues of Christmas decorating. Previously, she strung thousands of lights, standing atop 12-foot ladders on third floor landings to get the star placed "just so". And, more recently, when she felt one more string of lights was needed, another dozen strings were strung. This year, though, she opted for simplicity. Impressed by a display spotted last year, she surprised the family with this decree: "All I want this year is a cross, a cradle, a baby Jesus doll, a spotlight and a yard sign."

It sounded like a piece-of-cake request; her only addendum was that the cross needed to appear "aged and strong". I questioned, "You mean old and rugged?" She nodded.

Suddenly, I realized that she had described a "man" project. After all, she shouldn't have to shop for 2x6 lumber eight feet long, dig a hole two-feet deep, saw-and-hammer a crossbeam, string a heavy duty electrical cord, construct a cradle and implant a spotlight.

Maybe the most awkward part would be asking someone at the hardware store if they happened to have any weathered redwood. (Choosing "weathered" instead of "used" seemed to make me more credible.) This might be a daylong Saturday project to pass my wife's muster. I said a little Christmas prayer that all would be calm, and all would be bright.

The fateful Saturday came, and behold! In just six hours, all was in place. No blood had been shed, no fingers sawed, and no thumbs bludgeoned. The entire project was seamless!

My wife—long labeled a perfectionist by hubby and daughters—handed out "A-pluses". The towering cross was "center-bubbled" on the level test, the electrical cord properly obscured, the light beam perfectly adjusted and the little cradle properly placed, just as she had envisioned. Only a hand-lettered sign remained undone, and she'd handle that.

It had been a good day. Truth to tell, I gave myself a mental back-pat, caught up in the glow of a project that turned out well. After all, if good judgment had not prevailed, it could have been catastrophic.

The good judgment was mine. Upon learning what Brenda wanted, I called son-in-law Kyle Penney in Tyler. He can fix or build most anything, mechanical or otherwise. I invited him and his family for a weekend visit. He agreed, and my life grew simpler. When they arrived, I handed him the shopping list and a credit card. Then, I retreated to the den to watch multiple football games on TV, and to keep my long string of nap days intact. My waking from the day's final nap coincided with Kyle's project sign-off upon completion of the day handed off to him.

Within hours, all three daughters and sons-in-law, as well as six grandchildren, gave "thumbs up" to the Christmas scene. It is a sharp contrast to others in the neighborhood. They feature lights racing across rooftops and mechanical reindeer prancing across lawns. Inflatable figures must not be forgotten; no matter how carefully inflated, they invariably droop in various stages of deflation. Meanwhile, Brenda completed lettering on the little sign.

The simple message is paraphrased from John 3:16: "The baby came for this." The sign is centered, full light in front of the cross. I could have claimed a small role in the project if she had chosen something from Isaiah. She might have asked me to confirm the spelling. Spell check I can do.

One final thought: If you decide to bow out of next year's Christmas decoration competition, why not consider mounting a simple, lighted wire frame on your roof? Write the letters "Ditto" thereon, with an arrow pointing to your neighbor's house….(12-2011)

AN ACCOMPLICE FOR CUPID?...

David Hatala claims no kinship to Cupid, but as operator of a fondue restaurant where proposals of marriage are common, he's a willing accomplice upon request. Hundreds—maybe thousands—of suitors have popped the question in the intimate "lovers' lane" area tucked away inside The Melting Pot, an upscale eatery in Arlington.

He happily strives to accommodate guys who've put down a ton of money for an engagement ring. He spoke of a recent vignette that might qualify as a unique prelude to the upcoming Valentine proposal season. (Poets have written of such across the centuries. For example, Alfred, Lord Tennyson in 1835 chilled winter's grip, telling of a young man's springtime fancy turning to thoughts of love.) Romantics believe such thoughts are harbored by both men and women all winter long.

Anyway, the saga began on a Thursday, shortly after dark. Into the restaurant moseyed a cowboy-looking guy, guitar case in hand. (Call him Barney.) "There's going to be a mighty big moment in my life—if you can help me out," the visitor said. "I drove over two hours in heavy holiday traffic to get here 'cause I'm determined to 'get it right'."

Sensing he might be vital to "getting it right", Hatala snapped to attention, ready to assist. Barney explained that he'd been dating a woman for several years and was ready to propose. "I want to request her hand in marriage here come Saturday night."

"You'll get the corner booth in lovers' lane, and the most romantic melodies in our musical arsenal will waft through the air with the aroma of a wonderful dinner," the proprietor promised. "We won't need any 'canned music'," Barney countered. "I've composed music and lyrics for a special proposal. I'll leave my guitar here today, and when it's chocolate-dipping time, I'll wink at the waitperson to deliver it. Then, I'll get down on one knee to make my marriage proposal in song."

Hatala, impressed that a man would make a 300-mile round-trip to cover all preparatory bases, pledged to silence the house music at "wink time". Thus the proposal plan was in place. Just 48 hours later, the couple arrived, and was promptly directed to the promised booth.

Finishing 90 minutes of fonduing morsels of meats and veggies, the pair was ready for dessert. The chocolate repast was in place, and one wink led to delivery of the guitar and the elimination of house music.

After a single verse of the "proposal", potential for problems prevailed. "He was one-note Charlie as a guitarist," Hatala said. "His singing was worse and the lyrics were horrible." The owner knew if he didn't act quickly, other guests might choose exiting more important than eating.

On the second verse, the woman answered, yelling several decibels louder than her suitor's musical mess-up: "No way on God's green earth I'm gonna marry you!" Hatala acted quickly, making a timely turn-up of house music in a "return to regular programming". Some guests whispered in hushed tones, wondering about the commotion. (One thought a waiter had dropped a tray of dishes and was lamenting the loss in song.) The couple finished dessert in silence, then made a quick exit.

"At least they didn't ask for separate checks," the restaurateur said. "And I made sure to hand him his guitar case as they left." Hatala figures conversation was frosty at best—absent at worst—during the couple's 150-mile trip home. Reflecting on the experience, he's trying to figure out the whole scenario. "Maybe the guy was determined to propose at a fondue restaurant and ours was closest," he reasoned.

"Cupid's accomplice can only do so much," Hatala said, admitting the couple's relationship was at the "fork-sticking" stage. Sometimes,fondue becomes "fon-don't."

"Cupid's arrow doesn't always hit the mark," Hatala said. "But I'll keep on aiming to please." Two things for sure: If he sees the guy again up the way, he'll mumble something about a broken knob on the music system and that his insurance no longer covers guitar storage….(01-2012)

DIN IN THE DEN…

Our grandkids shred Christmas wrapping paper in seconds, joking about their dexterity in "baring gifts." Soon, though, they squirm with "indoor-itis." Crowded into our den, they are ready to put aside month-long warnings about "Santa Claus watching them." Their deportment grades plunge, ranging from "gremlin to grinch." (Grades typically peg to the right of the latter than to the left of the former.)

We have six "grands" ranging from ages 4-10. They still qualify as "electric Chihuahuas"—ever ready to dare and accept dares, as well as take on challenges involving speed, athleticism and dogged determination. Their competitive juices flow like Niagara Falls. When the "din in the den" jiggles the Richter scale or sounds like the dull roar used to describe tornados, the "chillun" face backyard banishment. There, all six are under the surveillance of a keen-eyed adult.

I was assigned to backyard duty recently. (That holiday afternoon, they waived the "keen-eyed" requisite.) The kids scattered like quail, except for 7-year-old Jonah. He remained on the patio to jump on his new pogo stick. Ten minutes later, he was still bouncing, albeit it with lessening control. The other five cousins gathered 'round, joining me in shock that this first-grader could be so tenacious.

"One thousand and 95 jumps," Jonah jawed joyfully. Nine-year-old Juliana, herself a gymnast, offered a slight correction. "I was counting, too, Jonah, and it was 1,093 jumps." One thing for sure and one "maybe." This goes down in my memory book, and four other cousins—Ben, 10; Brittin, 7; Kedren, 5 and Addison, 4—will "practice up" for next year's Christmas pogo stick-jumping event….(01-2012)

YELLOW DOG TALES…

It was a dream-like state with tales retold around 10,000 campfires, all of them—save one—meeting Smokey Bear's rigid standards. It was "come and go" for the afterglow as long-ago stories unrolled—many stretched—on recollections of biggest fish, deepest snow and ages of first bike rides, except for that one fire. Its flames licked skyward, lighting a thousand acres.

Firefighters and medics were on alert; signs offered $10 parking in adjacent pastures. Folks were drawn like moths, ever closer to the growing inferno. And nobody left.

They patiently took turns to share memories logged over many miles and many years of riding "yellow dogs"—a nickname for school buses. Unlike Las Vegas, where "what happens" stays, they "cut loose" with stories previously known only to witnesses either sworn to silence or too embarrassed to share. Some of the vignettes—dating back to 1960—beg to be shared. That's the background, fuzzy as it may be. However, I shall commence with reflection over the past dozen years of writing.

Prentice Martin, a football coach at Abilene Cooper High School, was highly organized; he had to be. There was much to do—even driving the team bus to out-of-town games. He heaped much on the student manager—call him Jimmy—always an eager helper. One managerial chore included "tie-downs" of uniforms and game paraphernalia on top of the bus.

Following one game, Martin asked Jimmy to hurry with tie-downs. After all, hamburgers awaited pick-up at the diner across the street, and there were many miles to cover before slumber. Jimmy scurried to the top, and players jumped on board as the bus rolled slowly from the stadium.

At once, pounding noises from the roof caused serious vibrations. "Jimmy, I thought I asked you to tie all the stuff down," the coach gruffed. A player, wondering if he should say anything, answered, "Sir, that *is* Jimmy!"…

Sul Ross State University, deep in West Texas, has always been challenged geographically. (If the earth were cube-shaped, Alpine would be one of the corners.) For many years, SRSU teams competed in the Lone Star Conference. The Lobos' nearest opponent was 325 miles away, and three were 600 miles down the road.

It was challenging to keep buses rolling. Once, a new transmission was ordered for the football team bus. The late Otilio Ramos, a "do-everything" mechanic/maintenance man at SRSU during most of his adult life, was bilingual, but sometimes his "take" on English was a bit "off." He was instructed to put the transmission in the bus prior to its departure on a 500-mile trip to Kingsville.

Outside of Del Rio, the bus ground to a stop, its transmission dead. Asked why he didn't put the new transmission in the bus, the eager-to-please Otilio responded, "I did. It's in the luggage compartment."…

Iraan High School, also in West Texas, has a "yellow dog" story from a memorable 1960 band trip. The always-careful driver was within a few hundred yards of the Alpine High School football field, where the 40-member band would perform.

As he approached a low-slung railroad trestle near the stadium, he slowed to a crawl, realizing that the vehicle—with large brass instruments atop the bus—would have no more than a two-inch clearance. Inching forward snail-like, he wiped sweat from his brow as band members exited the bus, eager to stretch after the 130-mile ride. The director announced a 30-minute "walk-through" of the half-time routine.

Figuring 30 minutes would give him enough time for re-fueling, the driver headed back to a service station in town. What he didn't consider was that buses are considerably taller when 3,000 pounds of students are removed. The trestle—its unforgiving clearance unchanged—wiped out most of the brass section. Needless to say, there were far more "trills" than "oompahs" from the IHS band that night, and nobody contacted remembers who won the game....

Still another coach remembers his first out-of-town trek as both coach and driver. Glenn Petty, retired athletic director of Abilene ISD, was a ninth grade coach at Big Spring early on. Jotting down driving directions to the stadium, he was puzzled by instructions to "take a right when the second rock hits the bus." Sure enough, two tough kids a block apart tossed rocks at the slow-moving bus. Petty took the next right, and there was the stadium....(03-2012)

DEEDS OF A 'BEST' SAMARITAN...

His smile said much and his words said even more, but good deeds during his "three score and ten" life trumped them both. Alzheimer's finally had its way with Hal Rowe recently, but during the seven-year ordeal, he was talked out of little—and had his way with much—in a life that inspired, delighted and encouraged.

More than 500 people gathered at his beloved Bacon Heights Baptist Church in Lubbock for a memorial service bathed in rich memories of one who did all he could for as many as he could for as long as he could. The sanctuary was awash in "Hal Rowe stories," none richer, though, than one of his final acts of kindness that tied a ribbon around an exemplary life. Four years before his death, he gave away a kidney.

When Hal learned that Randy Parsons—an acquaintance—faced a bleak future of blindness and dialysis without a kidney transplant, he offered "a perfectly good kidney". Family members agreed after medical professionals assured them that it was "Hal talking—not Alzheimer's". He wanted everyone to know that having Alzheimer's didn't rob him of his ability to help, and that Jesus' "doing unto others" instructions didn't stipulate "unless you get sick." In fact, he urged doctors to take a portion of his liver while they were "in there". Friends believe he would have given the other kidney away, too, had he known of a need.

At the funeral, laughs and tears got equal time. Words, music and videos provided warm remembrances. His admission of nervousness during his marriage proposal to Joyce—his wife of almost 50 years—was recalled. Under a tree at Howard Payne University, their alma mater, he jammed an engagement ring onto her finger without saying a word.

"Hal, I'll marry you, but please put the ring on my other hand," Joyce said. "I've never done this before," Hal stammered. "Besides, do you want a proposal from a 210-pound football tackle or a 130-pound poet?"

A deacon for several decades, he taught fifth-graders in Sunday school for more than 40 years. "Mr. Fix-It" was the "who-you-gonna-call" guy for hundreds of widows and widowers. Whatever was broken or needed replacement, he was the man, relentlessly taking on all projects. Some of 'em not even a former football tackle should tackle.

He was immersed in work—even as a preschooler—at his dad's service station in Temple, where he and Joyce were high school sweethearts. A natural salesman, he sold Bibles during summers of his college years. Some earnings went for that engagement ring.

He worked in retail for many years, and with a school-teaching wife, invested steadily in rental properties, all kept up by "Mr. Fix-It". Rowe always had time for others. Someone recalled the day he misdialed a church widow. The respondent was not to be spared Hal's warm spirit. "How're you doing?" he asked. She expressed frustration about failure to sell her house. You figure Hal bought it over the phone? That would be correct.

An outstanding college football player, Hal passed on a chance to play professionally with the Dallas Cowboys. Instead, he opted to teach in Comanche during Joyce's final college year. Soon, they were off to Lubbock, where she was an oft-honored teacher and Hal spent most days—and many nights—giving his life away. A member of the church orchestra, he "saxophoned" birthday greetings by phone to widows and widowers for many years.

A couple of years ago, as his memory started to fail, he told Joyce he wanted funeral attendees to be fed. He projected full meals, but settled for Blue Bell cups at the exits.(Pudgy as an adult, this dessert lover claimed to be a "recovering anorexic".)

What a model for others! Beloved by his wife, family and friends, he was an unwavering Christian stalwart. Even when his 20-year-old son was killed in an auto crash caused by a drunk driver, his faith was strong.

Hal personified Corrie Ten Boom's quote: "The measure of a life is not its *duration* but its *donation*." When he died February 19, that's really all he needed to do that day….(04-2012)

WHEN PIGS FLY…

Once a track coach, always a track coach. Some retirees still have stop watches close at hand—maybe even looped around their neck—and their daily life continues to be framed with references to time, height and distance. They still dream, but they're mostly "re-runs."

One such retiree is David Noble, who spent almost four decades coaching track and field at the high school and collegiate level. A quarter-century was spent at Angelo State University, where he taught young men and women about the sport—and even more about life. Throughout his career, he turned out champions, and the school's annual meet is named the David Noble Relays in his honor. (Settle down, I think to myself, having reached this paragraph without any mention of pigs.) Hang on.

Noble, who ranches, restores old cars and welds (including some items that don't need welding), has adjusted to retirement fairly well. He and wife JoAnn are doing "grandparent things," and the "life lap" they're currently on requires some pacing. They're now great-grandparents. In their 52nd year of marriage, the Nobles spend considerable time attending contests, performances and events involving their five grandchildren. Often, their "to-do" list includes attending FFA stock shows….

I'm closing in on pigs now. Sydney Hamlett, the Nobles' 15-year-old granddaughter, raises pigs as an ag project at Snyder High School. She's entered contests all over the state, and her bedroom is festooned with trophies and ribbons.

JoAnn, herself a retired educator, has maintained decorum throughout life. She's a model mom, grandmom and now great-grandmom. David has done the same thing—mostly. Sometimes, though, track thinking" takes over, drawing more attention than a dropped baton on the final lap, a hurdler who loses his rhythm or a jumper/vaulter who fails to clear the bar. One such vignette occurred when the Nobles were in Snyder for an FFA stock show to support Sydney, and her prize pig, Arnold....

As the youngsters assembled, one of the pigs broke free, racing at full speed toward the other end of the arena. "Well, let's go," Noble blurted, "That pig gets the blue ribbon—the rest of 'em will be running for second place." Once a track coach, always a track coach....

Noble still thinks in terms of inches, feet and yards, and may have had the stopwatch on Arnold. If the track and field world had listened to him, American enthusiasts for track and field would still be on the old measurement standard that served us well—until the NCAA went to the metric system. He still reddens with disgust, convinced that the decision was a virtual knock-out blow to fans whose minds can't—or won't—wrap around the new numbers. He and many other coaches wailed about the conversion, but their voices were drowned out by a few big-time coaches who thought otherwise.

"It would never have happened in football," Noble opines. "Can you imagine a football TV guy saying, 'it's third down and 3.4 meters to go?' Fans want YARDS!" He says that now, decades later, American sports fans are no closer to embracing the metric system than when it was first imposed on the sport. Sure, another century or two may make a difference, if the world is still spinning….

Noble, himself a star quarter-miler and half-miler in high school and college, never converted his times to the metric system. He ran them in yards, by gum, so it doesn't matter how many meters he covered.

His courage, conviction and dogged determination are rooted in associations with long-ago coaching giants, J. H. (Cap) Shelton and Joe Bailey Cheaney.

The latter was a beloved teacher and coach best known for his work as a race starter at Texas' top track meets. He always had a "mini-sermon" before firing the pistol. "Men, I don't know who is going to hit the string first, but I'm sure of one thing: We're all leaving here at the same time." That's the very thing that defines Noble's life, always fighting for "truth, justice and the American (not the metric) way", whether it's people or pigs….(05-2012)

UNRAVELING OF RIDDLES…

A silly riddle from bygone years: "Railroad crossing, look out for the cars. Can you spell THAT without any 'r's'?" Wow, that was a mountain to climb until older kids' explanations finally made sense. Eureka! Light dawned; there are no "r's" in "that."

Now, mention of railroads awakens preschool imagery of stops at crossings where train cars lumbered forward like so many elephants, each grasping the next tail. We grew dizzy trying to count them, so spelling anything—with or without any "r's"—was off our radar….

Those were "stop, look and listen" days. Now, it's "pause, glance and text". I can't remember the last riddle I heard—or overheard. Marquees, t-shirt messages and "tweets" have put riddles to rest. Consider Abilene Animal Hospital's sign: "It's all fun and games until somebody ends up in a cone." Passersby are snapping pictures, remembering vets' placement of megaphone-like cones around their pets' heads.

Makes one remember the childhood tag game called "got-you-last." Each tag got rougher. One-upmanship became two-up, then three-up before one or more participants broke into tears. We deserved to be handcuffed; cones would have only heightened our determination to get the last tag.

I came across a 90%-off sale on t-shirts the other day. There were reasons for the virtual giveaways. Some messages failed to resonate; others were hopelessly dated. I examined the shirts with eagerness equal to my wife's as she slams down multiple chocolates.

One had "two strikes" against it. First, it had a washtub full of "X's" in front of XL. Second, its message: "I Beat Anorexia." Another dated back to the American Revolution: "General Washington's Boat Will Never Make It Across the Delaware."

Long-time friends Will and Tracey Carrier have turned out millions of t-shirt messages at Willie's T's, a business they founded 22 years ago. Here are some of their favorites: "I Smile Because You're My Sister—I Laugh Because There's Nothing You Can Do About It.... To Save Time, Let's Just Assume I'm Always Right.... I'm Silently Correcting Your Grammar.... I'm Not Short—I'm Fun Size.... Mom Likes Me Best.... I'm Not Bossy—I Just Know What You Should Be Doing.... Bad Spellers of the World—Untie.... I Don't Suffer From Insanity; I Enjoy Every Minute of It!"

Here are a few more picked up here and there: "Photoshop: Helping the Ugly Since 1988..... He *IS* heavy, Father (Flanagan); He's My Brother-in-Law.... Spousal Question: Why Do I Love Your Mother-in-Law More Than I Love My Mother-in-Law?... Only Dead Fish Go With the Flow...I'm a Glove-findin', Uniform-washin', Gatorade-gettin', Carpool-drivin', Picture-takin', Always Cheerin' Baseball Mom!"... Drum roll, please, for my favorite: "Top 10 reasons to procrastinate: No. 1)."...

Before we were enfolded by t-shirt info, we depended on signage—billboards, for example—for humor enhancement. Somewhere along the way, neon light signs pierced the darkness, usually with brevity. (Them 'lectric signs were priced by the letter. Thus "Acme" became a generic name for an array of firms.)

One of my ill-fated business ventures (ill-fated seemed to fit all of 'em) was selling snow cones. My machine, cups, scoop and flavors were atop a table in a small gun shop.

You guessed it: The sign out front read "Snow Cones and Handguns."…

A public outrage erupted during World War II, when soft drink companies dared to increase the charge from five cents to six cents.

Grocers and restaurants alike tried to "soften" the blow with clever wall messages, such as "We Don't Know Where Mom Is, but We've Got Pop on Ice."

We aren't much good at public outrage anymore. Anyone else notice that soft drinks, iced tea and coffee now cost a minimum of $1.50 at restaurants? We've yawned instead of picketed.

We are in "ho-hum" modes, settled into "sock-it-to-me" postures. We fully expect daily "hits" by unidentified missiles from unexpected directions.

Radio's "Lum and Abner," one of the weekly "must-hear" shows of yesteryear, posted this door sign at their general store: "Open When We Get Here; Closed When We Leave." They unashamedly carved out fishing time daily and lived to ripe old ages….(06-2012)

A HEARTBEAT FOR HUMANITY…

Rarely does one meet such an individual with a heartbeat so strong for humanity and a "what's in it for others" attitude. His smile engages and he seems to ignore advancing years. He glows with good will, projecting unbounded love for others. No one better represents "The Greatest Generation".

You may think he's a giant Texan—one with life's papers neatly arranged into chapters, now a book destined for the best-seller list. And, you'd be wrong. He stands 5-6 and never weighed more than 165. He lied twice at age 15 to join the Navy, has embraced overcoming as a "way of life" and has never thought of himself as being extraordinary.

But he is. In Galveston, where he's lived 70 of his first 85 years, Eddie Janek is beloved. On the streets, fellow motorists honk their greetings; in stores, owners and custodians—and all in between—stop what they're doing to greet "Mr. Eddie".

Following are more than "howdies". Friends want to hug a man who has served them far longer than most know. Shucks, even short memories recorded his efforts for the common good during his 16 years as a county commissioner. And men whose hair is starting to gray remember life lessons learned from a man who coached Little League, Pony League and American Legion baseball teams for 34 years. Those closest to him know he put everything aside more than a decade ago to care for his beloved wife, Doris, when dreaded Alzheimer's laid claim.

That's the way Janek's wound. Words of the poet Emerson fit best: "When duty whispers down, 'thou must,' the youth replies 'I can'." Duty first "whispered down" to Eddie in 1942. A fatherless child of the depression, he spent most of his youth on a "hand-me-down" Hill County farm near West. His "fib of being 15" was found out, and the Navy sent him home. Undeterred, Eddie altered his Catholic confirmation records, and he was in "navy whites" again.

Perhaps the doctor who performed his Navy physical exam deserves a medal; had his findings been recorded more accurately, Janek wouldn't have been accepted. Somehow, his weight and height—one inch over five feet and 98 pounds—were entered as 5-2 and 105, to meet minimal requirements. "The Navy didn't seem to care that I stuttered," Eddie laughed. "And I still do."

The military provided many "firsts". including first uses of toothbrushes, telephones, light switches—and, uh, commodes. During four years in the Pacific, including landings at Leyte and Peleliu, he saw death up close. Strong in his memory are sounds of comrades praying at night for God's protection in the coming day.

Janek rightly treasures a sealed, glass-covered box that contains Presidential Unit Citations from the U.S., the Philippines and Korea—and 18 other awards. They were presumably lost forever when Hurricane Katrina ravaged the first floor of his high-rise home.

Survivor of two wars, a stroke, a heart overhaul and a blood disease, Eddie remains upbeat—cherishing his wife, three sons and six grandchildren—and lovingly tending his roses.

He's grateful to his son, Dr. Kyle Janek, who, as a State Senator in 2001, wrote legislation providing high school diplomas for WW II participants. Eddie proudly marched across the stage in Galveston where 58 were so honored—one posthumously, three in wheelchairs and two on crutches.

Eddie also is grateful to Texas A&M for the safe return of his medals! A few weeks after Katrina, some A&M personnel—cleaning up Pelican Island five miles across the bay from Janek's home—

found the box containing his military medals. A&M President R. Bowen Loftin called Eddie about the find. The medals were returned, now again proudly displayed in the Janek home.

Upon meeting Eddie recently in Galveston, we were inspired by his optimism and patriotism. Those who know him best aren't surprised that his most recently project benefited a Galveston resident who needed funds for sight-restoring eye surgery. He wrote a check, then 53 letters to friends. Within days, $42,000 was contributed, and the surgery is scheduled.

He's well on the way to restoration of flood-ravaged memorabilia. Eddie is at mass on Saturday afternoons, and attends family and naval reunions from time to time. Usually, though, he's at home. Doris needs him there.... (12-2012)

(Addendum: Eddie's beloved wife, Doris, died in 2014.)

BIGGER THAN LIFE…

It was, hands down, the most remarkable athletic feat I've ever witnessed. The scene was Dallas' American Airlines Center, where some 20,000 fans watched the Mavericks/Phoenix Suns NBA game on April 5, 2009. They saw a blow-out win by 26 points—and the Mavs' 140-point barrage could have been more. Memorable, too, was Josh Howard's 71-foot shot that beat the halftime buzzer.

Moments later, however, an intermission feature drew greater applause. Fisher Floyd, a man from the stands in street clothes, hit a lay-up, free throw, 3-pointer and half-court shots. Fisher's "swishers", made in 45 seconds, have never been duplicated. What are the odds?

His feat has gone viral on "YouTube" with 5.5 million "hits"—some 3 million the first year. I found him to be engaging, gracious and caring during a phone conversation later. He politely answered questions, but seemed most interested in whether I saw him "blowing kisses to Lindsey", his bride of a year. She was seated behind the Mavericks' bench, where several players—unaware that the kisses were directed slightly above their heads—blew them back!

Friends—and he had many—describe him only in superlatives. He was captain of his district champion Highland Park High School basketball team and was the league's offensive player of the year for 2000-2001. At the University of California-Santa Barbara, where he graduated with honors, he introduced a new game of Frisbees played with tennis rules.

Those who knew him best agree that his specialty was making virtually everything competitive, ever pushing closer to the edge. His adventurous spirit dates back to 1986, when *Top Gun* was a movie hit. Just four years old at the time, he was "hooked"—always probing, "what-iffing" and fixing whatever was broken.

Perhaps no one was ever more in love with life. His Christian principles and knack for making friends at warp speed were evident. His checklist of "things to do" included flying in a fighter jet....He won such a ride as the high bidder at a charity auction.

Dressed in aviation gear, he made three trips to a Lancaster airport for a flight with Noell Rather, himself a Highland Park High School graduate. (Rather flew 60+ missions in Vietnam and was a former Braniff pilot. He loved the Delfin L-29 aircraft he'd spent years restoring and frequently gave rides to charity benefactors.) Weather scrubbed the first two efforts, but Dec. 13 dawned bright and clear.

A friend accompanied Fisher to the airport. There were exchanges of phone texts until take-off and animated, first-hand descriptions were anticipated upon return. But it was not to be. There were no second or third-hand descriptions, either, or any kind of distress signals prior to the crash of the two-seater plane in Kaufman County, where both men perished in a crash about a half-hour after take-off. The tragedy is inexplicable. Again, what are the odds?

Fisher Floyd's memorial service was held at Highland Park United Methodist Church, where he, his wife and two sons—Ryder, 2, and Hudson, 1—had planned to become church members soon.

Real friends, it is said, are not counted on one hand, but in one heart. Fisher, a picture of humility whose spirit brought out the best in others, had a giant heart. It would have taken a facility the size of the AAC to contain the mass of mourners. Seating at the church accommodates about 1,000 people; some 1,600 were present.

The family received hundreds of condolences. One referenced Fisher's being "kind, decent, happy". It was signed "Averill Mitchell, usher, Sections 117-118, AAC". Another mourner said Fisher made friends more quickly than anyone he'd ever known, and he was "an even better husband and father".

Dallas Coach Rick Carlisle was among the eulogists. At the service—as well as at the Mavs' game the same evening—he chose the champagne-soaked red tie he'd worn when Dallas won the 2011 NBA title in Miami. "It won't be worn again," Carlisle said following the game. At the next Maverick game, a Fisher tribute preceded the contest, and his historic "four swishers" video was shown at halftime.

Much in life baffles, exceeding our understanding. We pray for clarity on the other side of the river....(01-2013)

(Addendum: In just over two years, the YouTube video of Floyd's making all four shots at American Airlines Center now has in excess of 10 million "hits".)

THE WALK AND THE TALK...

When life's talkin' lines up so closely with the walkin', light is shed on how joy can trump sadness at a funeral. That's my nutshell description of Dr. Mike Toby's memorial service, one he largely planned himself. At 80 minutes, it didn't seem protracted, though he might have disagreed. After all, he had included no allowances for senior staff ad-libbing, or for reflective pauses shared by an overflow crowd of almost 2,000 people at First Woodway Baptist Church, near Waco. He had been senior pastor for 35 years.

His life was a testimony, his stature obvious and his leadership consistent. Mike "stood tall" in the faith, and, at 6-5, towered over most congregants, his disarming smile projecting an "all is well" countenance. "Be a lighthouse" was the credo of this beloved pastor. He was the kind of man who "seized the day" at an early hour, ready to face the opportunities, challenges and demands that would surface later.

Mike felt numbness during an October sermon. He went to the doctor, sharing symptoms he found mystifying. Doctors feared and medical tests confirmed that brain cancer was entrenched.

Jackie, his wife of 45 years, sons Joshua and Scott and their families knew the course their loved one would take. Options of invasive surgery might have extended his life for about one year, or he could finish his life at home, with the probability of living two or three months.

He made a short video for a church service, explaining that he "wouldn't bargain with the Lord for 15 seconds beyond his allotted time." Mike spent November and December at home, medication keeping him comfortable. There, he said what he needed to say and did what he needed to do.

He had incurable cancer; it was trumped, however, by incurable optimism. Ever ready for the next step, he said, "If it were up to me, I'd be in the front seat of the next flight out." (His staff often kidded about his penchant for punctuality. "To be on time," one said, "was to be a few minutes late!") His ever-present sense of humor lightened the moment when the senior staff gathered at the Toby home to "nail down" memorial service details.

"I don't want a preacher doing my funeral," he insisted, turning to Rev. Terry Graham, Associate Pastor for the past 18 years, "I want you to do it." Chuckles erupted. This "God's man/family man/man's man"—his spiritual calling never questioned but prankster tendencies sometimes were—was a tender leader, tough only when situations demanded. In reality, his life work began almost a half-century ago while a student at Pasadena, TX, High School. Each morning, he offered prayer and devotionals on the intercom system. Relentless in athletic competition and a devoted outdoorsman, his experiences became life lessons for sermons.

Mike spent much time in reflection at home during the eight weeks prior to his death. Included were mission points in the Waco area and around the world. In his final hours, he told Jackie that he wanted to "take a puppy along". Puzzled, she recited all the dog names she could remember. He interrupted, "You know, the one we had when we moved to Waco." Then, she remembered.

To conclude the memorial service, the Toby's grandchildren walked with Rev. Graham in front of the casket. A trumpeter belted out *When We All Get to Heaven.* Behind the family were 50 or so children, "whosoever will" participants. All of them carried glow sticks. Congregational singing closed it out with lively singing of *I'll Fly Away.*

Putting the glow sticks away, the children—some of them as young as five—hastened to an adjacent room, where their parents were waiting. Though the church has grown to be large—from a membership of 1,000 to 4,600 during Toby's ministry—they know "the way". Dr. Toby spent the bulk of his life telling them about it.... (01-2013)

OUTSMARTED BY SMART KEY…

Introspection and retrospection should never be taken lightly; otherwise, we dwell on what might have been. On rare occasions, though, it is profitable to re-visit bad decisions, declare intent to avoid them in the future, and freely share details of painful experiences. Perhaps others can be helped to avoid pitfalls swallowing me up—uh, actually, down. I was "chewed up and spit out", and only recently can smile about an avoidable ordeal causing discharge of many tears—mine….

It was car-buying time, purchases we face no more than twice in a decade. A few details are "givens". My wife always wants a white vehicle that gets good gas mileage and has leather upholstery. I shoot for cars 2-3 years old with low mileage. Eureka! I found a hybrid that commonly delivers 40 MPG. It met all our specs. I whistled a happy tune.

If I had known then what I know now, I would have at least given pause to the seller's mention that the vehicle has just one "smart key". Assured that I could get another one, I gave the matter little thought.

First I had to learn what "smart keys" do. I found out they join horseshoes and hand grenades in "coming close" effectiveness. As long as a smart key is carried in pocket or purse, the car "knows" it's nearby. Locked cars are magically unlocked, and the ignition requires no key insertion. What a "smarty-pants" it is. "Smart key" and auto are in a state of harmonious "gee-haw", and the motor purrs at the push of a button. All the while, the "smart key" lays low in pocket or purse.

Even I knew at least one additional "smart key" would be needed, so I visited a locksmith to determine the cost of a duplicate. He was patient with me—mostly explaining that much has changed—it's no longer 1957. That was the year I bought my first car—a 1949 Nash Ambassador, just a dozen years younger than its buyer, then age 20. It had "plain" keys—three, as I remember. The car set me back $300, had a bloated appearance and almost no distinguishing features, save the fact that the front seat backs lowered to make a bed. I could have made my bed and lain in it, I guess, though I never did.

I digress. The locksmith, unable to help, suggested a visit to the dealership. There, I was stunned to learn that an additional "smart key" called for detailed programming on an expensive machine that had a $350 price tag—$50 more than my first car. If I wanted two, the cost would be $700, plus tax.

Had my wife been along, she'd have noticed face-reddening and asked if I'd taken my heart medication. "Get some 'smart keys' on the Internet", another shopper whispered. "Take 'em to a locksmith for programming and save a bundle." So I did. I should have listened to the first locksmith—the one who referred me to a dealer.

The Internet has many sites trumpeting availability of "blanks" for "smart keys". (No doubt some could provide "dumb keys", too.) The purchase was NOT seamless. The blanks ran $85 each, programming NOT included. I spent the equivalent of two full days, visited five locksmiths and drove more than 200 miles before finding a shop that would tackle the programming procedure. Woe is me! The first blanks I ordered weren't the right ones—my mistake—and only one in the second order worked.

Thankfully, Jay Reed, a Colleyville locksmith some 30 miles from our home, took pity. His work ran into hours, tying up the "super-duper" machine which programs "smart keys". The result, though, was TWO additional "smart keys". All told, the bill was well short of $700. This doesn't include, of course, two wasted days spent on the project, emailing/telephoning Internet supplier or the miles driven all over the Metroplex. My wife, though, summed it up: "What difference does the time make? You're retired." It's a line she uses often…. (05-2013)

CHILDREN AND 'GOOSE-GOOGLING'…

Perhaps it's a trivial thing, this business of "Goose" and "Google" beginning with the same three letters—or maybe not. The former—with "Mother" in front of her name—is a remnant from centuries past. For hundreds of years, printed words—and those from the lips of loving parents and others putting children to bed—have provided stories activating vivid imaginations. On the winds of what was, what is and what might yet be whirled through young minds swept up in "play-like" worlds of make believe.

The latter, "Google"—a word often attached at the hip to "it"—may play a more critical role than we realize. One day, "Google" likely will be responsible for gathering the remnants of what is remembered about "Mother Goose," fading, even now, in the ever-shortening days of youthful innocence. Here lately, she's "flown the coop," with her absence ever lengthening.

The mother called "Goose" was the property of no one—and everyone. A "feathery grandmother of make believe," she was known on many continents. Her verses were many and unquantifiable, a compilation of the thoughts of multiple minds. Her fables, verses and rhymes were products of many generations. Their words—some clever, or ridiculous or even absurd—seemed worth writing down, repeating and remembering. They're collected in that big memory repository now entrusted largely to "Google". It is a new century....

Her words were handy when time was allotted for getting children to bed. The old bird was on good terms with the Good Book, lovingly linked for bedtime application. Today, bedtime rituals call for technicians. Buttons are pushed to access sounds, and pages—formerly turned—slide silently across iPad screens as children drift off to dreamland. Alas, youngsters still in footed PJs are more likely today to recognize the AFLAC duck than the goose offering nursery rhymes.

Mother Goose, never "pushy", was more of a "go along to get along" type. She'd be saddened today in a world where fear dominates. Children furrow their brows now like their elders, rarely breaking into robust laughter like they used to.

Circumstances—something we've always lived "under"—are authors of fear. They grow ever more ominous, and we're afraid far more often than we're joyful. Children learn early in life to take too much too seriously.

The other day, I heard a quiet conversation by a couple of youngsters, perhaps second graders. I was surprised at their leisurely conversational pace, as well as the topic, "Humpty-Dumpty". I resisted the impulse to mention that this is one of the hundreds of "Mother Goose" poems. After all, I was waiting in the mall for my wife to finish shopping. Besides, these youngsters already had a grandfather in tow. The conversation grew serious. "I've heard Humpty-Dumpty was pushed," one said.

"Maybe so," said the other. "And I'm sad for the first responders. Don't you know they felt like they were walking on eggshells?" Wow, thought I. Here was a kid who "imagined", just as the old goose would hope.

My wife and I walked to our car, "clicking" the door lock a few feet away, then drove home, cruise control on and radio news blaring. My mind hearkened back to simpler days and my long-departed grandfather, a man ever proud of his Hamilton pocket watch. It was chained to a belt loop, lifted dozens of times daily from its pocket resting place. It was done methodically. Poppa stared at the time piece, usually saying nothing. It didn't even have a second hand, nor was one needed. He had seconds to spare, this man whose activities rarely involved "punching in". Quite simply, he worked from early 'til late, usually six full days a week.

He always seemed happy. Though uneducated, he learned life's hardships early on. Widowed at age 45, he was left with nine children, three of elementary school age. He had reason to be pensive, this man so very much at home in the cotton fields and on land dotted by cedar trees. It was his to pick the bolls of cotton, and, with his ax, turn the trees into cedar posts. As he stared at his watch, he was in deep thought. And we thought he was checking the time…. (09-2013)

DON'T SELL DOGS SHORT…

Dog-fanciers, present company included, have only themselves to blame. Our pets didn't ask to become family members. However, we have freely elected to include them, and they've accepted our invitation, happy to accept courtesies consistent with favored treatment. What gigs, they must think, their only "jobs" involve tail-wagging, eating. sleeping and barking more than occasionally, usually for reasons that wouldn't stand up in court, kangaroo or otherwise.

Initially, invitations were offered in inches; our canines have learned, however, that most of 'em can be stretched to miles. They've come a long way from a half-century or so ago when most dogs lived outdoors, subsisted on table scraps, chased small wild animals and considered pats on the head enough affection for a week.

My Uncle Mort remembers that during his youthful years of poverty, his family brought their dogs inside for the night when thermometers plummeted toward zero. "But this was self-serving," he admits. "When we shivered in bed, we simply pulled up another dog."

Ah, yes, our dogs do the "knickknack/paddywhack" things, consuming more than their share of bones along the way. Beyond this, they've keenly mastered—perhaps simply by observation of our habitual patterns—what our moves mean. In a flash, they know whether to head for the feed bowl, the car or the hills.

At the risk of raising the dander of cat lovers, I believe dogs are preferred by most pet owners. For starters, they are more demonstrative in expressions. Their eyes, velocity of tail-wags and volume of yips, yaps and whines say much. I can barely stand it when one of our rescue dogs "tucks tail" and retreats to another room, maybe even seeking under-the-bed darkness.

What can I do to make up? A treat maybe—when my wife isn't looking. (She's more concerned about their weight than mine, and that's saying quite a bit.) Or, maybe I'll invite them for a short ride in the car.

Little wonder, really, that dogs have taken what we've given them, always with paws out for more. Granted, their interpretative skills are many, and we haven't even mentioned their ears perking up when our conversations involve them. Often as not, their heads cock immediately sideways. They understand more than we know.

There is "mucho" trouble ahead if they learn to read, because exploits of talented pets splash regularly across pages of books and newspapers. And don't we always open those emails with "really special" dog pictures?

If they could read, dogs would have good reason to be "full of themselves" with far more than dog chow. They'd puff up with pride, bragging about the canine that pushed a wheelchair-bound woman to class, and others that sniff out drugs, guide the blind, round up farm animals and bark to high heaven when danger threatens—and sometimes when nothing threatens. At San Jose, CA, airport, they offer a roaming golden retriever whose ONLY job is to be available for folks who "need a buddy, a belly to rub or a paw to shake". We've come a long way from Lassie, and from that nameless doggie in the window who chewed the price tag off his collar.

If our dogs could read, they'd have insisted on participating in the "Harbor Howl-O-Ween" for "frightfully furry fun" at Lake Ray Hubbard. There, a "Lick-or-Treat" dog costume contest was featured. In Dallas, "blessings of animals" are conducted, with all species of pets invited. (Holding these ceremonies on the lawn of a mausoleum—and I don't mean a pet mausoleum—seems beyond the pale, however.)

Our pets—Sadie and Sailor—both are "rescues" of unknown parentage. The latter, though, looks more like a purebred dachshund than the former does a Jack Russell. Still, they suit us well in this season of life, vet bills be hanged.

The other day, they raced through my study with pads and pencils in clenched teeth. Immediately, I envisioned their drawing up plans for a "bobble-head dog." I followed them, but lowered expectations greatly. One had chewed the pencil down to a nub, and the pad looked like it had gone through a shredder. Sometimes, dogs will be dogs....(11-2013)

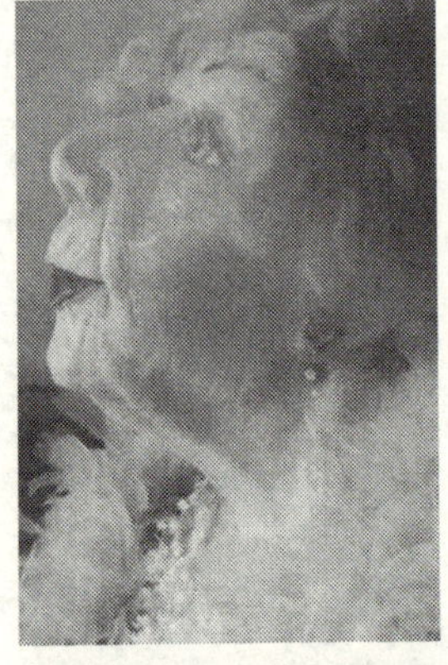

NO, IT IS NOT A LIKENESS OF MAUDE — You may have noted there is no likeness of Maude in this book. She said she hasn't made a good picture since Mort broke the Kodak. At left is her sister who ran away from home upon learning she had to go to school.

SHHHH! THEY THINK THEY'RE FAMILY
Our rescue dogs, Sailor, Dachshund (we think) and Sadie, mostly Jack Russell...

WESTJET'S CHRISTMAS MIRACLE...

Likelihood is great that airlines of the world—most of them maligned by flustered flyers venting their feelings when plans go awry—owe much gratitude to a single member of their flock. WestJet, a Canadian airline, has become a social media darling with a "feel good" Christmas video that has rocketed far to the right of "viral" on YouTube and other Internet sites.

For five minutes—brief and shining moments in multiple languages around the world—it's reaping tears of joy from multiple millions of viewers. It has promoted a sense of "oneness" for 150 airline employees whose joint efforts made the miracle possible, as well as a "lean-back" kind of satisfaction for those who dreamed it up. Results include awakened sugarplum imaginations, as well as re-commitment to seeking peace on earth, good will toward men….

Who can say it was not divine creativity that inspired August planners for a video in November that might warrant 800,000 YouTube "hits" during its December release? WestJet planners missed projections by light years. Since it was "unleashed", the numbers are growing by millions daily. Who knows how many hundreds of millions of viewers will eventually see the video? And, if it doesn't tug at your heartstrings, you need to get them tuned—maybe even re-strung.

A hurting world yearns for good news. The video provides exactly that. If you use a computer, you've likely already seen WestJet's Christmas Miracle. If you don't, arrange for someone with computer literacy to access it for you, and prepare to weep. If you don't shed a tear or two, *Forbes* magazine suggests you may need a "scrooge-ectomy". Planners' concepts were warm and cheery. Feature Santa Claus, give presents and throw in "ho-ho-ho's" every few words.

Settings were airports in Toronto and Hamilton for passengers booked on simultaneous flights—each 2,000+ miles—to Calgary. The flyers—125 at each terminal—saw the Santa set-up, then scanned boarding passes as requested. Next, they stood in front of the interactive Santa for what they thought was "seasonal conversation". Passengers were asked what they'd like for Christmas.

The merry old gent listened intently, whether passengers asked for big screen TVs, iPads, diamond rings or simply "socks and underwear." Each request was also noted by 150 "WestJetters" (the airline's employees) in Calgary. They raced to procure the items, defying the snow, shopping lines and whatever other obstacles they encountered.

They had just four hours for the whole deal, including wrapping each gift, affixing each name and getting the whole "kit-n'-kaboodle" to baggage claim carousel eight, where passengers claimed their luggage. Stunned, they first spotted gifts on the carousel. And Santa was in the midst of the crowd. A commercial venture or not, it provides a vignette of the way Christians believe our world should be.

It is a reminder that the ground at the foot of the cross is exceedingly level—that the same God intervening in the affairs of man throughout history is still in charge. It's also an example of His ongoing work in mysterious ways—His wonders to perform. Strive to remember WestJet's warm Christmas story—even when your flight is canceled, your luggage is lost or sent to the wrong continent, your carry-on is overweight by a pound or an inch too big, the snoring guy seated next to you has taken the armrest, the cabin temperature is not just right, or….Well, just breathe a prayer for the folks who came up with this idea. It reminds us that we shouldn't "give 'til it hurts, but 'til it feels good"….(12-2013)

ON THE MATTER OF MATTRESSES…

Goldilocks didn't realize it at the time, but she had it comparatively easy—lucky beyond measure—to find the "just right" bed on the third try. Within seconds of trying out The Three Bears' beds, she nestled comfortably, thinking—albeit erroneously—that all was right with her world.

Today we are challenged by dozens of eye-crossing choices offered by many firms, some with big ads proclaiming whatever day it is to be the best day ever to purchase a new mattress. Our first one was comfortable for nigh on to 40 years—until it buckled 14 years ago. When they removed it, a card fell out: "Re-Elect LBJ to the US Senate."

My wife and I thought we were careful shoppers back there at century's turn, hoping to buy another king mattress to take us to 2040 or later. After all, we bought from a reputable company. We learned, however, that mattresses today are designed to meet standards of comfort and hygiene for 7-9 years.

Young adults are largely to blame. Back when, mattresses were constructed with durability in mind; comfort was a distant second. Nowadays, it's all about comfort, bells, whistles and miscellaneous technology. Durability concerns rarely come up.

During my youth, our mattresses were cotton-filled and usually bought "used". When the cotton started escaping, we called Elmo Letbetter, who reconditioned with cotton refills. There were no warranties to deal with, since the mattresses—like most clothes—were hand-me-downs.

'Course most folks did far more physical labor in those days, so we could sleep anywhere—on pallets, cots, air mattresses or curled up in a wheelbarrow. Creek bank sleeping was fine should fishing be involved.

A few weeks back, we discovered mattress-sagging on both sides. Yep, it was time to shop for a new one—our fourth mattress since 2000. (I can live with my "matted hair", but not if it is caused by a bad mattress.) Brenda "deaf-eared" my suggestion to consider a gently-used, $17.50 mattress listed on Craigslist. So, we watched retail ads, read *Consumer Reports* and called various stores to find a king mattress that was "just right". We "lucked out" on the first store we visited.

I never thought I would admit it, but here goes: The salesman escorted to a computer-assisted mattress that provided important data. All we had to do was lie down and follow instructions. Within five minutes, the "Expert Match"™ had spit out information on our sleeping contortions, movement and more stuff, and then the nice man said it to be the mattress closest to meeting our needs. There was no pressure. We bought it—the one the guy and the computer agreed on, and one we could afford.

Our purchase was made from Aaron Simmons, who, while saying nice things about Simmons mattresses, regretted being from a limb on a different Simmons tree. He's a sleep expert, though, who has heard it all. (He spoke of one customer seeking a mattress for her pet pig. She insisted on steel coils; otherwise, her pet would "root" through the foam in short order. Another guy wanted a king bed with a matching, extra-long twin bed, the latter for his dog.)

The very next day, delivery men came. During the minutes before delivery, Brenda was readying our vacuum cleaner, ready to "attack" when the old mattress was removed. She told them she just couldn't imagine where all the dust came from; I'm sure it's been there since the last mattress was brought in….(01-2014)

HIGH ABOVE IT ALL…

Inside on TV news, talking heads described ravages of California wildfires raging across the landscape. Outside, my neighbor Josh was ready to climb into his pick-up, heading for his firefighting shift 40 minutes up away. Fresh from hearing descriptions of modern firefighting technology, I asked him to explain it so even I could understand. "Doc, firefighters just spray the wet stuff on the red stuff."

As he drove away, I gave myself a mental kick for missing the opportunity to thank him for his acts of saving lives and property. And the same goes for other emergency responders—men and women, professionals and volunteers—across the land. They deserve to be on pedestals, none of which is tall enough, broad enough or sturdy enough to hold them all.

Josh is a great neighbor, eager to help with chores that call for more strength and endurance than we can muster. His smile, gentle nature and acts of kindness underscore his goodness.

I asked him about life at the station. Are firefighters really good cooks? Are jokes shared? Does it seem like family? "Yes," to all three.

He said there's no other job where they "wake you up to go home", adding, "God made firefighters because police need heroes, too." (Law enforcement personnel may remember that this question can be re-phrased with the names reversed.)

Another firefighter—a "friend of a friend"—continues his "sunny side up" approach to life, despite having lost a leg in a freak accident at the station a dozen years ago. He remains an incurable optimist and continues on the job with a strong commitment to exercise. Within months of his accident, he put his prosthesis to the test, entering and completing the Turkey Trot and the Jingle Bell charity events in Dallas, both 5K races.

Regularly mounting his bicycle in Van Alstyne, his hometown, he often takes 25-mile rides. Sometimes a pack of three or four dogs gives chase. One day, a large three-legged boxer set the canine pace, getting way too close to Dan on his "real leg" side. He gave the dog a "can-we-talk"? look as he pedaled faster.

More than six decades ago, an ultra-conservative newspaper ran an editorial critical of public fire protection. The editor was strongly opposed, feeling that such protection should be offered only to individuals and businesses willing to pay for fire protection. A few days later, flames engulfed the newspaper offices. Thanks to the fire department, much of it was saved.

In the next edition, the editor profusely thanked the firefighters in a front-page piece. The final sentence, however, read: "However, we still don't believe in public fire protection."

When Josh reads this, I'll be pleased to consider his assistance, unless he wants me to tone it down some. And when he finishes reading, I hope he'll take a few minutes to take a look at our squeaking garage door….(02-2014)

ON RUMBLE SEATS AND RECALLS…

Just as his granddad and dad before him and more recently his own son, Dwain Bruner has depended greatly on fair play, business ethics, hard work and occasional blind hog luck. It was surprising, though, that one of his first problems in business would involve theology.

Some 45 years ago when he purchased the Stephenville Chevrolet dealership, he'd counted on the mechanic who'd been pivotal to his success in Wolfe City to join him there. Bruner was crushed with the mechanic's decision to "stay put". The man cited "theological differences"--not with Bruner, but with the Lutheran Church. "I hate to disappoint you," he said. "We made sure they had a Lutheran Church in Stephenville. They do, but it's the wrong synod."

Bruner Motors, founded by Dwain's granddad and "staffed" by his dad, was born in 1923 in Kerens, TX, as service station/repair business. There weren't that many cars to service then, so in 1928, they started selling Star automobiles. Soon, they sold Chevrolets, and big as "car show day" was, for the 1931 models, dad Vern missed it. In those days, dealerships nationwide planned much "whoop-de-do". They covered show windows for several days, removing the window coverings on the same day to reveal the new models. Vernon helped with the preliminaries, but on November 14, 1930—"car show day"—he wasn't in the showroom. Instead, he was in the waiting room near the Corsicana hospital delivery room awaiting the birth of the first of four sons. Dwain grew up in the car business.

During the summer of his 12th year, it was his daily "duty" to signal "high noon" to the thousand or so residents. He'd listen for the radio announcement: "It's 12 o'clock," then hasten outside to blow the whistle hooked up to the air compressor mostly used for the hydraulic auto lift "ups and downs".

The youth took piano to please his mother, and was permitted to take typing as a freshman—thanks to the superintendent's intervention. The class usually was only for juniors and seniors. With World War II raging, motorists were required to have certificates of need to buy new tires. Kerens' only option for the inspection was at the dealership, and no one there could type. As a freshman, Dwain "whipped out" the typed documents and paid 25 cents for each. Soon, he also was earning extra money as pianist for weddings and funerals. Later, he bought savings bonds that helped him scrape together money for his first dealership.

After finishing high school, he majored in accounting, played in the Baylor marching band and studied organ with the prof he'd met a few years earlier during installation of his church's pipe organ. Following discharge from the US Navy, he and Carolyn—his wife of 57 years—lived for seven years in Wolfe City. In Stephenville, where son Greg and daughter Gwyn were reared, he's been a member of the First Baptist Church choir, often serving as organist and pianist for weddings, funerals and programs. The family long has been at the forefront of the community's educational, civic and business projects.

Now, they've expanded to include a Brown County dealership serving Brownwood, Early and other communities. Greg is president of the all-new dealership. "Greg has a vision for continuing the business," Dwain said. And Dwain remains active at the Stephenville location.

More family help is anticipated soon, since grandson Kyle (Greg's son) is completing a BU master's degree in business. He is eager to start the family's fifth generation in the automobile business. And other grandchildren—Courtney, Megan and Amanda—could wind up in it as well.

At the dedication, reps from eight car manufacturers spoke of unique business services, including Wi-Fi in waiting areas, new auto features and cutting edge technology. "All the new stuff is dizzying," Dwain said. "Dad bragged about rumble seats on the '31 model, the six-cylinder engine and best gas mileage at 20 MPH."

I asked him to recall his most memorable sale. "First, don't say 'recall,'" he joked. "It was after my first day in Wolfe City. I made a joyous long distance phone call to my folks back in Kerens, telling them I'd sold A CAR!" It was a truly exciting day in my life… (06-2014)

IT ALL STARTED WITH STRINGS...

Books could be written about lives radically changed by introduction to strings. Before duct tape, string had endless uses, ranging from Yo-Yos to string cheese. This time, we'll limit fame's floodlights to individuals who—at ages 15 and 10, respectively—began pilgrimages toward major world venues—thanks to strings.

Of this "twosome," Everett (Bunny) Martin is farthest down the road. He defeated one hundred others to win the 1950 city Yo-Yo championship in Houston at age 15. This qualified him for the last World Yo-Yo Championship held the next year in Toronto, and he survived competition with 500 others from five countries, thus remaining as "defending world champion" at age 80. He and his preacher dad won the expenses-paid trip, and Bunny claimed the $2,500 cash prize.

Also remarkable is Chris Tomlin, arguably America's best-known praise and worship leader. This Christian music artist's career might never have occurred except for mononucleosis at age 10. Sentenced to a summer of indoor rest when he had planned Little League baseballer, Chris was devastated.

His dad, Connie, longtime Grand Saline, TX, druggist, asked what he thought was a throwaway question: "Chris, would you like me to teach you to play the guitar?" It was a distant second to Chris' "druthers", but it might make staying indoors more bearable, the youngster figured. His dad had an old guitar, and felt brief instructional times would be his only investment. There was one problem—Connie is right-handed and Chris, left. Ever the concept man, dad thought Chris could figure out a way to learn—be it with mirrors, head-standing and/or brain flip-flopping.

Christian music lovers offer "amens" to Chris repeatedly. He's a favorite in sold-out venues throughout the world and also is worship leader in an Atlanta church. His published works are used in thousands of churches throughout the land, and some 30 million Tomlin CDs have been sold to date.

They renamed Main Street "Chris Tomlin Boulevard" in Grand Saline, where 7,500 fans crowded into the football stadium to honor him on his 39th birthday, May 4, 2011. Looking back, Connie and wife Donna are thankful that mono—paired with Chris' perseverance—bode much good as a left-handed son learned from a right-handed dad.

Bunny knows the importance of strings, too, with extra yo-yo strings always in his pocket. His talents have taken him around the world and he, too, has chosen Christian venues. Many programs have been for Fellowship of Christian Athletes, where he's enshrined in the Hall of Fame. He has entertained thousands of times in prisons, churches, schools and on TV. As impressive as his mastery of entertainment and articulate testimony is his overcoming a serious speech impediment. "I was a classic stutterer until I was in college," he said. "When in high school, if I wanted to ask a girl out, my sister made the phone call. I was embarrassed to attend church youth meetings, fearing I'd be called on to pray or read a scripture."

He "wowed em" with a yo-yo performance early on at a state convention of magicians, where an 85-year-old member complimented him effusively. "Like nothing I've ever seen," he said. "But I have to be honest—a couple of times I could see the strings." Eyes rolling, Bunny—whose sandpapered Yo-Yo once lit a match clenched between Garry Moore's teeth on NBC's *To Tell The Truth*—promised he'd try to do better.

These two men have much in common besides strings. Bunny, now 80 and still in demand, resides in Dallas with Mary Etta, his wife of 56 years. Chris and wife Lauren live in Panama City, FL, with Ashlyn, 2. Another child is due soon. Fans know Martin and Tomlin to be "real deals," with no strings attached…. (09-2014)

A SABBATH REMEMBERED—AND KEPT HOLY…

Surely they weren't actual sounds from a flesh-and-blood ox with nostrils flared, disrupting the order of a Sunday morning. But the bellowing—imagined or not—sounded like a wounded beast reduced to his knees, surrendering to a "week that was". Yelling to be heard above the bellows, I informed my wife, kids and grandkids—all scurrying about to make church on time—that I'd remain at home.

Bone weary, I claimed "king's X"—ox in the ditch. It's a card I rarely play, remaining pajama-clad at home, coffee refills and Sunday morning sports pages at hand. I volunteered to have lunch ready, though—two truly giant pizzas….

Shakespeare warned of slips 'twixt cups and lips. Still, the perfect storm—which could have resulted in a house reduced to ashes—seemed severe penance for missing church.

My misadventure had such innocent beginnings. I was a bit careless placing the pizzas on the oven racks, not realizing that Aldi's giant pizzas are two inches wider than other brands. Therefore, each pizza must be placed perfectly on the rack. A three-inch overhang—out of view in back—can have serious consequences.

The family's return home coincided with smoke curling from the oven. That's when my world turned to mush—in fast forward mode. Quickly, I turned on the oven fan. This made the pizza drippings combust faster, and in the next couple of minutes, son-in-law Kyle scattered a box of baking soda over flames lapping from the oven's innards. He also emptied a fire extinguisher and ordered a call to the fire department. My wife dialed 9-1-1, the rest corralled dogs and kids, and I mostly wrung my hands.

Kyle subdued the fire about the time the Burleson Fire Department truck arrived, some three minutes after the call. The firemen inspected the area, congratulated him for expertly extinguishing the blaze, carried the stove into the garage and bade us farewell.

Massive cleaning of residue from surfaces began; an order was placed for take-out tacos. I rescued a couple of pieces of pizza—the ones I'd placed green olives on to replace the black ones—and urged others to join me. Alas, despite the pizzas' "done-to-a-turn miracle", their "nays" drowned out my "aye". There were mutterings about dangers of ingesting food where names could be written in the ash-coated residue.

It was a dreadful way to end a homecoming weekend, one in which my wife and I had crowded a half-century of memories into two days. We don't often have the opportunity to celebrate 125 years of anything, but so it was in Brownwood for Howard Payne University's observance.

A story provided by new friend Dan Russo (father in law of organ transplant surgeon, Dr. Tom Collins, who was cited as distinguished alumnus at homecoming) must be shared. A former FBI official who served 27 years—and knew five US presidents "up close"—Russo recounted a tale of legendary J. Edgar Hoover, the FBI's first director. Mr. Hoover redefined eccentricity. His foibles were many and well known by others in the Bureau. Few along his trail ever crossed him, and the few who tried did so at their peril. All FBI figures knew their director decreed that all correspondence sent to him must include wide margins, 1.5 inches at top, bottom and sides, to be exact. This allowed him room to make marginal notes before returning to sender. On one occasion, the Special Agent in charge of the Dallas Field Office sent a memo, momentarily forgetting about wide margins. It was, in fact, almost devoid of margins. Hoover returned it with this single notation: "Watch the borders." The agent sent 50 agents to the Rio Grande, where they awaited further instructions…. (11-2014)

OH, FOR A CHOCOLATE CHIP COOKIE…

Patrick Voith, an accomplished pilot who flies a sleek King Air 200 plane for M&F Western Products Company, Inc., in Sulphur Springs, would have stumped the panel had he ever appeared on the old TV quiz show, *What's My Line*? He could have claimed to be a "food taster" for Texas billionaire Ross Perot.

OK, maybe that's a stretch, but he did share a cookie with the 1992 independent presidential candidate and a Texarkana native and founder of mega-companies in the US, and is now a world-renowned philanthropist. Perot, who will be 85 on June 27, ate the "other half of the cookie" at his 81st birthday party. Background information is critical to understanding how such an unlikely chain of events could link up so seamlessly.

Patrick's mom, Nancy Voith—now living in her hometown of Knoxville, TN—joined EDS in 1979. She rose to Director of Communications during her 28-year career, working closely with Perot in both his business and political campaigns.

She returns to Dallas at every opportunity to visit Patrick, his wife Mandy and 15-month-old granddaughter Kennedy. Four years ago, she visited Perot on the occasion of his 81st birthday. (She visits him on or near his birthday annually, and typically takes him a gift.)

Anyway, she purchased the chocolate chip cookies at La Madeleine Restaurant, remembering how much he enjoyed them. Why not purchase three monster cookies, thought she, and "fancy up" the La Madeleine cookie box with a birthday ribbon? A piece of cake, she figured….

The plan looked great on paper. When she returned to her son's home, she placed the box on the kitchen table, planning to attach the ribbon later upon departure for Perot's home. Minutes later, however, Patrick walked through the kitchen. He, too, is something of a "cookie monster", particularly when the marked box is a dead giveaway as to contents. The master of his house, he did what most American males would do. Quietly, he lifted the lid, spying the three giant cookies.

Unadvised that the cookies were for Mr. Perot, he showed considerable restraint, breaking off one-half of one cookie. Salivating liberally with each jaw movement, he slowly chewed each bite. Then he closed the box and went on his way.

Minutes later, his mom whipped through the kitchen, attached a festive bow to the cookie box and headed out. During the greeting, Perot—like Patrick earlier—spotted the unmistakable La Madeleine box. He, too, salivated, and he, too, couldn't wait.

Tearing the ribbon away, he spotted the half-cookie. Repeatedly, he alternated stares, first at the cookie, then at Nancy. He lifted the partial cookie from the box for her to see, then took a bite might near as big as the young pilot's chomp a few hours earlier.

For Nancy, as one might guess, time stopped. Immediately, she was 100% certain where the missing half of the cookie had wound up. Then she—in 50 shades of red—tried to explain what probably happened as Perot finished consuming the cookie. It all made for a wonderful laugh.

It's a vignette often shared. Patrick's boss, M&F President Mickey Eddins insists on hearing again and again, sometimes at 25,000 feet. (Mickey and wife Linda have three sons, and now consider Patrick—a 2001 Richardson HS graduate and a 2005 graduate of Embry-Riddle Aeronautical University—a member of the family. Patrick became M&F company pilot in 2010.)

Nancy, who will have a grandson to visit when she comes to Dallas in September, likely will wind up at the Perot home to help him celebrate another birthday one of these days. Count on creative juices to flow freely when she shops for another gift. There is little likelihood that it will be edible. Perot and his "taster" will be the losers…. (05-2015)

LIFE'S UPS AND DOWNS…

I have reached that place in life when virtually all I see, hear or do reminds me of something that's already happened, often decades ago. As an example, when whisked to the top of a skyscraper recently by a state-of-the-art elevator, I thought of its association with music we liked to joke about in another century. Elevator music was scoffed at—often disparaged, rarely praised. It has gone the way of the wild goose, what with most elevators now devoid of music, friendly small-talk of riders and the gentle patter of usually-older men or women at the controls.

Gone, too, are elevator jokes, such as the one shared a zillion times about the Baylor graduate who dreamed he'd died, then faced St. Peter in an elevator. The grad assumed, of course, that the car would zoom skyward. Instead, it began a rapid descent into colder and colder climes. It was a frozen encasement, and when the door opened, he beheld a wintry wonderland. "Oh, my," he exclaimed, "Baylor must have beaten Texas."

That's pretty much the way it was when storied Coach Grant Teaff came on the Baylor University scene in the 1970s. He preached and lived the "yes-we-can" approach, and both the Bears and their fans believed him. Sure enough, the 1974 Bears, piloted by All-American quarterback Neal Jeffrey, won the Southwest Conference.

Most memorable was the Bear's 34-24 comeback win over UT, despite being on the short end of a 24-7 halftime score. (First win over UT in 17 years; first SWC championship in 50 years.)

Coach Teaff invited me to address the Bears and their faithful at the euphoric post-season banquet. Happiness ruled and was contagious. It mattered little what I said. That night, I was privileged to meet Jeffrey.

A longtime staff member at Dallas' Prestonwood Baptist Church, Neal is widely-known for his amazing pilgrimage of service, inspiration and encouragement. His career is amplification of the credo engrained by Teaff and by the late James Jeffrey, his dad. (In the early going of the Fellowship of Christian Athletes, James was executive director for almost a decade.)

Neal has addressed audiences of all sizes and types since his BU years, often with, "It's good to see you again" openings.

He begins by saying he stutters extremely well. Prayerfully dealing with the condition across the years, Jeffrey has long since cleared the hurdle of embarrassment that once ensnared. Audiences relax, realizing he's comfortable with stuttering that caused football signals to be "sung" during his BU years. Hearers, in fact, pull for him during long pauses that still occur sometimes in current presentations. During his verbal hang-ups, he explains that whatever he intended to say will happen soon.

Neal's endorsements are many. Masterful motivator Zig Ziglar said, "Brace yourself! You're about to be charged and challenged." Similar accolades are from Andy Pettitte, all-star pitcher for the New York Yankees; Dr. Kenneth Cooper, founder of the Cooper Clinic and Aerobics Center, Dallas; legendary broadcaster Pat Summerall, and Lovie Smith, coach of the NFL's Tampa Bay Buccaneers.

In both pulpits and at lecterns, Jeffrey speaks unashamedly of his Christian walk, and when he's putting words together—verbally or in print—he's an energetic encourager for both the here and the hereafter.

He has no greater fans today than Sheila, his wife of 39 years, as well as three children and their families. The Jeffreys have eight grandchildren and counting, with a ninth on the way.

A while back, we both were speakers at a regional senior adult conference in Amarillo. I was humbled; what could I say that Neal couldn't say better? Nothing. I did mention, however, that if we were ever on the same program again, I'd stay at a different hotel, kidding that I was wakened several times by a stuttering snorer—or vice versa. And we were on different wings of the hotel, four floors apart....

Whatever, no one is happier than Neal that the Bears' current football resurgence has put those "put down" stories to rest. He's a walking testimonial to Teaff's claims. 'Course, Neal's dear old dad got in the first formative shots. And if heaven has a glass bottom, there's a smiling father, mighty proud of his son....(04-2015)

IN HARNESS WITH A PREACHER...

It's hard to believe I had a genuinely cordial "argument" involving a birthday observance, a $91 gift check, and a couple driving 3,000+ miles to spend two days with the honoree. I confess to igniting the gentle disagreement, but the principal figure is Ethelyn Smith, a resident at Redstone Park in Brownwood, TX—where some residents round off—or round down—their ages.

With right hand-on-a-Bible solemnity, she claimed to be age 90 upon my expression of good wishes "at the beginning of her 91st year". She balked. "Ethelyn, birthdays mark the year of completion, not the beginning," I reminded. She wouldn't budge, saying, "A year from now, you'd be right, but for now, I'm just 90."

Oh, the $91 check. It was in a birthday greeting card from Mr. and Mrs. David Shing, whose wedding was the second performed by the late Dr. Robert Smith early in his 15-year pastorate at Pompano Beach First Baptist Church. (Mrs. Shing now has taught children's Sunday school classes there for 53 years.) The check, Ethelyn said, was for each year since birth, with $1 to grow on—"nothing to do with a 91st year."

Ethelyn taught newly-marrieds throughout the 1970s, and the class grew exponentially, since most members didn't want to join the next age group. So they didn't.

Bill and Judi Skeen's first-ever road trip to Texas was a birthday highlight. They—like many others—were impacted by Ethelyn's "alongside" guidance and friendship. Such friends marvel at this seemingly indestructible woman who faces whatever comes next with grit, humor, energy and above all, Christian commitment. Throw in the sufficiency of His grace, and she's enabled to smile through it all.

"She and her son are making us smile at Redstone," said Executive Director Janie Harper, noting Ethelyn's sparkling personality and genuine, overarching appreciation. Plus, around 4 p.m. most days, Ethelyn plays hymns on the parlor piano, often attracting two-dozen of the 61 residents from their rooms. Son Robert, a resident just two doors down, often is there, too, unless he's helping plant flowers, or on his electric scooter/delivery cart. Himself a "cheerer-upper," he moved to the assisted living center early this year, soon after his mother sustained three broken vertebra in a backyard fall.

For several days, she was in critical condition, the outlook bleak. She had worked alongside her late husband, whose previous pastorates included First Baptist Churches of Pine Bluff, AR, then Houston, TX. We've all heard stories of preachers hired because their wives could play the piano. Ethelyn plays the organ, too, and has worked nobly during her husband's pastorates, as well as his 25-year tenure as Professor of Preaching at Howard Payne University. She also assisted him with the Smith Sunday school class at Brownwood First BC, where he taught until age 85, when mounting health issues loomed. She has been the "family driver" for several years, and still makes short trips in their specially-equipped van so Robert Jr. can have an outing, too.

When her husband's macular degeneration wouldn't turn loose, she held up poster boards with big, black letters of his teaching outline. The "marriage made in heaven" phrase seems perfect for this couple who missed their 70th wedding anniversary by just four months. She envisioned widowhood in their home with Robert Jr., who has lived there most of his life. Her accident, some three months after her husband's death, changed her plans.

Life is measured, someone said, by how we handle the rebounds. For Ethelyn—described by daughter Judy Bynum George as "Jesus with skin"—rebounding calls for shooting the ball again, usually from three-point range.

She's a "smiler" and a "do-er", always committed to looking her best. Upon regaining consciousness when her string of life seemed short and frazzled, she asked Judy to fetch her lipstick and wrinkle cream. Sustained by deep faith and rehab, she's walking again. Hymns describe her. She knows whom she has believed, and is persuaded that He is able….Ethelyn knows she's never alone, in the garden or any place else. Currently, though, she's miffed by her new driver's license photo that "looks like an old woman." Expect her to see if retouching is an option…. (08-2015)

(Addendum: An account I chose not to include in the column in original release. However, the lives of Ethelyn and Robert Jr. in the Red Stone Assisted Living Center deserve more detail. Here 'tis: It was during the years of her teaching the young-marrieds in Sunday school at Pompano Beach. A member alerted her one morning of a woman who was living with her daughter in an old clunker at the beach. The woman was invited to Sunday school.

Soon after, with hurricane warnings up, Ethelyn chanced to see the woman, learning she still was living on the beach. She insisted that the woman and daughter move in with the Smiths "for a while". (It would be eight months.)

Turns out, the woman was, uh, a dancer in an adult entertainment district. A brass pole and scant clothing, really, is all that needs be said. One Christmas Eve, it was learned that the woman's second husband was being released from prison. Robert and Ethelyn invited him to join them at Christmas dinner. Present also was another Sunday school member who was a peace officer. It was unknown to the Smiths that the offender, seated across the table from the "good guy", had vowed to shoot him if ever given the opportunity.

Landing there the same weekend was the dancer's first husband, who had vowed to kill the second husband. After Christmas lunch, Ethelyn asked her if she wanted to toss any clothes into a load of washing. She did. A tiny item—my wife said I could call it her "work clothes"—became lost, perhaps under the agitator.

Well, no one got shot, the item was found and the holiday continued. Bottom line, the woman was restored, attended a community college and is now a hair-dresser. The daughter befriended by the Smiths for those eight months is doing fine, too.

I've never known a finer family than the Robert Smiths. Early on, they believed the ground at the foot of the cross is exceedingly level. And neither ever noticed any shift. May their kind increase....)

FINALLY, THE WIND-UP...

Fulton Lewis, Jr., the national radio network newsman we heard daily during the tough days of World War II always began evening newscasts with these words: "There's good news tonight." He was a leading spokesperson for the "sunny side up" crowd. (A critic said he was a "disaster's best friend," since he tried to extract good news from tons of it not so good.)

We're never quite sure whether our stories—mine and/or Mort's—have such "bent" as well, but this is our sincere intent. So, please forgive us if stories, situations or "news twists" are stretched beyond the breaking point.

Whatever, we hope very much some of these accounts—whether lumped into the categories of absolute yarns or otherwise—provide smiles along the way in a world running way short on smiles. And hopefully, I'll be able to extract some outright laughter—sometimes in "soggy" efforts to seek humor even if it means suggestions involving umbrellas. There are no guarantees that any smiles induced will keep you dry if depended upon to serve as parasols. I know the song suggests we can "let a smile" be our umbrella, on a rainy, rainy day, as the song suggests. Still, there's something to be said for smiling, even if the likelihood of the world smiling along with us is a long shot. We can, though, hope for the best.

"Further deponent sayeth not," as they say in the courts of law, seems now in order. It's pretty much time to say "adios," or simply to cease and/or desist. Speaking of time, the hour has arrived when I typically enjoy a brief interlude of repose. I hope to see you on the other side of slumber. I think Madam Morpheus expects a positive response to her invitation daily. And she's certain—this goddess of sleep—that Sadie and Sailor will find their spots with me in the big lounge chair, one under the blanket, the other on top, just in case. Simply stated, it would be a better world if we'd all take "time out" for short afternoon snoozes. And if there happens to be a chill in the air at your house, I hope there's another blanket or afghan within reach. If there's not, canine warmth is mighty hard to beat, today and evermore....

STING 'EM, JACKETS!

OK, so that sounds a bit collegiate, but it makes as much since as a bear's menacing claw extended--index and little fingers held aloft--or a red wagon sweeping down the Oklahoma plains to suggest the cavalry has won, or soon will. At Howard Payne University, we are "Yellow Jackets," fearing no possibility of lobbyists protesting in behalf of these tiny insects.

We, therefore, feel it likely they will exist into perpetuity. Hoisting their "pinkies"--as they did in college days of yore at games and other events where the alma mater is sung--are our daughters, all proud HPU alumnae, left to right, Jana (Mrs. Kyle) Penney; Julie (Mrs. Bryan) Choate and Jeanie (Mrs. Ryan) McDaniel, not so many years ago. It seems like yesterday. We realize the grandchildren's picture opened the book, and their moms are shown above. Isn't that the way it is supposed to be?...

Made in the USA
Charleston, SC
04 September 2015